Complex Pictures of Poverty and Multiple Paths of Poverty Alleviation in Ethnic Areas of China

Xiaomin Liu

Complex Pictures of Poverty and Multiple Paths of Poverty Alleviation in Ethnic Areas of China

SSAP

Springer

Xiaomin Liu
Institute of Ethnology and Anthropology
Chinese Academy of Social Sciences
Beijing, China

Translated by Wenchao Li and Xiangnan Wei

Polished by Wanyun Liu

ISBN 978-981-97-4132-8 ISBN 978-981-97-4133-5 (eBook)
https://doi.org/10.1007/978-981-97-4133-5

Jointly published with Social Sciences Academic Press
The print edition is not for sale in China (Mainland). Customers from China (Mainland) please order the print book from: Social Sciences Academic Press.

This book is published with financial support of the Chinese Fund for the Humanities and Social Sciences.

This Springer imprint is published by the registered company Springer Nature Singapore Pte Ltd.
The registered company address is: 152 Beach Road, #21-01/04 Gateway East, Singapore 189721, Singapore

Overview

I chaired the CASS (Chinese Academy of Social Sciences) Key Project 2010 "An Investigation of Poverty and Social Security in Ethnic Minority Areas in Southwest China" and took charge of the CASS Key Project 2013 "An Investigation of Poverty and Social Security in the Pastoral Area at the Source of the Yangtze River: A Case Study of Zhiduo County." Between 2013 and 2014, I worked with an NSSF-sponsored key project "A Study of Poverty and Anti-Poverty in Ethnic Minority Areas in China: Anti-Poverty Social Security Programs." I have been since 2013 working on an NSSF-commissioned project "A Survey on the Economic and Social Development in Ethnic Minority Areas in China in the Early 21st Century." Therefore, I have made study trips to ethnic minority concentrated areas all these years. This book draws on the primary sources I've obtained in my field work. It outlines and looks into the complexity and causes of rural poverty in ethnic minority concentrated areas in China, illustrating the status quo of poverty and anti-poverty efforts in those areas. The book finds out the shortcomings of anti-poverty policies and measures in the areas in question and explains why. In this way, it puts forth suggestions on how to improve the anti-poverty policies, measures, and efforts in ethnic minority concentrated areas, as reference for related authorities.

The book concludes that like other areas across China, ethnic minority concentrated areas have been relieved from poverty thanks to the Central Government's anti-poverty strategies. However, in addition to the common features of poverty shared with other areas, ethnic minority concentrated areas have suffered the complexity of poverty caused by geographic, historical, and cultural factors. For instance, an ethnic area is more vulnerable to poverty and suffers from multidimensional poverty. In some cases, we have seen ethnic poverty. Years' anti-poverty efforts in ethnic minority concentrated areas have made notable progress, over the process of which we have accumulated experience. However, many problems remain for poverty reduction programs, including under-counting of poor people, ill-advised choice of strategy and tactics, inadequate funding, under-performance of poverty-alleviation programs for poor and low-income populations, mismatch between grand strategies and conditions on the ground, and weak supporting policies. Furthermore, slower growth of China's economy under the new normal makes it more challenging to lift ethnic minority concentrated areas and populations out of poverty. As General Secretary Jinping Xi puts it, "China's battle against poverty has entered the toughest stage." As a result, we must incorporate poverty alleviation into the strategy of economic and social development in ethnic minority concentrated areas, to achieve inclusive development shared by all and see poor and low-income people enjoy equal opportunities for economic and social development. We must also work on new working mechanisms and take targeted measures, to lift the poor population in ethnic minority concentrated areas out of poverty by the target date.

Contents

Chapter 1
Introduction: Anti-poverty Efforts and Building a Moderatel Prosperous Society in All Respects

1 Background

Poverty has been an issue of international concern. Reducing poverty is a major way to promote and indicator of social justice, fairness, and equality. The United Nations declared, in *The 2030 Agenda for Sustainable Development*, to "end poverty in all its forms everywhere." China is the largest developing country in the world and has spared no efforts to fight poverty. *The Communist Party of China Central Committee's Proposal for Formulating the 13th Five-Year Plan for National Economic and Social Development (2016–2020)* made clear new targets in building a moderately prosperous society in all respects. One target was "to raise out of poverty all those defined by current standards as rural poor, raise out of poverty all those counties designated as poverty-stricken, and eliminate overall regional poverty by 2020." Poverty and anti-poverty issues are and will be of common concern of human beings.

The Chinese government has always made poverty reduction an important goal since it adopted the policy of reform and opening up. Ever since 1978, China's anti-poverty efforts have largely undergone five stages, namely structural reform for poverty reduction (1978–1985), large-scale development-oriented poverty alleviation campaign (1986–1993), tackling key problems of poverty relief (1994–2000), new development-oriented poverty alleviation program (2001–2010), and battle against poverty (2011 up to now).[1] China has advanced its anti-poverty programs step by step largely by three means, namely economic growth, development-oriented poverty alleviation, and social assistance. In the early days of reform and opening up, economic growth was boosted in China's rural areas thanks to structural reform, and rural poverty was relieved. Afterwards, large-scale development-oriented poverty alleviation programs were launched and the subsistence allowance system introduced to the rural areas, and China made notable progress in poverty reduction. By

[1] China-style Poverty Alleviation in the Fifth Stage: Focus on the 14 Contiguous Impoverished Areas and Inter-provincial Coordination. In *Dongfang Zaobao*, July 5, 2012; State Council Information Office (2001). *The Development-oriented Poverty Reduction Program for Rural China.*

X. Liu, *Complex Pictures of Poverty and Multiple Paths of Poverty Alleviation in Ethnic Areas of China*, https://doi.org/10.1007/978-981-97-4133-5_1

the standard of China's poverty line at 2,300 yuan per year at the 2010 prices, the number of rural poor fell from 770.39 million to 16.6 million between 1978 and 2018; that is, 753.79 million have been raised from poverty, or roughly 19 million a year on average. The incidence of poverty has dropped by 95.8% points, from 97.5% in 1978 to 1.7% in 2018, with an annual decrease of 2.4% points.[2] China has achieved a miracle in the history of poverty reduction. But we must understand that as China enjoys rapid economic growth and social progress, it also suffers increasingly widened gaps between regions, urban and rural areas, and social strata, thus weakened effects of poverty reduction, economically and socially. That is, poverty reduction in China presents a diminishing marginal tendency.[3] What's more, the strategy of development-oriented poverty alleviation sometimes under-performs. Many key projects do not deliver the intended benefits to the target poor population, including region-specific poverty-alleviation projects (e.g. rehabilitating projects in impoverished counties and comprehensive development-oriented poverty reduction in villages) and group-targeted poverty-alleviation projects (e.g. poverty reduction with industrialization, low-interest loans for the poor, poverty relief through science and technology, and training of labor force). Therefore, the projects have fallen short of expectation. It many cases, it is the non-poor population or those households living in poverty-stricken areas but that are fairing reasonably well that end up benefitting. This has limited the effecaciousness of development-oriented poverty-alleviation projects.[4] Furthermore, in most places, there are always those who are poorly endowed and suffer chronic poverty, and thus need long-lasting social assistance; and there are those who fall into temporary poverty due to economic restructuring and fluctuations, and thus require temporary social assistance. The central and local governments must readjust anti-poverty strategies and policies, adapting to changes in rural poverty issues. The Chinese government has been doing so all these decades.

[2] A calculation drawing on data from *China Statistical Yearbook 2018* and A Fall in the Chinese Rural Poor by 13.86 Million in 2018. http://www.stats.gov.cn/tjsj/zxfb/201902/t20190215_1649231.html. Accessed February 15, 2019).

[3] Zheng Changde (ed. 2013). *Report on Economic Development in China Minority Region (2013)*. Beijing: China Economic Publishing House.

[4] For instance, no more than 3% of poverty-stricken families with labor capacity received financial support for poverty reduction in 2009. Department of Household Surveys NBS (2011). *Poverty Monitoring Report of Rural China 2010*. Beijing: China Statistics Press.

Ethnic minority concentrated areas[5] have long been less developed due to inadequate resources and geographic, location, and cultural restraints. Since the founding of the People's Republic of China in 1949, the Chinese government has adopted preferential policies for these areas to address the long-existing inter-ethnic problems in multiethnic China.[6] Thanks to such policies, ethnic minority concentrated areas in China have witnessed economic growth and social progress, and ethnic groups in the country have enjoyed better living conditions. Nonetheless, ethnic minority concentrated areas remain restricted by historic conditions and see a large population sink in poverty. The Chinese government has stepped up its support for those areas. When the Chinese government adopted the full-scale development program for the western regions in 2000, all the five autonomous region, 30 autonomous prefectures and an overwhelming majority of 120 autonomous counties were included in the program. Favorable policies and measures were drawn up for the autonomous counties not included in the program. In 2005, the CPC Central Committee convened the first working conference on ethnic issues in the twenty-first century. On the conference, the CPC Central Committee promulgated the Decision of the CPC Central Committee and State Council on Stepping Up Efforts for Ethnic Issues and Accelerating the Economic and Social Progress for Ethnic Groups and in Ethnic Minority Areas (CPC Central Committee [2005] No. 10). Favorable policies for economic and social progress for ethnic groups and areas followed, for frontier provinces and autonomous regions like Tibet, Xinjiang, Ningxia, Guangxi, Guizhou, and Yunnan, and for Tibetan areas in provinces like Qinghai. Preferential policies were formulated for trade in ethnic minority concentrated areas and manufacturing of special items for ethnic groups.[7] The policies and measures were carefully drawn and applicable to targeted groups in a wide range of areas and conducive to the leapfrog development in ethnic minority concentrated areas and to boosting economic and social progress in those areas and lifting poor population there out of poverty. The Chinese government has made it its top priority to address poverty in the ethnic minority concentrated areas in western China, "putting emphasis on the old revolutionary bases in the central and western regions, areas inhabited by ethnic minorities, border areas and destitute

---

[5] Generally, an ethnic minority concentrated area refers to an area majorly inhabited by ethnic minorities rather than the Han people. That is to say, ethnic minority concentrated areas include all the ethnic autonomous regions, leagues, counties (banners), townships (towns), and villages. Ethnic minority areas are alternatively called the ethnic areas in western China, as they are concentrated in the western part of the country. It is academically agreed that Xinjiang Uyghur Autonomous Region, Ningxia Hui Autonomous Region, Guangxi Zhuang Autonomous Region, Inner Mongolia Autonomous Region, and Xizang Autonomous Region, and Yunnan, Guizhou, and Qinghai provinces with relatively large ethnic populations, are collectively called the eight ethnic provinces and autonomous regions. The term is an alternative name of ethnic minority concentrated areas.

[6] Wei Houkai, Cheng Aihua and Zhang Dongmei (2012). A Study on the Chinese Government's Favorable Policies for Ethnic Minority Concentrated Areas. In *Journal of South-Central University for Nationalities (Humanities and Social Sciences), 1.*

[7] Yang Jing (2011). Report of the State Council on Efforts to Accelerate Economic and Social Progress for Ethnic Groups and in Ethnic Minority Concentrated Areas (*Communiqué of the Standing Committee of the 11th National People's Congress, January 2011*).

areas"[8] and launching poverty-alleviation programs for ethnic minority concentrated areas. In addition, training has been conducted for the labor force from poor families in ethnic minority concentrated areas, to enhance their job-hunting capabilities, and developed provinces and municipalities in the eastern regions, large businesses, and social organizations have been encouraged to help ethnic minority concentrated areas out of poverty. Ethnic groups have thus seen economic and social progress in all aspects and made notable progress in poverty reduction. By the cutoff for poverty line adopted by the Chinese government in 2008, the rural poor population in the eight ethnic provinces and autonomous regions decreased from 31.44 million in 2000 to 10.34 million in 2010, and the incidence of poverty in rural ethnic minority concentrated areas dropped from 23 to 7% over the same period; that is, the gap between the incidence of poverty in rural ethnic minority concentrated areas and the national average incidence of rural poverty narrowed from 12.8% points in 200 to 5.9% points in 2010.[9] By the standard of China's poverty line at 2,300 yuan per year at the 2010 price, from 2010 to 2017, the rural poor population in the eight ethnic provinces and autonomous regions decreased from 50.40 million to 10.32 million, with the incidence of poverty falling from 34.1% to 6.9%.[10]

Despite the tremendous progress we have made in economic and social development and poverty alleviation in the ethnic minority concentrated areas in the western regions, we can't underestimate the gap between those regions and developed eastern regions and national average. The poor population in China is still concentrated in the ethnic minority concentrated areas in the western part, and the rural poor population there takes up an increasingly high ratio in the total rural poor of the country. By the standard of China's poverty line set in 2008, the proportion of poor population in the eight ethnic province and autonomous regions in the total poverty-stricken population grew from 33.4% in 2000 to 38.5% in 2010,[11] an increase of 5.1% points. And by the standard of China's poverty line adopted in 2010, the proportion of rural poor population in the eight ethnic province and autonomous regions in the total rural poor population grew from 30.4% in 2010 to 33.9% in 2017. Especially, the proportion figure of 2017 was 3.8% points higher than the year's average incidence of rural poverty and twice the proportion of rural population in the eight ethnic provinces and autonomous regions in the total rural population of the year. Over the period from 2012 to 2017, the eight ethnic provinces and autonomous regions saw 20.3%, 17.9%, 13.9%, 17.8%, 22.1%, and 26.9% of the rural poor lifted out of poverty in the corresponding year, while the figures for the national average over the years were 19.1%, 16.7%, 14.9%, 20.6%, 22.2%, and 29.7% respectively. That is, the eight ethnic provinces and autonomous regions did a better job than the national average in

[8] Outline for Poverty Reduction and Development of China's Rural Areas (2001–2010).

[9] Department of Household Surveys NBS (2012). *Poverty Monitoring Report of Rural China 2011*. Beijing: China Statistics Press.

[10] Poverty Monitoring in China's Rural Ethnic Minority Concentrated Areas 2017. http://whxcs.seac.gov.cn/seac/xxgk/201808/1101635.shtml. Accessed August 17, 2018.

[11] Poverty Monitoring in China's Rural Ethnic Minority Concentrated Areas 2017. http://whxcs.seac.gov.cn/seac/xxgk/201808/1101635.shtml. Accessed August 17, 2018.

2012 and 2013, but they were not as good in other years of the period in question. On the whole, poverty alleviation in the rural ethnic minority concentrated areas in the western regions has undergone fluctuations and slowed down. Anti-poverty efforts are facing new challenges.

2 Fighting Poverty in Ethnic Minority Concentrated Areas and Building a Moderately Prosperous Society in All Respects in China

The 18th National Congress of the Communist Party of China set forth the goal of completing the building of a moderately prosperous society in all respects by 2020. General Secretary Jinping Xi has put forth new ideas, judgments, and requirements, and addressed major issues to achieve this goal. He pointed in the report delivered at the 19th National Congress of the CPC, "As socialism with Chinese characteristics has entered a new era, the principal contradiction facing Chinese society has evolved. What we now face is the contradiction between unbalanced and inadequate development and the people's ever-growing needs for a better life." We must pay attention to "unbalanced and inadequate development" when striving to build a modern, moderately prosperous society in all respects. The problem is particularly prominent in ethnic minority concentrated areas, with the inadequacy to be addressed, difficulty to be solved, and priority to be focused on. It is a strategic choice of China to address unbalanced and inadequate development by stepping up efforts to fight poverty in ethnic minority concentrated areas, boosting economic and social development in those areas and helping them catch up with developed eastern regions. The CPC Central Committee with Comrade Jinping Xi at the core has vowed to "ensure that the people in severely impoverished areas lead a moderately prosperous life like people in other parts of the country." The Party and government will "work hard on achieving the goal of building a moderately prosperous society in all respects and fulfill new demands of all the people." We will "never leave a single member of ethnic groups or a single ethnic area behind on our way to a moderately prosperous society in all respects." And we will "help accelerate economic and social progress in ethnic minority concentrated areas." As is indicated in these judgments, poverty in poor ethnic minority concentrated areas hinders China in its efforts to build a moderately prosperous society in all respects by 2020. We cannot achieve the goal unless we lift the rural poor, including those in poverty-stricken ethnic minority concentrated areas, out of poverty as scheduled.

Thirty years' anti-poverty efforts in ethnic minority concentrated areas have made notable progress, over the process of which we have accumulated experience and explored diversified anti-poverty programs. Nonetheless, poverty reduction in the areas has been also crippled by prominent issues, such as under-counting of the poor, inadequate case-sensitive selection of the anti-poverty path, insufficient funds for poverty alleviation, inaccessibility of poverty-alleviation programs to poor and low-income populations, anti-poverty strategies failing to address specific complexities, and weak supporting policies. What's more, China's economic growth has slowed down in the new normal. Therefore, it is challenging to lift ethnic minority concentrated areas and populations out of poverty through rapid economic growth. thus, ethnic minority concentrated areas must adapt themselves to the new normal, shake off poverty as soon as possible, and lead a moderately prosperous life like people in other parts of the country by following a new vision of development, transforming the way of development, and setting up and improving the modern system of social security, to build up an effective anti-poverty strategy and mechanism of multiple dimensions, channels, and levels. We must understand the complexity of rural poverty in ethnic minority concentrated areas and see into its unique features and differences across ethnic minority concentrated areas. We must fully review the problems in our past anti-poverty efforts in ethnic minority concentrated areas and be clear about the condition of rural poverty in those areas and new issues arising in anti-poverty practice. By this, we are able to readjust and improve the anti-poverty strategy and mechanism for ethnic minority concentrated areas. As a result, it is academically and practically important to go deeper into poverty issues and anti-poverty efforts in ethnic minority concentrated areas.

3 Data Sources and Methodology

3.1 Source

The data and materials in this book are mainly from four sources.

1. Official statistics, documents, and interviews from the CASS (Chinese Academy of Social Sciences) Key Project "An Investigation of Poverty and Social Security in Ethnic Minority Areas in Southwest China." The data was collected by the project team in Yunnan, Guangxi, Hunan, and Guizhou in October 2011 and in June and July 2012. The team held interviews with persons-in-charge from county (township) governments and related authorities, farmers and herders, and staff from specialized rural cooperatives in the areas in question, to understand the local economic and social progress, anti-poverty strategy and practice, social security system, and status quo of poverty-stricken farmer and herdsman families. More than 200 were interviewed, with the situation satisfactorily illustrated.
2. Statistics, documents, and interviews from the CASS Key Project "An Investigation of Poverty and Social Security in the Pastoral Area at the Source of the Yangtze River: A Case Study of Zhiduo County." The data was collected between 2010 and 2013 by the project team in the field study in Yushu Tibetan Autonomous Prefecture, Qinghai Province, and from questionnaire survey co-conducted by the project team and Kegawa Herders Cooperative of Zhiduo County, Yushu Tibetan Autonomous Prefecture, Qinghai Province. More than 60 locals were interviewed in the same way as under the aforementioned project launched in

Yunnan, Guangxi, Hunan, and Guizhou. For the questionnaire survey, four townships and towns under the jurisdiction of Zhiduo County were selected by the standards of economic and social progress. Farmer and herdsman families in the four sample towns and townships were either invited to group or individual interviews, depending on the concentration pattern of households. Two hundred families were interviewed in total. The survey was painstaking since herdsman families scattered across the grassland and moved as seasons changed. It was time-consuming to follow their way.

3. Chinese Household of Ethnicity Survey (CHES) data collected in 2012 in Xinjiang, Inner Mongolia, Ningxia, Qinghai, Guangxi, Hunan, and southeast Guizhou by the CASS Institute of Ethnology and Anthropology and the project team of Economic and Social Progress in Ethnic Minority Areas in Western China under the School of Economics, Minzu University of China. CHES questionnaire survey followed the NBS's sampling method for rural households and selected randomly 7,257 sample households (31,671 people in total) from 757 administrative villages in 81 counties. The samples were statistically reliable for representativeness (see Sample Analysis in Chap. 7).
4. The questionnaire survey under the NSSF-commissioned CASS Major Innovation Project "A Survey on the Economic and Social Development in Ethnic Minority Areas in China in the Early 21st Century." The project team conducted the questionnaire survey in 18 municipalities and counties in Inner Mongolia, Jilin, Zhejiang, Hubei, Guangxi, Sichuan, Tibet, Qinghai, Ningxia, and Xinjiang in 2014, thus the name the Survey of Ethnic Minority Areas 2014. Stratified random sampling was in use. In the 18 municipalities and counties, urban and rural communities were selected by standards of (high-, medium-, and low-level) economic development and distribution of ethnic groups, as well as urbanization rate. Then sample households were selected from the communities or administrative villages. The number of sample households was 400–500 for each municipality or county, totaling 7,341 sample households in the 18 municipalities and counties. The questionnaire illustrated the sample household's basic information and the interviewee's opinion on the local economic development, social progress, and ethnic culture, policy and relations, and public security, and level of social harmony.

3.2 Methodology

Applicable quantitative analysis and econometric models were adopted for a thorough analysis of the data collected in the questionnaire surveys. Qualitative and literature study was applied to organizing the official statistics, local documents, and in-depth interviews, evaluating related policies and measures and their effects, and elaborating on the result of quantitative research. On the whole, the research, facilitated by the aforementioned methods, outlined the status quo and features of rural poverty in China's ethnic minority concentrated areas, investigated major economic, social, and culture factors in rural poverty in the areas in question, and evaluated and analyzed the poverty-alleviation strategy and practice in ethnic minority concentrated areas, the social security system in rural ethnic minority concentrated areas, and the anti-poverty effects of related policies. Based on all this, the study aims to explore new ideas, strategies, and models to boost economic and social progress and better apply anti-poverty strategy and measures in ethnic minority concentrated areas in new situation, so that people in those areas can lead a moderately prosperous life like people in other parts of the country.

4 Synopsis and Research Framework

The book aims to understand the new developments of rural poverty and new challenges anti-poverty efforts facing in China's ethnic minority concentrated areas by investigating the complexity of rural poverty in the areas in question and conducting quantitative analysis. The research consequently detects and analyzes inadequacies of the anti-poverty policies and measures adopted in ethnic minority concentrated areas. By this, policy suggestions are formed for future anti-poverty efforts in ethnic minority concentrated areas, for reference of related authorities. The content is arranged as below (Fig. 1.1).

The book presents rural poverty scene and anti-poverty efforts in China's ethnic minority concentrated areas in eight chapters. Chapter 1 outlines the background, topic and objective of the research, and reveals the relationship between anti-poverty efforts in ethnic minority concentrated areas and China's goal to build a moderately prosperous society in all respects. The chapter also explains the sources, methodology, and framework of the research.

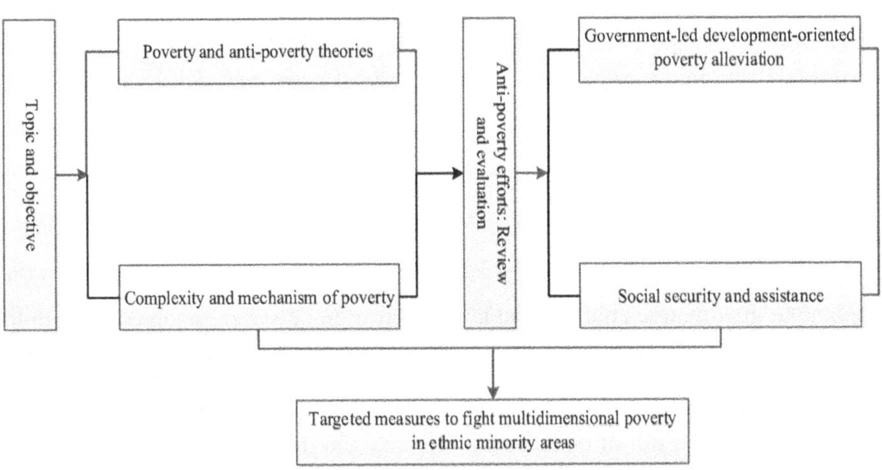

Fig. 1.1 Research framework

Chapter 2 studies poverty and anti-poverty theories both at home and abroad and puts them into three categories. The first category deals with meanings, types, causes, and measurement methods of poverty. The second evaluates poverty and anti-poverty efforts. And the third investigates anti-poverty strategies. The literature review shows that there has been in-depth academic research on rural poverty and rural poverty issues in ethnic minority concentrated areas in western China which draw increasing attention. However, research projects largely focus on local cases, or conduct qualitative analysis upon rural poverty in ethnic minority concentrated areas in western China. Quantified measurements and poverty mechanism on the microscopic level are in need for rural poverty research in ethnic minority concentrated areas. Also, there has been no comparative study of rural poverty and anti-poverty efforts across ethnic minority concentrated areas, let alone the research delving into poverty phenomena that are in multiple dimensions, diversified and complicated, in those areas. The book draws on primary surveys and data and Chinese and foreign theories of poverty, and applies empirical methods to the status quo of rural poverty and anti-poverty efforts in China's ethnic minority concentrated areas. It aims to better understand how severe and complicated the poverty issues are in ethnic minority concentrated areas. It also expects to elaborate on the distinctive features of anti-poverty strategy and policies for ethnic minority concentrated areas and stress how important it is to have comprehensive, structural, and applicable strategy and policies of the kind. By this, the research is expected to be helpful to formulate effective poverty-reduction policies.

Chapter 3 investigates the complexity and causes of poverty in China's ethnic minority concentrated areas. It first looks at the status quo and potential of economic and social progress in the areas in terms of the geographic and ecological conditions, natural resources, distribution of ethnic population to economic development and structure, industrialized and urbanized level, farmers' income, and anti-poverty efforts. In a word, ethnic minority concentrated areas take up a large proportion of China's territory and home to river sources. They stand as ecological barriers with distinctive cultures and rich resources, and are of strategic significance to the country. At the same time, ethnic minority concentrated areas are economically and socially underdeveloped and suffer widespread poverty.[12] Then, the chapter has an overview of the mosaic of rural poverty in ethnic minority concentrated areas. In those areas, a large rural population is stuck in diversified forms of poverty, and the poor population is concentrated in ecologically fragile areas. Large numbers of ethnic people in the areas suffer poverty, and the poverty-stricken ethnic population takes up a high proportion. Poor families are evidently more vulnerable to risks. In some rural ethnic minority concentrated areas, there is mass poverty. Besides, rural poverty is expected to spread across ethnic minority concentrated areas in China for a long time due to economic slowdown in the country and around the globe. Lastly, the chapter sees into details of the complexity and causes of rural poverty in ethnic minority concentrated areas. In general, geographic conditions, social and cultural traditions, family models, policies and institutional factors all lead to rural poverty in the interviewed

[12] *New Ideas from the CPC Central Committee's Working Conference on Ethnic Issues*. http://www.seac.gov.cn/art/2015/6/1/art_143_228925.html. Accessed March 9, 2017.

ethnic minority concentrated areas. Things like geographic conditions may not be changed overnight, whereas others may get improved with external help and efforts of poverty-stricken farmer families.

Chapter 4 makes a review of the achievements of poverty alleviation campaign in ethnic minority concentrated areas since the 11th Five-year Plan period. It first examines special poverty alleviation programs in the areas. Comprehensive development-oriented poverty reduction in villages plays the key part and is supplemented by poverty alleviation with industrialization and training of poverty-stricken labor force. After that, the chapter investigates poverty reduction through industrial development and social involvement in poverty alleviation in ethnic minority concentrated areas, by seeing into performance of specific programs and development-oriented poverty alleviation. It examines the restraints and challenges such efforts are faced with. Then, problems in the poverty-alleviation programs and how these problems came into being are discussed. Accordingly, suggestions are put forth.

Chapter 5 goes down to individuals' opinions on development-oriented poverty reduction in ethnic minority concentrated areas. It draws on the surveys conducted in the areas in question and looks at to what extent the target groups are satisfied with specific programs and how and why the results differ. An academic framework of satisfaction is established to evaluate the performance of policies for development-oriented poverty reduction in rural ethnic minority concentrated areas. Path analysis is adopted to find out the factors that affect the evaluation of satisfaction, and to see how the contributory factors have worked in the evaluation process.

Chapter 6 focuses on the role of subsistence allowances for rural residents in ethnic minority concentrated areas. It illustrates the positive role the subsistence allowance system plays before comparing the effects the system has across ethnic minority concentrated areas, to reveal how and why the effects vary. Then, the chapter examines how and why the effects of subsistence allowance system vary on different types of poverty-stricken rural families across ethnic minority concentrated areas. Following this, the chapter compares the subsistence allowances for rural poor residents in ethnic minority concentrated areas, revealing how and why the allowances are different across ethnic minority concentrated areas, to help correct the errors in the system. Lastly, the chapter looks at how the subsistence allowance system has helped income distribution in rural ethnic minority concentrated areas, particularly its positive role in reducing income inequality. The results are on the whole positive.

Chapter 7 examines how targeted measures perform to fight multidimensional poverty in China's ethnic minority concentrated areas. It draws on the first six chapters and aforementioned surveys and adopts a multidimensional approach to poverty established by the Oxford Poverty and Human Development Initiative (PHDI) under Amartya Sen. Thus, it presents a panoramic view of multidimensional poverty in rural ethnic minority concentrated areas and draw a more accurate map of poverty in the areas, i.e. the status quo and actual degree of poverty. Policy suggestions are put forth accordingly.

Drawing on the above theoretical and empirical studies, the book conducts case studies on three counties and municipalities, to reveal the causes of rural poverty in ethnic minority concentrated areas and show the anti-poverty efforts with local characteristics. By this, the book aims to find effective anti-poverty models and mechanisms applicable to rural ethnic minority concentrated areas and evaluate the effects. Case Study One examines the degree and causes of poverty in rural pastoral areas based on the study of Zhiduo County in Yushu Tibetan Autonomous Prefecture, Qinghai Province. Case Study Two investigates development-oriented poverty reduction in semi-farming, semi-pasturing areas based on the study of Wuqia County, Xinjiang Uyghur Autonomous Region. Case Study Three looks at Jingning She Autonomous County, Zhejiang Province. The county has made notable progress in poverty reduction and eradication through targeted measures to fight poverty. Jingning County makes a model of targeted poverty alleviation in rural ethnic autonomous areas. And the county's practice and experience is applicable to similar places or of reference value for them. In a word, the three case studies go deep into poverty and anti-poverty issues in rural ethnic minority concentrated areas of different types and reveal complicated, area-specific features of rural poverty across ethnic minority concentrated areas. The study also urges us to address rural poverty in ethnic minority concentrated areas through situation- and case-sensitive strategy and measures.

Chapter 2
Theories of Poverty and Anti-poverty

Poverty hinders sustainable development, and it is particularly true in developing countries.[1] It is a global challenge to eradicate poverty. Poverty and anti-poverty issues have been an academic topic in China and around the world. I have studied poverty and anti-poverty theories both at home and abroad and put them into three categories. The first category deals with what poverty is. The second evaluates poverty and anti-poverty efforts. And the third investigates anti-poverty strategies.

1 Definitions of Poverty

Poverty is a global challenge and has been defined and redefined all through the years. I have made literature review and put the definitions into five categories.

The first is income poverty or primary poverty; that is, the household income cannot cover primary expenses for subsistence.[2] The second focuses on lack, from lack of food, housing and other materials[3] to lack on social, spiritual, and cultural levels.[4] The third looks at poverty from the perspective of social exclusion. Social exclusion is defined as "a shorthand label for what can happen when individuals or areas suffer from a combination of linked problems such as unemployment, poor

---

[1] Chen Guangjin (2008). Rural Poverty in China and Its Contributory Factors. In *China Rural Survey, 9.*

[2] Seebohm Rowntree (1902). *Poverty: A Study of Town Life.* Edinburgh: Thomas Nelson and Sons, pp. 169–172.

[3] World Bank (1980). *World Development Report 1980.* Beijing: China Financial and Economic Publishing House.

[4] Bai Renpu (1990). A Study on Poverty Line and Its Measurements. In *Issues in Agricultural Economy, 8*; Wang Sangui (1994). *Poverty and Economic Policy.* Beijing: Rural Readings Press; Tong Xing & Lin Mingang (1993). A Study of China's Poverty Line. In *Social Science in China, 3*; Kang Xiaoguang (1995). *Poverty and Anti-Poverty Theories in China.* Nanning: Guangxi People's Publishing House.

X. Liu, *Complex Pictures of Poverty and Multiple Paths of Poverty Alleviation in Ethnic Areas of China*, https://doi.org/10.1007/978-981-97-4133-5_2

skills, low incomes, poor housing, high crime environments, bad health and family breakdown."[5] The fourth is from Amartya Sen who sees poverty as capability deprivations more than income deprivations.[6] And the fifth, known as multidimensional poverty, draws on Sen's capabilities approach to poverty. Sen sees capability deprivation as the primary manifestation of poverty in addition to a lack of income and wealth. Capabilities deprived are seen in premature deaths, malnutrition, chronic disease, illiteracy, and other aspects.[7] United Nations Development Programmes (UNDP) declared in its *Human Development Report 1997*, "Poverty can mean more than a lack of what is necessary for material well-being. It can also mean the denial of opportunities and choices most basic to human development—to lead a long, healthy, creative life and to enjoy a decent standard of living, freedom, dignity, self-esteem and the respect of others."[8] By the UNDP's definition, human poverty is multidimensional. It is more than a lack of income. Poverty affects every aspect of human survival and development.

The understanding of poverty has grown richer.[9] First of all, the way poverty is defined in developing as economy and society have advanced. It has grown from an issue of material well-being to one about capabilities, rights, and human development. Second, poverty is defined in a wider scope. It was in early days considered as merely an economic issue; that is, poverty means a lack of income and wealth and an absolute inadequacy. More indicators have been used to measure poverty, including social indicators of education, health, and living environments in addition to the income indicator. Third, higher requirements have been integrated in measurement of poverty, as economic and social development steps into a higher level; that is, poverty means unfulfilled demands on higher levels. Fourth, the complexity of causes of poverty is justified. Poverty was at first seen as the result of material inadequacies. However, it persists despite higher productivity and material abundance. Accordingly, it is held that poverty may be in forms of material inadequacies or a lack of income. But poverty might be caused by things like capability and right deprivations. Evidently, income poverty and deprivations of capabilities and rights have correlational linkages.

[5] Peter Saunders (2003). Can Social Exclusion Provide a New Framework for Measuring Poverty? In *SPRC Discussion Paper No. 127*; Guo Xibao & Luo Zhi (2008). Trade Liberalization, Economic Growth, and Poverty Alleviation: An Empirical Study Based on Data from Provinces of China. In *Management World, 2*.

[6] Amartya Sen (1976). Poverty: An Ordinal Approach to Measurement. In *Econometrica, 2*, pp. 219–231.

[7] Amartya Sen (2011). Wang Yu & Wang Wenyu (trans.). *Poverty and Famines*. Beijing: The Commercial Press; Amartya Sen (2012). Ren Ze & Yu Zhen (trans.). *Development as Freedom*. Beijing: China Renmin University Press.

[8] Jin Fengfeng (2005). Poverty Alleviation in Developing: Financial Policies to Fight Rural Poverty in Relatively Developed Areas. Shanghai: Joint Publishing.

[9] Zhu Xiamei (2010). A Study on Anti-Poverty Theories and Efforts: A Perspective of Human Development. A doctoral dissertation. Shanghai: Fudan University.

2 Poverty Assessment and Anti-poverty Assessment

2.1 Poverty Assessment

Poverty assessment generally includes two parts: identification and measurement.

Identification refers to the setting of the "poverty line" at a reasonable level, which critically depends on the choice of calculation method. In practice, people tend to use one or more social and economic indicators highly relevant to poverty that are observable, measurable and commensurable to define the poverty line. There are now more than ten specific calculation methods using either income or expenditure to determine who is poor. These include calorie consumption, Engel's coefficient, shopping basket method, income-to-poverty ratio, deprivation indicators, Martin Ravallion's Method and integrated method.[10]

Poverty indicators are introduced to measure the scope, depth, dynamics and geography of poverty. Metrics used in existing studies include the Foster–Greer–Thorbecke (FGT), Sen, Watts, SST and Atkinson indices.[11] The FGT measures consist of the headcount ratio, the poverty gap index and the squared poverty gap index. Compared with other poverty measures, the FGT measures are additively decomposable. This allows us to see clearly to what extent a component of the FGT family would affect poverty, and thus take focused measures to reduce poverty. The FGT measures are widely used at present.

Using Amartya Sen's concept of capabilities, and his multidimensional poverty theory, Sabina Alkire and James Foster have proposed a method of multidimensional poverty identification, aggregation and decomposition, namely, the Alkire Foster (AF) method for calculating the Multidimensional Poverty Index (MPI).[12] The United Nations Development Program (UNDP) has adopted the AF method to carry out multidimensional measurement of global poverty and has since 2010 published the result in the *Human Development Report*. The MPI consists of 10 indicators in three dimensions, namely, education, health and living standards.

The MPI model evidently measures poverty in a more integrated and scientific manner than an income-based measurement does. However, in practice, it remains open for discussion what relevant factors are included and how to determine the poverty thresholds of relevant factors. Thus, the operability of MPI and its application may be affected. It is noteworthy that the Chinese academic circle focuses more

[10] Zhuang Tianhui. Investigation and Assessment of Poverty and Anti-poverty in Poverty-stricken Ethnic Autonomous Counties in Southwestern China. (Beijing: China Agriculture Press, 2011).

[11] Sen and Watts poverty indexes are two distribution-sensitive poverty measures. The Sen index combines measures of the number of the poor, income and income distribution. It focuses on the income distribution among the poor. Watts index reflects how social welfare changes. Both indexes indicate the positive correlation between income distribution and poverty. See Yang Guotao and Wang Guangjin, "Measuring and Simulating Poverty in Rural China: 1995-2003", in *China Population Resources and Environment*, 2005 (6).

[12] S. Alkire, J.E. Foster. "Counting and Multidimensional Poverty Measures", OPHI Working Paper 7, *Oxford Poverty and Human Development Initiative*. (University of Oxford, 2007).

on multidimensional poverty and some scholars already begin to explore and try to establish the MPIs suitable to China's conditions, and conduct empirical study accordingly.[13] This study is one of them.

2.2 Anti-poverty Assessment

1. Defining "anti-poverty"

First coined by the Swedish economist Gunnar Myrdal,[14] the notion of "anti-poverty", as in conceptualized in three different ways Poverty reduction is to reduce the number of the poor by guaranteeing their survival and subsistence; it is the process-oriented aspect of anti-poverty. Poverty alleviation refers to the means adopted to achieve the fair distribution of income, narrow the wealth gap and alleviate the depth of poverty. Poverty eradication aims to secure the poor's rights and safeguard their dignity by enhancing their development competence. It is the ultimate goal of anti-poverty to eradicate material and spiritual poverty. Over a period of time, transient and absolute poverty can be partly eradicated with efforts of the government, society and the poor; relative poverty will always exist, though. It is a universal vision and goal to eradicate poverty.

It is noteworthy that in the anti-poverty practice in China, the widely-used term "Support the Poor" illustrates a specific action of anti-poverty, i.e. to help the rural poor (and poverty-stricken rural areas) shake off poverty through development. Thus, "Support the Poor" is a specific method and way of anti-poverty.

2. Anti-poverty assessment

The globally-recognized understanding of anti-poverty indicates a measurement of anti-poverty well beyond the dimensions in terms of funds and material. Wellbeing-based anti-poverty measurement focuses more on the welfare increase beyond the

---

[13] Wang Xiaolin and Sabina Alkire, "Multidimensional Poverty Measurement in China: Estimates and Policy Implications", in *Chinese Rural Economy*, 2009 (12); Feng Hexia, Wang Xiaolin and Xia Qingjie, "Income Poverty and Multidimensional Poverty", in *Studies in Labor Economics*, 2015 (Vol.3, Issue 6); Wang Xiaolin. *The Measurement of Poverty: Theories and Methods*.(Beijing: Social Sciences Academic Press (China), 2012); Zou Wei and Fang Yingfeng, "The Dynamic Multidimensional Study of Poverty in China", in *Chinese Journal of Population Science*, 2011 (6); Guo Jianyu and Wu Guobao, "Measure- and Weight-based Measurement of Multidimensional Poverty: A Case Study in Poverty-stricken Counties in Shanxi Province", in *Chinese Rural Economy*, 2012 (2); Yang Long and Wang Sangui, "The Measurement and Decomposition of Multidimensional Poverty of Peasant Households in Poverty-stricken Regions: An Analysis of the Relevant Data from the Poverty Monitoring in Rural China in 2010", in *Population Journal*, 2015 (2); Zhang Quanhong, "Dynamics of Multidimensional Poverty in China: 1991-2011", in *Journal of Finance and Economics*, 2015 (4); and Hu Angang, Tong Xuguang and Zhu Dandan, "Measurement of Four Types of Poverty: A Case Study of Poverty Reduction and Alleviation in Qinghai Province (1978-2007)", in *Social Sciences in Hunan*, 2009 (5).

[14] Myrdal. *The Challenge of World Poverty: A World Anti-Poverty Program in Outline*. Gu Chaoyang et al. (trans.). (Beijing: Beijing College of Economics Press, 2010).

period material gains. According to Prof. Allister McGregor from the University of Sussex, U.K., anti-poverty is measured at three different levels. Material gains are the "primary" outcome of an anti-poverty program, i.e. the direct effects of the program's fund on the recipients' material life. Social gains, or the anti-poverty input-resulted augmentation of the recipients' social (or community-relevant) status and of welfare-acquiring capability, such as the vocational training for the unemployed and even beggars, the financial aid for financially-troubled families on the verge of bankruptcy and the dropout subsidy, help enhance family wellbeing in terms of social relations. Subjective or psychological gains, i.e. the anti-poverty input-resulted augmentation of the recipients' subjective and psychological wellbeing, refer to the recipients' feelings about their material gains or the "secondary" outcome of an anti-poverty program, or to the recipients' feelings about their social gains or the "third- or higher-level" outcome of an anti-poverty program.[15] The augmentation of any of the gains and welfare may change the social dynamics of a target community and have a feedback effect on policy-making and implementation of anti-poverty strategies and policies, thus is of long-acting effects on the economic and social development and augmentation of living standards of the target communities and groups of anti-poverty programs.

Anti-poverty assessment is conducted in the following three forms in an empirical study.

(1) Assessment of economic growth

According to the *World Development Report 2000/2001*, economic growth is the major means to reduce poverty. The scenario of poverty in a country has changed in step with the economic growth in the past two decades. For example, Indonesia saw a lift of living standards during the 1970's and 80's when the country enjoyed a high-speed economic growth. The incidence of poverty went down from 60% in the 1970's to below 20% in the early 1990's. Sub-Saharan Africa has long been plagued with deteriorating poverty largely due to the chronic weak economic growth.[16] The studies in the relationship between economic growth and poverty reduction have kept increasing at home and abroad. Researchers have reached an agreement that while economic growth itself affects the scenario of poverty, the nature and pattern of economic growth (i.e. what benefits different groups have drawn from economic growth) and the original inequality affect the effects of economic growth on anti-poverty.[17] Over more than three decades, the number of the rural poor has got substantially smaller and rural poverty has been well relieved, thanks to the high-speed

[15] J. A. McGregor, "Researching Human Wellbeing: From Concepts to Methodology", in I. Gough and J. A. McGregor (eds.), *Well-Being in Developing Countries: New Approaches and Research Strategies*. (Cambridge University Press, 2007).

[16] Yu Fangdong, "The 'Poverty Reduction' in Developing Countries", in *China National Conditions and Strength*, 2002 (3).

[17] Lu Xi, "Economic Growth Doesn't Necessarily Lead to Reduced Poverty: A Refutation to the World Development Report 2001", in *Foreign Theoretical Trends*, 2001 (5); Chen Shaohua and Wang Yan, "Economic Growth and Poverty Reduction in China: A Study of the Trends 1990-1999", in *Journal of Finance and Economics*, 2001 (9); Feng Sujie and Chen Shuo, "On Relative Poverty in the High-speed Economic Growth", in *Modern Finance and Economics-Journal of Tianjin University*

growth of the national economy and to the government-led development-oriented poverty reduction strategy. However, the gap in economic and social development has got wider over a long period of time across regions, urban and rural areas and social strata, while China sees a fast economic growth. The ever-deteriorating inequality keeps crippling economic growth's positive role in poverty reduction and alleviation, so that poverty reduction and alleviation tends to be marginally diminishing, despite the economic growth in rural China.[18]

(2) Assessment of poverty alleviation and development projects

The World Bank made a full investigation and assessment of China's poverty alleviation and development strategy in 2009 and reached the conclusion that China has made extraordinarily remarkable achievement in reducing absolute poverty in the country over the last quarter century, while the task of poverty reduction continues and in some respects has become harder. According to international standards, the number of poor remains high in China. Also, as poverty alleviation progresses in China, the poor get more geographically dispersed and area-based poverty reduction programs may lose the advantage over household-oriented approaches. Development inequality deteriorates and rural families have the ever-heavier burden of education and health expenditures. Thus, sustainable development and capability-building of poor areas is a long-term goal of the national policy.[19] The domestic studies in China widely agree that poor rural areas in China have seen an all-around economic and social development and achieved substantially in reducing poverty, thanks to the support from the government-led poverty alleviation and development projects. However, deviations have been detected in the implementation of poverty alleviation and development policy and strategy. As a result, it is usually the non-poor or less-poor in poor areas who have been benefited by a poverty reduction program, while the poor and the destitute in particular have hardly received any direct benefits. Thus, poverty alleviation and development has been less successful.[20]

---

of Finance and Economics, 2006 (1); Hu Angang, Hu Linlin and Chang Zhixiao, "Economic Growth and Poverty Reduction in China (1978-2004)", in *Journal of Tsinghua University (Philosophy and Social Sciences)*, 2006 (5); Hu Bing, Hu Baodi and Lai Jingsheng, "Effects of Economic Growth and Income Distribution on Rural Poverty", in *Journal of Finance and Economics*, 2005 (8); Lin Yifu, "Poverty, Growth and Equality: China's Experience and Challenge", in *China National Conditions and Strength*, 2004 (8).

[18] Zheng Changde. *Report on Economic Development in China Minority Region (2013)* (Beijing: China Economy Publishing House, 2013).

[19] World Bank. From Poor Areas to Poor People: China's Evolving Poverty Reduction Agenda, 2009.

[20] Such a problem has been detected in a program of village-based poverty reduction, poverty reduction-oriented industrial development, poverty reduction discounted loans, technology-aided poverty reduction and labor training and transfer. For instance, no more than 3% of poor households able to work received poor-aiding funds (Department of Household Surveys, National Bureau of Statistics of China. *Poverty Monitoring Report of Rural China 2010*. Beijing: China Statistical Press, 2011). It is because poor peasant households usually have a poor capability of economic participation, and on the other hand, the distribution pattern is problematic in a poverty alleviation program. The rate of subsidies remains too low in a poverty alleviation program, due to inadequate

(3) Assessment of social security

Assessments on the effect of social security on poverty alleviation have been widely conducted at home and abroad. Since the late 1990's, Latin American and Caribbean countries have introduced CCT (conditional cash transfers) social assistance programs, such as Mexico's "*Progresa*", Columbia's "*Familias en Acción* (Family in Action)", Honduras's "*Programa de Asignación Familiar* (The Family Allowance Program)", Jamaica's "Program of Advancement Through Health and Education (PATH)", Nicaragua's "The Social Protection Network" and Brazil's "*Bolsa Família* (Family Allowance)". Conditional cash transfer (CCT) programs provide cash aid to poor families on conditions of verifiable human capital investment, such as enrolling children into public schools and using basic medical service. As is proved by various assessments, CCT programs have substantially reduced poverty in the program-launching countries.[21]

R. H. DeFina and K. Thanawala conducted a research gauging how public transfers affect poverty alleviation in 17 OECD countries by examining the relevant LIS (the Luxembourg Income Study) data. In addition to poverty indexes like headcount rate and poverty gap, the authors adopted "income inequality among the poor" in their research. As is demonstrated by the research, public transfers for low-income earners reduce the average headcount rate by 61% among the 17 OECD countries, with the figure measuring at 29.5%for the U.S., 56.1% for Canada and 85.6% for Sweden. Public transfers towards low-income groups not only reduce poverty, but also have an effect on the macro-level distribution, in particular income redistribution.[22]

Chinese scholars have carried out studies of how the subsistence allowance system has reduced poverty and ameliorated social equality in rural China. Four conclusions have been drawn. First, the rural subsistence allowance system has been tremendously beneficial by "providing social security for those in true need" to the maximum, thus

---

funds; thus, poor households can hardly receive any substantial financial support from the program. Shuai Chuanmin. *Research on Poverty Alleviation and Development Methods and Efficiency in Rural China*. (Beijing: People's Publishing House, 2010); Liu Xiaomin, "A Study on the Effect of Poverty Alleviation and Development in the Rock Desert in Yunnan, Guangxi and Guizhou: A Case Study of Kaili in Southeast Guizhou Province", in *Journal of Yunnan Agricultural University*, 2014 (8).

21 See J. Hoddinott. *Conditional Cash Transfer Programs*. (Washington, DC: International Food Policy Research Institute, 2000); L. B. Rawlings, "A New Approach to Social Assistance: Latin America's Experience with Conditional Cash Transfer Programs", in *International Social Security Review*, 2005 (58), pp. 133–161; S. Parker, E. Skufias. *The Impact of PROGRESA on Work, Leisure, and Time Allocation*. (Washington, DC: International Food Policy Research Institute 10 (2000); Y. T. Yap, G. Sedlacek, P. Orazem. *Limiting Child Labor through Behavior-based Income Transfers: An Experimental Evaluation of the PETI Program in Rural Brazil*. (Washington, DC: World Bank, 2001) P. J. Gertler. *The Impact of PROGRESA on Health*. (Washington, DC: International Food Policy Research Institute, 2000).

22 See R. H. DeFina, K. Thanawala, "International Evidence on the Impact of Transfers and Taxes on Alternative Poverty Indexes", in *Luxembourg Income Study Working Paper Series* No.325 (2002); S. Allegrezza, G. Heinrich & D. Jesuit, "Poverty and Income Inequality in Luxembourg and the Grande Région in Comparative Perspective", in *Socio-Economic Review*, 2004 (2), pp. 263–283; K. Hölsch, M. Kraus, "European Schemes of Social Assistance: An Empirical Analysis of Set-ups and Distributive Impacts", in *International Journal of Social Welfare*, 2006 (5), pp. 50–62.

alleviated poverty to some extent, ameliorated the income distribution in rural areas and narrowed the income gap between the poor and other groups in rural areas.[23] Secondly, the effectiveness of the rural subsistence allowance system varies greatly among different provinces and regions, with evident differences and on varying levels. Progress has been made, but much more needs to be done before everybody who needs subsistence allowance receives it.[24] Thirdly, deviations and target omissions are detected in the rural subsistence allowance system. The poverty line is set too low and the eligibility requirement for subsistence allowance is even lower, which means the income of the rural poor stays low even when subsistence allowance is factored in. As a result, too few people are covered by the system and many low-income families are not eligible to receive the benefits. Also, the poor's needs are inadequately met and the efficaciousness of poverty alleviation remains limited. In the destitute rural areas in western China, in particular, local governments usually take aggregate control in the rural subsistence allowance system, due to inadequate financial resources, so that not all the rural poor meeting the criteria for the subsistence allowance can be covered. In summary, the rural subsistence allowance system is plagued with problems, such as low poverty line, small subsistence allowance and inadequate coverage of the poor.[25] And lastly, despite heavy spending by government at all levels toward the rural subsistence allowance system, the effect has fallen short of expectations. This further leads to "the negative incentive effect", or welfare dependency.[26]

---

[23] Tong Wanheng, "Surveys and Thoughts on the Subsistence Allowance System Fully Run in Fujian Province", in *Issues in Agricultural Economy*, 2005 (1); Xie Dongmei. *Research on Distributive Effectiveness and Targeting Efficiency of the Rural Minimum Living Standard Security System.* (Beijing: China Agriculture Press, 2010); Dai Weidong, "An Analysis of the Fiscal Expenditure of the Rural Subsistence Allowance System: Based upon the Comparison Between Negative Income Tax and Deficiency Payments", in *Henan Social Sciences*, 2010 (5); Department of Household Surveys, National Bureau of Statistics of China. *Poverty Monitoring Report of Rural China 2011.* (Beijing: China Statistical Press, 2012), p.36.

[24] He Hui & Deng Dasong, "An Assessment of the Performance of the Subsistence Allowance System in Rural China", in *Jiangxi Social Sciences*, 2010 (11).

[25] Li Xiaoyun, Dong Qiang & Liu Qiming, "An Analysis of the Operation and Targeting of the Rural Subsistence Allowance System", in *Issues in Agricultural Economy*, 2006 (11); Wang Zengwen, "An Empirical Analysis of the Poverty Alleviation Effect of the Rural Subsistence Allowance System", in *Guizhou Social Sciences*, 2009 (12); Niu Qin, "On the Problems and Countermeasures Concerning the Rural Subsistence Allowance System in the Western Part of China", in *Journal of Anhui Agricultural Sciences*, 2011 (10); Wang Lihua & Meng Xianghong, "China's Social Assistance Scheme in an Anti-poverty Perspective", in *Gansu Social Sciences*, 2012 (2).

[26] Wang Zengwen, "An Empirical Analysis of the Poverty Alleviation Effect of the Rural Subsistence Allowance System", in *Guizhou Social Sciences*, 2009 (12); Li Shengji, Lv Kangyin and Zhu Jinxia, "An Analysis of the Poverty Alleviation Effect of the Rural Subsistence Allowance System", in *Taxation and Economy*, 2014 (3).

3 Studies of Anti-poverty Strategies

As for anti-poverty strategies, the Harrod-Domar model and Rostow's take-off theory in development economics both stress the decisive role of capital in the economic development of a developing country and state that the scarcity of capital lies as the root cause of rural poverty in a developing country.[27] According to Theodore Schultz, capital consists of "normal capital" and "human capital" and it is key to increase human capital, to shake off poverty.[28] As new institutional economics rises, scholars shift their focus to institutions in the study of rural poverty. Peter Townsend, a British scholar and representative of the study of institutional poverty holds that poverty is resulted from the lack of political resources. Swedish economist Gunnar Myrdal fully investigates the root of poverty in South and Southeast Asia from political, economic and social perspectives and proposes "circular and accumulative causation" theory (see the above), holding that the institutional factor is the root cause of poverty in a developing country and the government's intervention is necessary. Myrdal's anti-poverty model opens a new perspective and horizon for the world's anti-poverty strategy theory and pattern. Amartya Sen was awarded the Nobel Memorial Prize in Economics Sciences for his original study of poverty. Sen puts forth a new theory of measuring poverty with capabilities and income, going beyond the conventional concept that equates poverty with low income. This new theory broadens the horizon of understanding poverty. According to Sen, poverty means deprived basic capabilities and lost opportunities, instead of low income alone; income is an important means to acquire capabilities that in turn help an individual gain more income; good education and health guarantee a better life and stronger capabilities to gain more income and shake off poverty; and poverty and deprivation may be interpreted with the life and freedom one gets. Sen's poverty theory starts with rebuilding an individual's capabilities to avoid and eradicate poverty.[29]

China's anti-poverty strategy used to focus on chronic poverty, which has substantially reduced thanks to economic growth and on-going poverty alleviation campaigns and development initiatives. However, transient poverty remains a prominent problem, largely attributable to the combination of weak rural economy, inadequate rural social security system and the rural population's vulnerability to risks. Rural residents are easily stuck in poverty once again when they are hit by natural calamities and human foes. Both chronic and transient poverty requires ample attention, as the latter may have negative impacts on the former. According to Jyosna Jalan and Martin Ravallion, a sound social security system helps rural residents

[27] M. P. Todaro. *Economic Development in the Third World*. Yu Tongshen *et al.* (trans.). (Beijing: China Renmin University Press, 1988); Yujiro Hayami. *Development Economics: From the Poverty to the Wealth of Nations*. Li Zhou (trans.). (Beijing: Social Sciences Academic Press (China), 2009).

[28] Theodore W. Schultz. *Investment in Human Capital*. Wu Zhuhua *et al.* (trans.). (Beijing: Beijing College of Economics Press, 1990).

[29] Amartya Sen. *Poverty and Famines*. Wang Yu and Wang Wenyu (trans.). (Beijing: The Commercial Press, 2011); Amartya Sen. *Development as Freedom*. Ren Ze and Yu Zhen (trans.). (Beijing: China Renmin University Press, 2012).

survive temporary income volatility, thus addresses transient poverty; and it needs to increase capital accumulation, investment in human capital, infrastructure and public services, to address chronic poverty and reduce poverty in a long run.[30] According to Armando Barrientos and some others, be they in transient or chronic poverty, people face risks and are vulnerable. Thus, Barrientos holds that social security is the key to addressing poverty and developing countries should adopt social security in a broader sense to reduce both chronic and transient poverty.[31]

Chinese and foreign scholars make in-depth analysis of the anti-poverty policy and pattern in western China and propose new suggestions on innovative anti-poverty strategies from varying perspectives. In the study conducted by Xiaoguang Yang, Chuansheng Wang and Kerong Sheng, seven county-based zones are demarcated in the poverty-stricken areas in western China, namely the zone along the upper streams in northeast Qinghai-Tibet Plateau, the headwater region in the hinterland of Qinghai-Tibet Plateau, the upper and middles reaches of the Yalu Tsangpo River, the gully zone on the loess plateau, Xinjiang zone, the limestone area in the southwest, and the Hengduan Mountains and border area in south Yunnan. They also set up four development patterns in accordance with regional policies, namely the eco-migration based development, the ecology-based moderately-concentrated development, the state-supported infrastructure construction-based regional development, and the state-supported capability-oriented development.[32] Scholars like Scott Rozelle hold that poverty funds may greatly help in the economic growth in poor areas, but do little to increasing farmers' per capita net income, as most of the funds go to township businesses and state-owned enterprises. Thus, the household-oriented approaches in poverty alleviation and development are the best way to increase farmers' income. In addition, the government's education investment earns the highest return among all the public investments and substantially promotes the productivity; education plays a role in reducing poverty and narrowing regional gap by facilitating the educated with richer employment opportunities in non-agricultural sectors; the investment in agricultural technology ranks second in terms of poverty reduction, while the investment in rural infrastructure construction creates more job opportunities in non-agricultural sectors and augments migrant workers' wages, to materialize the goal of poverty reduction; and the investment in irrigation has little effect on the agricultural growth and even less on reducing poverty and narrowing regional gap.[33] According to Sangui Wang, a better efficiency of poverty investments is resulted from institutional

[30] Jyosna Jalan and Martin Ravallion, "Transient Poverty in Post Reform Rural China", in *Journal of Comparative Economics*, 1998 (26),pp. 338–357; "Is Transient Poverty Different? Evidence for Rural China", in *Economic Mobility and Poverty in Development Countries*, 2002 (3), pp. 82–100.

[31] Armando Barrientos, David Hulme and Andrew Shepherd, "Can Social Protection Tackle Chronic Poverty", in *The European Journal of Development's Research*, 2005 (3), pp. 8–23.

[32] Yang Xiaoguang, Wang Chuansheng and Sheng Kerong, "A Study of the Natural- and Cultural-factor Based Zoning and Development Patterns in China's Less-developed Regions", in *Journal of the Graduate School of the Chinese Academy of Sciences*, 2006 (1).

[33] Scott Rozelle, Albert Park, Vincent Benziger and Changqiang Ren, "Targeted Poverty Investments and Economic Growth in China", in *World Development*, 1998 (12), pp. 2137–2152; Zhang Xinwei. *Marketization and Anti-poverty Paths* (Beijing: China Social Sciences Press, 2001); Fan Shenggen,

innovations, such as the establishment of grassroots agricultural development banks, a sound non-commercial agriculture-dedicated banking system, a complete poverty monitoring and supervision system, the intensified power of local governments, a coordinated use of poverty investments, the streamlined government organization, and more education and agriculture subsidies for poverty-stricken counties.[34] Xinwei Zhang makes a conclusion that the market-oriented anti-poverty policy at present may focuses on enhancing the labor division in poor areas, to reduce transaction fees and enhance transaction efficiency. The anti-poverty policy may also establish and develop the market system and organizations in poor areas and promote the restructuring of traditional industries through the commercialization of agricultural produces, to realize a continuous economic growth in poor areas, and relieve and shake off poverty.[35]

Many scholars have in recent years investigated multidimensional poverty in China and made recommendations targeting different levels. Jianyu Guo and Guobao Wu saw into multidimensional poverty in Shanxi Province by analyzing the household data of the poverty-stricken counties in the province and made their conclusion and recommendations: To better illustrate the diversity and depth of poverty in rural China, multidimensional poverty indexes may added into the traditional income-based poverty identification; region-specific poverty measures and weights are selected to fully illustrate multidimensional poverty in a region in a more accurate manner and lay the fact-based foundation for a better-focused poverty relief work and a better effect of poverty relief policy in practice; region-specific poverty alleviation policies and measures are recommended.[36] With the data for the 2011 China Health and Nutrition Survey (CHNS) and the Alkire Foster (AF) method, Hexia Feng, Xiaolin Wang and Qingjie Xia analyze the link and differences between income poverty and multidimensional poverty. They recommend the poverty standards covering both income poverty and multidimensional poverty, to cover the shortage of income poverty measurement and illustrate a complete picture of the complicated issues of poverty, so that poor people receive higher income and better education and live a healthier and better life and government departments launch targeted measures for poverty alleviation in a more effective way.[37] Long Yang and Sangui Wang measure multidimensional poverty in poor rural areas with the data from the rural poverty monitoring survey and decompose the multidimensional poverty indexes. As is shown in their study, low-income peasant households suffer

Zhang Linxiu and Zhang Xiaobo. *Economic Growth, Regional Gap and Poverty: A Study of the Public Investments in Rural China* (Beijing: China Agriculture Press, 2002).

[34] Wang Sangui, "Institutional Innovations Needed for a Better Efficiency of Poverty Investments", in *Forestry Economics*, 1997 (4).

[35] Zhang Xinwei. *Marketization and Anti-poverty Paths* (Beijing: China Social Sciences Press, 2001).

[36] Guo Jianyu and Wu Guobao, "Measure- and Weight-based Measurement of Multidimensional Poverty: A Case Study in Poverty-stricken Counties in Shanxi Province", in *Chinese Rural Economy*, 2012 (2).

[37] Feng Hexia, Wang Xiaolin and Xia Qingjie, "Income Poverty and Multidimensional Poverty", in *Studies in Labor Economics*, 2015 (6).

more severe multidimensional poverty and rural residents in poor areas in rural China face more serious drinking water problem than income augmentation. Accordingly, the authors suggest relieving multidimensional poverty suffered by the population in absolute poverty by way of human capital investment, health amelioration and infrastructure construction, in the poverty alleviation and development projects launched in rural areas in future; and more is to be invested to build medium- and small-sized water conservancy facilities in poor rural areas, to provide ample and qualified drinking water for poor peasant households.[38]

In a summary, the public policy based upon income poverty tends to reduce poverty with a single income-support policy, while the social policy based upon multidimensional poverty addresses poverty through compound policies. Without the matching social policies for basic capability building, those who shook off poverty easily slide back to poverty. In contrast, the social policy for basic capability building, such as the ones to ameliorate education and medical services, reduce the possibility that those who shook off poverty and enjoy comparatively good human capital fall into poverty again. The Chinese government may try to understand and reduce poverty from an angle of multidimensional poverty in the future anti-poverty practice, in poor rural areas inhabited by ethnic groups, in particular.

There are a number of domestic and international in-depth studies of rural poverty. The issue of poverty in rural areas with large concentrations of ethnic groups in western China are drawing more attention. But such studies mostly either focus on the local conditions, causes, problems and countermeasures concerning poor farmers, or make quantitative macro-analyses of poverty in areas with large concentration of ethnic populations in western China, without any methodological micro-analyses of poverty measurement and poverty-producing mechanism, or any comparative analysis of poverty and anti-poverty across areas with large concentration of ethnic populations, let alone the study of multidimensional poverty in those areas. That may be due to the lack of comprehensive relevant data on areas with large concentration of ethnic populations on the micro level. That's why we managed to successfully apply for the CASS (Chinese Academy of Social Sciences) projects for the national conditions in 2011 and 2013. Under these two projects, we made a number of field surveys on poverty and anti-poverty in the areas with large concentration of ethnic populations in southwest and northwestern China and collected a great deal of individual cases and questionnaire data, including the data of the 2011 Chinese Household of Ethnicity Survey (CHES 2011) from 31,671 persons of 7,257 sample households in 757 administrative villages of 81 counties in Xinjiang, Inner Mongolia, Ningxia, Qinghai, Guangxi, west Hunan and southeast Guizhou. The book is based upon first-hand survey materials and data and domestic and international poverty theories and conducts an empirical research on recent poverty and anti-poverty issues in areas with large concentration of ethnic populations, so that the public has a full understanding of severe poverty suffered by people in areas with large concentration of

[38] Yang Long and Wang Sangui, "The Measurement and Decomposition of Multidimensional Poverty of Peasant Households in Poverty-stricken Regions: An Analysis of the Relevant Data from the Poverty Monitoring in Rural China in 2010", in *Population Journal*, 2015 (2).

ethnic populations and enhances the awareness of the significance of region-specific anti-poverty policies targeting different areas with large concentration of ethnic populations. The author hopes to provide solid evidence for policy-makers to work out effective poverty alleviation policies.

Chapter 3
Multiple Scenarios and Causes of Poverty in Ethnic Minority Concentrated Areas

China is a united multi-ethnic country, inhabited by totally 56 ethnic groups. According to the sixth census, the aggregated population of the 55 ethnic minority groups is about 133,792,200, accounting for 8.49% of the population of the Chinese mainland. The area of ethnic autonomous regions accounts for 64% of the national total, with most of border regions and western regions being ethnic minority concentrated areas. This basic situation of China has decided the critical status of the development of ethnic minority groups and ethnical minority areas in China's overall social and economic development.

"Building a moderately prosperous society" is an important historic mission of the Communist Party of China. The key to "building a moderately prosperous society in all respects" lies in "all aspects". That is to say, without the moderate prosperity of ethnic minority groups and ethnic minority concentrated areas, the "moderately prosperous society in all respects" of the whole country is impossible. In pursuit of the moderately prosperous society, poverty alleviation plays a critical role. If the ethnic minority groups and ethnic minority concentrated areas cannot be lifted out of poverty, the "moderately prosperous society in all respects" will not be realized for these groups and in these areas, nor will it be realized in the whole country. Therefore, it is of great academic value and practical relevance to observe the multiple scenarios of rural poverty in ethnic minority concentrated areas, understand the uniqueness, complexity of poverty and the heterogeneity of different ethnic minority concentrated areas, analyze the causes of poverty, assess the effect of anti-poverty policy adopted in these areas, and precisely identify new challenges to anti-poverty campaigns in these areas, with a view to seeking targeted policies for lifting impoverished population in these areas out of poverty on schedule. This chapter will observe the multiple scenarios and causes of rural poverty in ethnic minority concentrated areas from both macroscopic and microscopic perspectives.

X. Liu, *Complex Pictures of Poverty and Multiple Paths of Poverty Alleviation in Ethnic Areas of China*, https://doi.org/10.1007/978-981-97-4133-5_3

1 Features of Poverty in Ethnic Minority Concentrated Areas

Due to the influence of specific natural geographical, location, historical and culture factors, China's ethnic minority groups and areas have their own features. First, ethnic minority peoples live in compact communities, while these communities are mixed together in a large inhabited area. And their inhabited areas are mainly in remote arid regions, alpine regions and grassland, which are distant from central cities, suffering inconvenient transportation and poor natural conditions.[1] Second, as the society and economy of ethnic minority groups and areas have been underdeveloped, these areas witness the most concentrated and serious poverty in China. Third, wide development gaps not only exist between ethnic minority concentrated areas and non-ethnic minority concentrated areas, between ethnic minority groups and Han people, but also among different ethnic minority groups and areas.[2] It can be seen that unbalanced and inadequate development of ethnic minority concentrated areas is the key barrier affecting China building itself into a moderately prosperous society. Compared with eastern China and other regions, ethnic minority concentrated areas have demonstrated different poverty features due to their different economic, social and cultural structures.

1.1 Large Impoverished Population of a Broad Coverage

Table 3.1 shows the distribution of impoverished population and poverty headcount ratio of eight ethnic minority provinces and regions and of the whole country in 2000–2017. From this table, it can be seen that from the year 2000 to 2017, great achievements were made in poverty alleviation in ethnic minority concentrated areas; but compared to national average level, these regions have large impoverished population in broad areas. We divide this period into two phases.

In Phase I, that is, from the year 2000 to 2010, according to the then poverty line, rural impoverished population in the eight ethnic minority provinces and regions reduced from 31.44 million to 10.34 million, but its proportion to national total rural impoverished population rose from 33.4% to 38.5%. Moreover, this proportion had always been twice as large as the proportion of these regions' aggregated rural population to national total rural population. In the same period, poverty headcount ratio reduced from 23% to 8.7%, but this figure was still 5.9% points higher than the national average.

[1] Fei Xiaotong: "Now ethnic minority groups settle on plateaus, grasslands, valleys and arid land, where Han ethnicity cannot get used to or cannot get access to. In other words, in these places, the "agriculture-oriented" Han ethnicity cannot leverage their advantage." Fei X.T. 2004. *On Anthropology and Cultural Consciousness*. Beijing: Huaxia Publishing House, p. 148.

[2] Guan K.(2007). *Ethnic Politics*. China Minzu University Press, pp. 20–21.

Table 3.1 Distribution of impoverished population and poverty headcount ratio of eight ethnic minority provinces and regions and of the whole country in 2000–2017

Year	Poverty line[a] (yuan)	Impoverished population (10,000)			Poverty headcount ratio (%)		
		The eight ethnic minority provinces and regions	The whole country	The proportion of the eight provinces and regions to the whole country (%)	The eight ethnic minority provinces and regions	The whole country	Comparison between the eight provinces and regions and the national average (percentage points)
2000	865	3144	9422	33.4	23	10.2	12.8
2001	872	3077	9029	34.1	22.2	9.7	12.5
2002	869	2986	8645	34.5	21.5	9.2	12.3
2003	882	2771	8517	32.5	19.8	9.1	10.7
2004	924	2601	7587	34.3	18.5	8.1	10.4
2005	944	2338	6432	36.3	16.4	6.8	9.6
2006	958	2090	5698	36.7	14.6	6	8.6
2007	1067	1695	4320	39.2	11.8	4.6	7.2
2008	1196	1585	4007	39.6	11	4.2	6.8
2009	1196	1451	3597	40.3	12	3.6	8.4
2010	1274	1034	2688	38.5	8.7	2.8	5.9
2011	2536	3917	12,238	32.0	26.5	12.7	13.8
2012	2625	3121	9899	31.5	20.8	10.2	10.9
2013	2736	2562	8249	31.1	17.1	8.5	8.6
2014	2800	2205	7017	31.4	14.7	7.2	7.5
2015	2855	1813	5575	32.5	12.1	5.7	6.4
2016	2952	1411	4335	32.5	9.4	4.5	4.9
2017	2952	1032	3046	33.9	6.9	3.1	3.8

Source of data The data of 2000–2008 are collected and calculated based on *Poverty Monitoring Report of Rural China 2011*, compiled by Department of Household Surveys of National Bureau of Statistics of China and published by China Statistic Press in 2012. The data of 2009 come from *National Ethnic Affairs Commission Released the Rural Poverty Monitoring Result of Ethnic Minority Regions 2014* by the Economic Development Department of National Ethnic Affairs Commission (http://www.seac.gov.cn/art/2015/4/15/art_31_225897.html). The data of 2010–2017 come from *Rural Poverty Monitoring Result of Ethnic Minority Regions 2017* by the Economic Development Department of National Ethnic Affairs Commission, August 17, 2018 (http://whxcs.seac.gov.cn/seac/xxgk/201808/1101635.shtml)

[a]After 1978, China successively adopted three poverty lines, respectively 1978 line, 2008 line and 2010 line. The three lines represented different living standards, with changes in the same indicator mainly showing different price levels. In this paper, the poverty line for 2000–2010 is 2008 line, and that for 2011–2017 is 2010 line. *Poverty Monitoring Report of Rural China 2015*, China Statistics Press, 2015

In Phase II, that is, from the year 2011 to 2017, because the central government decided to largely raise the poverty line in 2011, rural impoverished population and poverty headcount ratio of the whole country, including the eight ethnic minority provinces and regions, witnessed a dramatic increase. In 2011, national poverty headcount ratio was 12.7%, 9.9% points higher than that in 2010. Poverty headcount ratio in ethnic minority regions was 26.5%, 17.8% points higher than that in 2010 and 7.9% points higher than the national increment. This means that in ethnic minority regions, both impoverished population and low-income population living slightly above the poverty line are large. As a result, raising the poverty line made the increment of impoverished population much higher than the national average. Moreover, from 2011 to 2017, rural impoverished population reduced from 39.17 million to 10.32 million, and the proportion to national impoverished population rose with fluctuations, from 32% to 33.9%. This proportion had always been twice as large as the proportion of these regions' aggregated rural population to national total rural population. Poverty headcount ratio dropped from 26.5% to 6.9%, but had always been more than 3.8% points higher than the national average.

1.2 Highly Coincident Impoverished Areas and Ecologically Fragile Areas

Domestic and overseas studies show that poverty is always accompanied by fragile ecological environment. In China, the impoverished population mostly live in remote areas with adverse ecological environment, and thus impoverished areas are coincided with ecologically fragile areas.[3] As is mentioned above, ethnic minority regions have complicated landforms since large basins, large deserts, large canyons, major water sources and national ecologically fragile belts are all in these regions. With fragile ecological environment, these regions are important ecological protective screens for the whole country, while at the same time, they are prone to natural disasters. Earthquake, hail, gale, frost, floating dust, rainstorm, drought, mud flow, landslide and other disasters occur frequently. It can be said that impoverished ethnic minority regions are highly overlapped with ecologically fragile areas.

1.3 Obvious Vulnerability of Rural Poverty

Due to the influence of natural geographical, location, social and economic factors, rural residents in ethnic minority regions are exposed to diverse risks, including

[3] Pearce D.W. & Warfold J.J. (1996). *World Without End: Economics, Environment, and Sustainable Development*. China Financial & Economic Publishing House. Wei Xiaowen & Zhu Xinlin. (2012). Anti-Poverty Research on Tibetan Farmers and Herdsmen from the Perspective of Environment Resources. *Technoeconomics Management Research (vol. 2)*.

natural risks, diseases, financial risks and volatile international economic landscape. Deficiency in multiple capabilities of impoverished population in ethnic minority regions leads to their low resilience to risks. And because of such obvious vulnerability, they are likely to return to poverty even after being lifted out of poverty. For example, once a natural disaster happens, 60% of the population lifted out of poverty in southwestern and northwestern China may return to poverty. In some areas in northwestern China, people returning to poverty even once outnumbered people getting rid of poverty.[4]

1.4 Ethnic Poverty in the Rural Areas of Some Ethnic Minority Regions

Some scholars proposed such a definition of ethnic poverty: ethnic poverty refers to the poverty of some ethnic minority groups caused by historical reasons related to living environment, way of production, lifestyle, culture, faith and custom. This type of poverty exists in some ethnic minority regions in China, mainly in border regions and alpine regions.[5]

1.5 Chronical Poverty

According to the definition proposed by the State Council Leading Group Office of Poverty Alleviation and Development, impoverished areas comprise "contiguous poor areas" and "key counties included in the national plan for poverty alleviation through development". Among the 14 contiguous poor areas and all the key counties, those in ethnic minority regions suffer chronical poverty.

According to the *List of Key Counties Included in the National Plan for Poverty Alleviation through Development* and *List of Counties in Contiguous Poor Areas*, China now has 666 key counties, including the 592 state-designated poor counties included in "key counties of poverty alleviation in the new era" and the 74 Tibetan counties designated after Tibet was identified as contiguous poor area on the 4th Tibetan Affairs Work Conference. Among them, 306 counties are in the eight ethnical minority provinces and regions, accounting for 45% of the national total. Among the 680 counties in the 14 contiguous poor areas, 330 are in the eight ethnic minority provinces and regions, accounting for 48.53%. All these counties have the features of chronic poverty. For instance, Qiandongnan is one of the poorest prefectures in Guizhou province, which is an ethnic minority concentrated area in southwestern China stricken hard by poverty. Due to natural and historical factors,

---

[4] Huang S.W. (2004). Thoughts on Anti-Poverty in Ethnic Minority Regions in Western China. *Academic Forum (vol. 4)*

[5] Wang S.G. (2011). Poverty and Anti-Poverty in China. *Rural Economy (vol. 3)*

most of the counties in Qiandongnan prefecture have been living in serious poverty. Therefore, since the first batch of key counties included in state poverty alleviation through development plan (331 counties) was designated in 1986, most of the 16 counties in Qiandongnan prefecture have been included by such plans. As of now, 15 counties except Kaili city have been designated as key counties or covered by the contiguous poor area of Yunnan-Guizhou-Guangxi stony desertification. This means that basically, Qiandongnan prefecture is in universal and chronic poverty.

2 Complexity and Micromechanism of Rural Poverty in Ethnic Minority Concentrated Regions

From what is mentioned above, it can be seen that ethnic minority regions still face underdeveloped economy and society, and current rural poverty in these regions still show high coincidence between impoverished areas and ecologically fragile areas, and large difficulty in getting rid of poverty. Then, what are the scenarios of rural poverty in these regions? What reasons have caused the rural population here? Apparently, rural poverty in these regions has both the common features of the poverty in all areas and its unique features. This part analyzes the microscopic mechanism that has caused the rural poverty in these regions on the basis of the survey of the research group and the CHES big sample micro-data, so as to explore the basic pathway of anti-poverty in ethnic minority regions.

2.1 Methodology and Strategy

In *World Development Report 2000/2001*, the World Bank defined "human poverty", and pointed out that poverty has three features: the poor lacking opportunities to participate in economic activities; having no saying in major decisions that are related to their own future; and being prone to economic and other impacts, in other words, being highly vulnerable. Vulnerability refers to the possibility that individuals or households are exposed to some risks and thus suffer losses in wealth, or thus their living standards drop to be below a certain level that is widely acknowledged in the society. Impacts leading to vulnerability comprise multiple categories, almost covering all aspects of society, economy and politics. For a specific region, common impacts include natural disaster, environmental crisis, economic fluctuation, policy change, racial conflict and so forth. For households and individuals, apart from the direct influences of the aforementioned impacts, losses in household wealth and drop in living standard can also result from diseases, unemployment and accidents. The concept of vulnerability also includes lack of resilience against impacts. For impoverished population, they not only become victims of impacts right after these impacts happen due to their vulnerability, but also find it hard to return to the former living standard without external assistance after the impacts, such as flood and other natural disasters. In particular, due to the dropping welfare level caused by impacts, households reduce their input in children, and this will undermine the health and education of the next generation. As a result, they will fall in a vicious cycle: vulnerability—poverty—higher vulnerability—deeper poverty.[6]

Domestic and overseas studies have shown that poverty is always accompanied by ecological fragility. In China, most of the impoverished population live in remote regions with adverse ecological environment. Of course, the poverty of one region can be attributed to the interaction of multiple factors. The rural poverty in the ethnic minority regions of western China is not only intertwined with fragile ecological environment, but also with specific ethnic background and regional features. Donghui Yang, Shenggen Fan and Suping Shen (2010) have conducted empirical studies on the poverty of Blang people, an ethnicity which evolved from primitive society directly to socialist society, through the survey on farmer households in Blang Shan township of Menghai county, Yunnan province. They found that rural residents in southwestern border regions live in serious poverty, with a large income gap among them.[7]Xiaolin Wang (2012) has conducted comparative analysis on the poverty of Tibetan, Qiang, Hui and Han ethnic groups from ethical, gender and education perspectives, on the basis of a survey on farmer households in 13 counties of Aba prefecture, and found that the probability of ethnic minority groups falling into poverty is 2.5% higher than that of Han people.[8] Tianhui Zhuang (2011) has systematically analyzed the current situation and features of poor counties in ethnic minority regions in southwestern China, and pointed out that poor counties in these regions had their uniqueness: with a relatively high poverty headcount ratio, poverty in these regions always coexists with fragile ecological environment, diverse ethnic cultures, complicated relationship among ethnic minority groups in border region and high possibility of returning to poverty. This paper thus proposed to pursue an anti-poverty development pathway that suits regional and ethnic characteristics, in combination with protecting the ecological environment, carrying on and developing ethnic cultures and maintaining national solidarity and border stability.[9] Quangong Chen and Xi Cheng (2014) have regarded the mountainous areas inhabited by ethnic minority groups as a special regional unit in their research. They thought that the poverty of these areas was mainly chronical poverty. Compared with other regions and Han ethnicity, the poverty in

[6] Han Z. (2004). Fragility and Rural Poverty. *Issues in Agricultural Economy (vol. 10).*

[7] Yang D.H., Fan S.G. & Shen S.P. (2010). Studies on Income Gap and Poverty in Ethnic Minority Regions That Evolved from Primitive Society Directly to Socialist Soiety—Analysis Based on Surveys on Farmer Households in Blang Shan Township, Menghai County, Yunnan Province. *Public Policy and Rural Poverty in Western China*, edited by Fan S.G., Xing L. & Chen Z.G., Beijing: China Science Publishing & Media Ltd. Yang D. H. (2009). Income Gap and Poverty in Rural Areas Inhabited by Ethnic Minority Groups: Taking Surveys on Residents in Blang Shan Townshi, Yunnan Province for Example. Doctor Disseration. Chinese Academy of Agricultural Sciences.

[8] Wang X.L. (2012). *Poverty Measurement Theory and Method*. Beijing: Social Sciences Academic Press.

[9] Zhuang T.H. (2011). Poverty and Anti-poverty Survey and Assessment in Ethnic Minority Poor Counties in Southwestern China. Beijing: China Agriculture Press.

these areas was more serious and it was more difficult to lift ethnic minority groups in these areas out of poverty. Poverty in these areas is caused by intertwining multiple factors, such as adverse natural geographical conditions, handicaps in institutional reform, market impact and deficiency in self-development capability.[10]

From this brief literature review, we can see that a lot of researches have been conducted on rural poverty in the ethnic minority regions in western China, but most of these researches focus on the current situation, causes, problems and countermeasures of local poverty, or give macroscopic and quantitative analysis on poverty in these regions. Existing literature lacks comprehensive and systematic microscopic analysis on rural poverty in ethnic minority regions, and lacks comparative analysis on poverty and anti-poverty issues among different ethnic minority regions. The reason may be attributed to lack of comprehensive microscopic data of ethnic minority regions. In the following part, we will conduct empirical studies on the features and influencing factors of rural poverty in ethnic minority concentrated areas on the basis of CHES big sample micro-data and overseas and domestic poverty theories, so as to explore the basic pathway to accelerate the anti-poverty process in rural ethnic minority concentrated areas.

Based on the literature review mentioned above, we adopt the following strategy in qualitative analysis.

1. Poverty measurement

In this chapter, poverty is measured by income level. In measurement, FGT index will be used as follows[11]:

$$P\alpha = \frac{1}{\mathrm{N}}\sum_{i=1}^{\mathrm{q}}\left(\frac{\mathrm{z}-\mathrm{y}_i}{\mathrm{z}}\right)^{\alpha} \tag{1}$$

In Eq. (1), P_α represents poverty index; α ($\alpha \geq 0$) represents social poverty aversion coefficient; N is total population; z represents the poverty line; y_i represents the income of person No. i; and q represents the number of persons whose per capita income is below the poverty line.

When $\alpha = 0$, P_α is poverty headcount ratio coefficient H. Poverty headcount ratio is the ratio of poor population to total population in a country or region, reflecting the broadness of poverty.

When $\alpha = 1$, P_α is poverty gap index PG, which measures the gap between the average income of poor population and the poverty line and reflects the depth of poverty. When PG is small, most of the poor population live slightly below the poverty line. At this moment, poverty alleviation can achieve obvious effects in a short term with low cost. When PG is large, most of the poor population live far

10 Chen Q.G. & Chen X. (2014). Studies on Chronical Poverty in Mountainous Areas Inhabited by Ethnic Minority Groups and Policies of Poverty Alleviation Through Development. Beijing: China Science Publishing & Media Ltd.

11 James Foster, Joel Greer, and Erik Thorbecke: "A Class of Decomposable Poverty Measures". *Econometrical* 3(1984): 761–766.

above the poverty line, and poverty alleviation campaigns will not achieve obvious effect in a short term. Poverty alleviation at this moment may be time-consuming and takes place at a high cost.

When $\alpha = 2$, P_α is square poverty gap index SPG, which reflects the intensity of poverty. This indicator is acquired from the weighted average of PG index. Poor population is given higher weight so that the income gap within the poor population can be better reflected.

2. Inequality measurement

This chapter uses Gini coefficient to measure the general situation of inequality, which is widely used in academic researches, and uses Theil index and its decomposition to analyze the component of inequality. The Gini coefficient is:

$$Gini = 1 - \frac{1}{N}\sum_{i=1}^{N}(x_i - x_{i-1})(y_i + y_{i-1}) \quad (2)$$

In Eq. (2), x_i represents the cumulative percentage of population; y_i represents the cumulative percentage of income (consumption). Gini coefficient comes from Lorenz curve. Its value ranges from 0 to 1, with smaller value meaning higher equality in income distribution. The formula for calculating the Theil index is:

$$GE(\alpha) = \frac{1}{\alpha(\alpha - 1)}\left[\frac{1}{N}\sum_{I=1}^{N}\left(\frac{y_i}{\overline{\overline{y}}}\right)^{\alpha}\right] - 1 \quad (3)$$

In Eq. (3), y represents the income (or consumption) of each individual; $\overline{\overline{y}}$ represents the average of per capita income (or consumption); and α is a weight ranging from 0 to 1, given to per capita income or consumption deviation distribution. When $\alpha = 0$, α is Theil L index. When $\alpha = 1$, α is Theil T index. When $GE = 0$, the income distribution is absolutely fair; and larger GE value means more unfair income distribution. Theil index can be decomposed to inequality within the group and inequality among groups, and such decomposition can be referred to in measuring the contribution of these two types of inequality to general inequality.

3. Model of poverty determination

This chapter uses the Probit model with binary dependent variables as the model of poverty determination.[12] Variables comprised by the model include all the variables of the aforementioned three types of capital. The model is:

$$(P(\text{poverty} = 1|x) = G\beta_0 + \beta_c X_c + \beta_h X_h + \beta_e X_e + \beta_s X_s) \quad (4)$$

[12] Probit model can be used when the dependent variable has selective bias and thus is partially unobservable. This is one of the reasons why social sciences researchers prefer Probit model, and the reason why this paper chooses to use Probit model as poverty determination model.

In this equation, "poverty" represents poverty, with 1 meaning the impoverished household and 0 meaning the non-impoverished household. X represents farmer household feature vector; X_h represents human capital possessed by households (and the using model of these capital); X_e represents economic capital possessed by households; and X_s represents social capital possessed by households. Moreover, X_c is a controlled variable, including the ethnic identity of the head of household and the natural, economic and social features of the locality where the surveyed household lives in.

2.2 *Rural Poverty Distribution in Surveyed Areas*

In 2012, the Institute of Ethnology and Anthropology of Chinese Academy of Social Sciences and the School of Economy of Minzu University of China jointly conducted a "Chinese Household Ethnicity Survey" (CHES). This survey was conducted in Xinjiang, Inner Mongolia, Ningxia, Guangxi, Qinghai, Guizhou and Hunan, covering the urban and rural communities and households in these provinces and regions. By using urban–rural stratified random sampling method of National Bureau of Statistics, CHES focused on the survey on households of major ethnic groups in each region, and also took into account the differences between concentrated areas of ethnic groups and non-concentrated areas, in natural geographical conditions and in socioeconomic development levels. Finally, in terms of rural households, CHES took 7,257 sample households (with 31,671 residents) from 757 administrative villages in 81 counties, and surveyed their income in 2011. According to international routine, based on the per capita net income of rural households defined by the NBS, the per capita net income of rural households used in this chapter also counts in per capita estimated rental of privately owned houses.[13]

In the following part, the distribution of impoverished population in the surveyed regions is analyzed based on CHES (2011) data for rural areas. As poverty is a family condition, the following part regards households as the objects of study, with ethnicity-specific data referring to households of ethnic minorities. This chapter

[13] This survey covered seven provinces and regions: Inner Mongolia, Ningxia, Xinjiang, Qinghai, Guangxi, Hunan and Guizhou. Among them, Inner Mongolia, Ningxia, Xinjiang, Qinghai, Guangxi and Guizhou belong to ethnic minority regions in western China, and Hunan province has Tujia-Miao Autonomous Prefecture of Xiangxi, Shaoyang city, Yongzhou city and Huaihua city as surveyed areas, most of which are ethnic minority regions. For the sake of convenience, this paper calls the seven surveyed provinces and regions as "surveyed ethnic minority regions", Inner Mongolia, Ningxia, Xinjiang and Qinghai as "the four northwestern provinces and regions", and Guangxi, Hunan and Guizhou as "the three southwestern provinces and regions" (despite the fact that Hunan is in central southern China rather than southwestern China). This paper has processed the data when calculating the rural household per capita net income based on the definition of this concept by the research group. The details of CHES database and its data processing method can be found in Li Keqiang, Long Yuanwei and Liu Xiaomin (2014), *Chinese Household Ethnicity Survey 2013*, Beijing: Social Sciences Academic Press. In addition, all the data with no special note of the source are from CHES.

defines households with 50% and above of the members belonging to ethnic minority groups as ethnic minority households, and other households are Han households. Among ethnic minority households, those with 50% and above of the members from certain ethnicity are defined as a household of this ethnicity. The poverty line used in this chapter is the poverty line newly identified by the central government in 2011, which is 2,300 yuan (in the constant price of the year 2010).[14]

Table 3.2 shows the FGT poverty index of rural households in the surveyed ethnic minority regions, and the measurement is based on the newly identified poverty line of 2011.[15] From this table, it can be seen that the poverty headcount ratio of surveyed regions is 16.98%. If we look at the data of southwestern China and northwestern China separately, we can find that the poverty headcount ratio of rural households in the three southwestern provinces and regions is 23.68%, 6.7% points higher than the average of all surveyed regions; and the poverty headcount ratio of rural households in the four northwestern provinces and regions is 11.6%, 5.38% points higher than the average of all surveyed areas. If we zoom in the focal distance to see each province or region, we can see that Hunan, Guangxi and Xinjiang have a higher poverty headcount ratio, respectively 39.04%, 22.52% and 16.48%; and that Inner Mongolia, Qinghai and Guizhou have a lower poverty headcount ratio, respectively 7.22%, 10.12% and 11.83%. Ranked by ethnicity, Tujia, Uyghur and Salar ethnic groups have a higher poverty headcount ratio, respectively 40.11%, 31.69% and 32.84%; and Kazak, Mongol Han and Tibetan ethnic groups have a lower poverty headcount ratio, respectively 4.92%, 8.84%, 8.96% and 9.06%.

Generally speaking, the poverty headcount ratio, poverty gap and square poverty gap of rural households in the surveyed regions vary for different regions and different ethnic groups. And regions and ethnic groups with higher poverty broadness also have higher poverty depth and intensity. In particular, among all the seven surveyed provinces and regions, the three southwestern provinces and regions have more severe problems than the four northwestern provinces and regions. Compared with others, Hunan and Guangxi have more severe problems of rural household poverty, and the problems in Inner Mongolia, Guizhou and Qinghai are less severe. Compared with others, surveyed households of Tujia, Uyghur and Salar ethnic groups are poorer, and the surveyed households of Kazak, Mongol, Han and Tibetan ethnic groups are less poor.

[14] The new poverty line is set at 2,300 yuan (constant price of the year 2010). Calculated according to rural CPI, 2,300 yuan under the constant price of 2010 amounts to 2,536 yuan in 2011. *National Ethnic Affairs Commission Released the Rural Poverty Monitoring Result of Ethnic Minority Regions 2011*, the website of National Ethnic Affairs Commission, November 28, 2012.

[15] Based on the per capita net income of rural households defined by the NBS, the per capita net income of rural households used in this chapter also counts in per capita estimated rental of privately owned houses according to international practice. In other words, total income of rural households includes income from wage and salary, income from household business operation, income from property, transfer income, estimated rental value of privately owned houses and miscellaneous income. If the surveyed household cannot provide the estimated rental value of its house, this value will be counted as 6% of the net value of its house. Therefore, there is some discrepancy between the poverty headcount ratio calculated using CHES income data and that released by the NBS.

Table 3.2 FGT poverty index of rural households in surveyed ethnic minority regions

Region	Poverty headcount ratio H * 100	Poverty gap PG * 100	Square poverty gap SPG * 100
The three southwestern provinces and regions	23.68	8.49	4.62
Among them: Hunan	39.04	15.10	8.47
Guangxi	22.52	8.97	5.26
Guizhou	11.83	2.56	0.84
The four northwestern provinces and regions	11.60	4.34	2.53
Among them: Ningxia	12.80	3.68	1.76
Qinghai	10.12	2.94	1.42
Xinjiang	16.48	8.45	5.78
Inner Mongolia	7.22	2.37	1.18
Average of surveyed regions	16.98	6.20	3.47
Han ethnicity	8.96	3.04	1.61
Mongol ethnicity	8.84	3.17	1.51
Hui ethnicity	14.83	4.10	1.79
Tibetan ethnicity	9.06	2.39	1.18
Uyghur ethnicity	31.69	16.60	11.35
Miao ethnicity	25.30	8.58	4.48
Zhuang ethnicity	29.20	13.21	8.48
Dong ethnicity	18.36	5.03	2.30
Yao ethnicity	22.56	5.86	2.07
Tujia ethnicity	40.11	15.53	8.78
Kazak ethnicity	4.92	3.05	2.28
Salar ethnicity	32.84	9.32	3.57
Others	28.81	11.09	6.16

2.3 Complicated Scenarios of Rural Poor Households in Ethnic Minority Regions

After analyzing and comparing the distribution of poor households in surveyed regions, we describe multiple socioeconomic features of these households in the following part based on the literature review in Chapter Two. Given that China's poverty alleviation practice takes national poverty line as the standard, in the following part of this chapter, we divide all surveyed households into impoverished households and non-impoverished households according to the national poverty line.[16] To better reflect the socioeconomic features of impoverished households, we take non-impoverished households as the reference in the research. In addition, to analyze the ethnicity differences of poverty, we also conduct comparative analysis on the socioeconomic features of ethnic minority households and Han households.

1. Natural geographical and social features of rural impoverished households in ethnic minority regions

Analysis on CHES shows that among all the surveyed households, those living in mountainous areas account for the largest proportion, reaching 56.79% (Table 3.3), the second largest proportion is comprised by those living on plains, reaching 24.73%, and the proportion of those living in hilly areas is the smallest, standing at 18.48%. Comparatively, the proportion of ethnic minority households living in mountainous areas is much larger (32.09% points) than that of Han people living in mountainous areas; the proportion of ethnic minority households living on plains is much smaller (11.61% points) than that of Han households living on plains; the proportion of impoverished households living in mountainous areas is much larger (14.92% points) than that of non-impoverished households living in mountainous areas; and the proportion of impoverished households living on plains is much smaller (9.74% points) than that of non-impoverished households living on plains.

In the three southwestern provinces and regions, more than 80% surveyed households live in mountainous areas while less than 2% surveyed households live on plains. From the perspective of ethnicity, all ethnic minority households live in mountainous or hilly areas, and none of them lives on plains. The proportion of ethnic minority households living in mountainous areas is as high as 88.03%, 30.69% points higher than Han households living in mountainous areas. The proportion of impoverished households living in mountainous areas is 8.4% points higher than the proportion of non-impoverished households living in mountainous areas; and the proportion of impoverished households living on plains is 1.87% points lower than the proportion of non-impoverished households living on plains.

In the four northwestern provinces and regions, more than 40% surveyed households live on plains, and less than 40% live in mountainous areas. Compared with Han households, more ethnic minority households live in mountainous areas and on plains, and less live in hilly areas. Compared with non-impoverished households, more impoverished households live in mountainous areas and on plains, and less live in hilly areas.

From Table 3.3, it can also be seen that among the rural households in surveyed regions, compared with Han households, ethnic minority households are more likely to live in ethnic minority regions far from suburban areas; and compared to non-impoverished households, impoverished households are more likely to live in ethnic minority regions far from suburban areas.

[16] Households with per capita net income lower than national poverty line are defined as impoverished households; otherwise, they are non-impoverished households. The national poverty line identified in 2010 is 2,300 yuan; and if converted into the constant price of the year 2011, it should be 2,536 yuan.

Table 3.3 Living environment of surveyed rural households

		Terrain of village			Suburban areas or not		Ethnic minority regions or not	
		Plain	Hill	Mountain	Yes	No	Yes	No
General	General	24.73	18.48	56.79	7.89	92.11	68.59	31.41
	Impoverished households	16.61	14.17	69.22	5.28	94.72	81.08	18.92
	Non-impoverished households	26.35	19.35	54.30	8.42	91.58	66.08	33.92
	Han households	32.04	30.88	37.08	8.74	91.26	27.62	72.38
	Ethnic minority households	20.43	10.40	69.17	7.31	92.69	94.78	5.22
Southwest	Three southwestern provinces and regions	1.57	17.72	80.71	8.15	91.85	82.84	17.16
	Impoverished households	0.13	12.72	87.15	6.02	93.98	85.27	14.73
	Non-impoverished households	2.00	19.25	78.75	8.79	91.21	82.10	17.90
	Han households	6.73	35.94	57.34	10.91	89.09	43.88	56.12
	Ethnic minority households		11.97	88.03	7.18	92.82	94.83	5.17
Northwest	Four northwestern provinces and regions	43.63	19.11	37.27	7.69	92.31	56.96	43.04
	Impoverished households	44.65	16.63	38.72	4.05	95.95	73.98	26.02
	Non-impoverished households	43.50	19.42	37.08	8.15	91.85	54.79	45.21
	Han households	41.38	29.01	29.61	7.95	92.05	21.60	78.40
	Ethnic minority households	46.73	8.38	44.89	7.47	92.53	94.72	5.28

Note In statistical description of database in this chapter, the missing values in database were not processed. As some variables, such as ethnicity, household registration, gender, age and education level were missed to different extent, the studied samples grouped by ethnicity, urban–rural areas, gender, age and education level are different from general samples. But such differences do not affect our analysis on the general situation of surveyed regions. The following tables in this chapter may have the same issue, and this note is also applicable

To sum up, from the perspective of living environment, compared with the four northwestern provinces and regions, the southwestern provinces and regions have a larger proportion of surveyed rural households living in mountainous areas and ethnic minority regions, far from the suburban area. Compared with Han ethnicity, ethnic minority groups have a larger proportion of households living in mountainous areas and ethnic minority regions, far from the suburban area. Compared with non-impoverished households, a larger proportion of impoverished households live in mountainous areas and ethnic minority regions, far from the suburban area. Apparently, this conclusion is coincident with the conclusion on poverty distribution mentioned above. Compared with the surveyed households in the four northwestern provinces and regions, those in the three southwestern provinces and regions suffer larger poverty broadness, depth and intensity. Compared with Han households, ethnic minority households suffer larger poverty broadness, depth and intensity. This conclusion, to some extent, can prove that the poverty distribution in rural areas is highly relevant to geographical condition.

The reasons of such relevance are: first, natural geographical condition directly influences the rural productivity and yield, which is significantly related to the occurrence of poverty. Second, mountainous areas with fragile ecosystem lack necessary conditions for large-scale industrial operation, and are prone to high ecological risks. This constrains the development of these areas, and constraints in local economic development undermine poverty alleviation actions. Third, fragile ecosystem is likely to cause natural disasters, and frequent natural disasters can lead to a vicious cycle of "disaster-recovery-disaster". Based on the aforementioned poverty vulnerability and poverty dynamism theory, natural disasters are not only the main reason for temporary poverty of households in ethnic minority regions, but also the reason for difficulties in getting rid of chronical poverty. Especially against the backdrop of global climate change, disasters and extreme weather events happen more frequently than before, and some disasters are unprecedented in decades or even in one century. This aggravates the vulnerability of impoverished population, and makes them less likely to get rid of poverty or more likely to fall into severe poverty.

Economic geographical factors have greater impacts than pure geographical factors.[17] Table 3.4 shows that in contrast with non-impoverished households, impoverished households always live in underdeveloped villages, far from cities, towns and stations. In other words, impoverished households are concentrated in regions with fragile infrastructure and poor conditions for production and life. These are also reasons for difficulties in getting rid of poverty. First, impoverished households live far from public service institutions, which makes it hard for them to get access to public goods and public services. This leads to multiple forms of poverty. Second, because impoverished households are isolated from market economy system, poverty will be further "consolidated" and become chronical poverty. Third, the improvement of ecological and socioeconomic situation is time-consuming, and thus impoverished regions may remain unchanged for a long period.[18]

[17] China Development Research Foundation. (2007). *Eliminating Poverty Through Development*. Beijing: China Development Press.

[18] Central China Normal University & International Poverty Reduction Center in China. (2013). *China Anti-poverty Development Report 2012*. Wuhan: Huazhong University of Science & Technology Press.

Table 3.4 Economic and geographical conditions of the inhabited areas of surveyed rural households

		Per capita net income per year of the village (yuan)	Wage for temporary jobs in the township (yuan/day)	Household poverty rate in the village (%)	Distance of the village from the nearest county (kilometer)	Distance of the village from the nearest township government (kilometer)	Distance of the village from the nearest station/wharf (kilometer)
General	General	4501.35	83.45	16	31.52	7.00	10.03
	Impoverished households	3711.75	79.58	48	35.73	7.01	10.25
	Non-impoverished households	4662.03	84.24	9	30.67	7.00	9.99
	Han households	5293.27	87.65	8	30.60	6.72	8.39
	Ethnic minority households	4002.28	80.90	20	32.25	7.18	11.10
Southwest	Three southwestern provinces and regions	3446.34	74.12	21	33.63	6.96	10.97
	Impoverished households	3363.49	72.76	52	36.73	7.33	11.50
	Non-impoverished households	3472.30	74.55	12	32.69	6.85	10.81
	Han households	3512.09	75.73	14	30.84	5.17	8.58
	Ethnic minority households	3420.85	73.69	24	34.75	7.51	11.70
Northwest	Four northwestern provinces and regions	5350.89	90.97	11	29.79	7.03	9.25

(continued)

Table 3.4 (continued)

		Per capita net income per year of the village (yuan)	Wage for temporary jobs in the township (yuan/day)	Household poverty rate in the village (%)	Distance of the village from the nearest county (kilometer)	Distance of the village from the nearest township government (kilometer)	Distance of the village from the nearest station/wharf (kilometer)
	Impoverished households	4303.63	90.90	41	34.05	6.48	9.40
	Non-impoverished households	5484.40	90.98	7	29.24	7.09	8.14
	Han households	5943.20	91.98	6	30.51	7.29	8.31
	Ethnic minority households	4736.34	90.12	16	29.04	6.76	10.31

In this aspect, ethnic minority households and impoverished households have something in common in economic, natural and geographical conditions. In other words, the reason why ethnic minority households are poorer than Han households is highly related to the fact that ethnic minority households live in localities with adverse environment and underdeveloped economic and social conditions. This means that the ethnicity difference between impoverished and non-impoverished population comes from differences in local conditions.

2. Human capital features of rural impoverished households in ethnic minority concentrated areas

Based on our survey, generally speaking, on average rural households in surveyed regions have 4.88 members (as is shown in Table 3.5), 1.62 times the national average (3.02 members/household).[19] The average elderly dependency ratio of surveyed households is 9.48%, 2.79% points lower than national average; the average children dependency ratio of surveyed households is 25.35%, 3.22% points higher than national average; and the total dependency ratio of surveyed households is 34.72%, slightly higher than national average.[20]

According to Table 3.5, in terms of whether the household is impoverished or not, the scale, children dependency ratio, elderly dependency ratio and total dependency ratio of impoverished households are all higher than the average of all surveyed households, and is even higher than those of non-impoverished households. In terms of ethnicity, the scale and all types of dependency ratio of Han households are lower than those of ethnic minority households.

Furthermore, if we look at the number of members, number of children, and physical condition and years of education of household owners, we can see that (in Tables 3.6, 3.7 and 3.8) compared with non-impoverished households, impoverished households have more members and more children; and that the physical condition of impoverished household owner is poorer, elder, and less educated.

Generally speaking, impoverished households have a large number of members, a large number of children, a heavy family burden and poor physical condition, and the household owner is elder and less educated. In terms of demographic features, ethnic minority households and impoverished households have something in common. In other words, the reason why ethnic minority households tend to be poorer than Han households is related to such demographic features as more members, more children, heavier family burden, poorer physical condition, elder age and less education of the household owner.

3. Economic capital possession of rural impoverished households in ethnic minority concentrated areas

Analysis results of the survey demonstrate that in 2011, the original value of per capita productive fixed assets of surveyed households is 4,596.75 yuan (as is shown in Table 3.9); per capita actually operated land is 17.39 *mu*; the proportion of domestic

[19] *China Statistical Yearbook 2012*. (2012). Beijing: China Statistics Press.

[20] *China Statistical Yearbook 2012*. (2012). Beijing: China Statistics Press.

Table 3.5 Demographic features of surveyed households 1 unit: person, %

Region	Average scale (person/household)	Age mix					
		Proportion of members aged 0–14	Proportion of members aged 15–64	Proportion of members aged above 65	Children dependency ratio[a]	Elderly dependency ratio[b]	Total dependency ratio[c]
All surveyed ethnic minority regions	4.88	18.73	74.23	7.04	25.23	9.48	34.72
The three southwestern provinces and regions	5.01	17.48	74.46	8.06	23.48	10.82	34.31
The four northwestern provinces and regions	4.76	19.83	74.03	6.14	26.79	8.29	35.08
Impoverished household	5.55	22.03	69.12	8.86	31.88	12.82	44.69
Non-impoverished household	4.71	17.90	75.52	6.58	23.71	8.71	32.42
Han	4.52	16.22	77.27	6.49	20.99	8.40	29.39
Ethnic minority groups	5.09	20.19	72.59	7.24	27.81	9.97	37.79

[a]Children dependency ratio is the ratio of children in non-working-age population to working-age population, meaning how many children are dependent on every 100 working-age persons. This concept is also called children dependency coefficient.

[b]Elderly dependency ratio is the ratio of the elderly in non-working-age population to working-age population, meaning how many elderly persons are dependent on every 100 working-age persons. It is one of the indicators reflecting the social influence of aging population from the perspective of economy. This concept is also called elderly dependency coefficient or "elderly coefficient" for short.

[c]Total dependency ratio is the ratio of non-working age population to working-age population. It measures the number of non-working age population supported by each working-age person.

Table 3.6 Demographic features of surveyed households 1 Unit: %

		Number of members				Number of children				
		One	Two	Three	More than three	0	One	Two	Three	Four and above
General	General	0.54	8.59	18.37	72.50	46.93	29.74	18.90	3.73	0.69
	Impoverished households		3.30	8.99	87.72	33.64	31.16	26.13	7.42	1.65
	Non-impoverished households	0.65	9.66	20.27	69.42	49.62	29.46	17.43	2.99	0.50
	Han households	0.75	13.85	24.23	61.17	55.07	28.09	14.20	2.25	0.39
	Ethnic minority households	0.42	5.12	14.70	79.76	41.81	30.59	21.99	4.70	0.91
Southwest	Three southwestern provinces and regions	0.47	5.09	14.73	79.71	46.71	30.80	19.04	2.73	0.71
	Impoverished households		1.45	8.30	90.25	36.89	32.54	24.90	4.74	0.92
	Non-impoverished households	0.61	6.21	16.71	76.47	49.74	30.26	17.24	2.11	0.65
	Han households	0.54	5.52	16.69	77.25	46.66	30.82	19.58	2.32	0.62
	Ethnic minority households	0.46	4.89	14.27	80.38	47.64	30.01	17.09	4.17	1.08
Northwest	Four northwestern provinces and regions	0.60	11.42	21.31	66.67	47.11	28.89	18.78	4.54	0.68
	Impoverished households		6.39	10.13	83.48	28.19	28.85	28.19	11.89	2.86
	Non-impoverished households	0.68	12.07	22.75	64.50	49.55	28.90	17.56	3.60	0.40
	Han households	0.83	16.85	26.95	55.37	57.75	27.39	13.16	1.55	0.15
	Ethnic minority households	0.37	5.41	15.26	78.96	35.55	30.30	25.11	7.76	1.28

Note "Children" refers to population aged 0–14

cash crop planting area to actually operated land is 19.67%; per capita household financial asset balance is 3,578.60 yuan; and the proportion of per laborer non-agricultural working hours to total household working hours is 27.31%. All these indicators are lower than the national average.

Compared with surveyed households in the four northwestern provinces and regions, those in the three southwestern provinces and regions have lower original value of per capita productive fixed assets, less per capita actually operated land, lower proportion of domestic cash crop planting area to actually operated land, lower per capita household financial asset balance and lower proportion of per laborer

Table 3.7 Demographic features of surveyed households 2 Unit: %

		Physical condition of household owner		
		Without disability	With disability but work, study and life not affected	With disability and work, study and life affected
General	General	94.87	3.53	1.60
	Impoverished households	94.07	3.76	2.17
	Non-impoverished households	95.03	3.48	1.49
	Han households	94.65	3.69	1.66
	Ethnic minority households	95.05	3.36	1.59
Southwest	Three southwestern provinces and regions	94.94	3.58	1.48
	Impoverished households	94.39	4.01	1.60
	Non-impoverished households	95.11	3.45	1.44
	Han households	93.07	4.48	2.45
	Ethnic minority households	95.54	3.24	1.22
Northwest	Four northwestern provinces and regions	94.81	3.48	1.70
	Impoverished households	93.54	3.34	3.12
	Non-impoverished households	94.98	3.50	1.52
	Han households	95.22	3.40	1.38
	Ethnic minority households	94.42	3.52	2.06

non-agricultural working hours to total household working hours. Compared with Han households, ethnic minority households have lower original value of per capita productive fixed assets, less per capita actually operated land, lower proportion of domestic cash crop planting area to actually operated land, lower per capita household financial asset balance and lower proportion of per laborer non-agricultural working hours to total household working hours. Compared with non-impoverished households, impoverished households have lower original value of per capita productive fixed assets, less per capita actually operated land, lower proportion of domestic cash crop planting area to actually operated land, lower per capita household financial

Table 3.8 Demographic features of surveyed households 3 Unit: %

		Age			Years of education				
		Youth household	Middle-age household	Old-age household general	0–2	3–6	7–9	10 and above	General
General	General	24.19	59.65	16.16	10.13	34.73	43.80	11.34	10.13
	Impoverished households	21.45	54.79	23.76	12.06	37.47	41.04	9.43	12.06
	Non-impoverished households	24.75	60.64	14.62	9.75	34.18	44.35	11.72	9.75
	Han households	22.04	63.14	14.82	7.65	30.10	50.24	12.01	7.65
	Ethnic minority households	25.61	57.35	17.04	11.71	37.88	39.63	10.78	11.71
Southwest	Three southwestern provinces and regions	20.14	60.34	19.52	6.07	36.01	46.81	11.11	6.07
	Impoverished households	15.17	59.10	25.73	8.02	37.09	45.92	8.97	8.02
	Non-impoverished households	21.67	60.71	17.61	5.47	35.68	47.08	11.77	5.47
	Han ethnicity households	17.54	59.11	23.35	5.23	37.15	48.45	9.18	5.23
	Ethnic minority households	20.82	60.85	18.33	6.19	35.90	46.31	11.59	6.19

(continued)

Table 3.8 (continued)

		Age			Years of education				
		Youth household	Middle-age household	Old-age household general	0–2	3–6	7–9	10 and above	General
Northwest	Four northwestern provinces and regions	27.47	59.10	13.43	13.40	33.70	41.38	11.51	13.40
	Impoverished households	31.94	47.58	20.48	18.82	38.10	32.88	10.20	18.82
	Non-impoverished households	26.89	60.58	12.52	12.72	33.14	42.46	11.68	12.72
	Han ethnicity households	23.65	64.59	11.75	8.50	27.63	50.87	13.00	8.50
	Ethnic minority households	31.80	52.84	15.36	18.82	40.42	31.01	9.74	18.82

Note "Old-age household" has an owner aged above 60, "middle-age household" has an owner aged 40–60, and "youth household" has an owner aged below 40

Table 3.9 Economic capital possession and labor economic activity structure of surveyed households

Region		Original value of per capita productive fixed assets (yuan)	Per capita actually operated land (mu)	The proportion of domestic cash crop planting area to actually operated land (%)	Per capita household financial asset balance (yuan)	The proportion of per laborer non-agricultural working hours to total household working hours (%)
General	General	4596.75	17.39	19.67	3578.60	27.31
	Impoverished households	2217.61	5.00	17.69	1715.11	25.06
	Non-impoverished households	5033.40	19.90	20.07	3916.23	27.75
	Han households	6762.49	17.60	20.54	4748.23	28
	Ethnic minority households	3130.93	17.55	19.31	2733.41	27.88
Southwest	Three southwestern provinces and regions	1832.57	3.28	17.81	2497.22	26.66
	Impoverished households	1329.44	3.12	18.8	1603.36	24.38
	Non-impoverished households	1981.17	3.33	17.51	2772.02	27.33
	Han households	2419.90	2.87	17	3312.51	26.37
	Ethnic minority households	1671.97	3.40	18.2	2271.24	26.7
Northwest	Four northwestern provinces and regions	6885.53	28.81	21.24	4445.30	27.86
	Impoverished households	3988.70	8.15	15.76	1954.79	26.23
	Non-impoverished households	7188.48	31.47	21.95	4685.23	28.06
	Han households	8209.27	22.91	21.87	5184.73	28.59
	Ethnic minority households	5214.63	35.80	20.82	3404.26	27.03

asset balance and lower proportion of per laborer non-agricultural working hours to total household working hours.

It is fair to say that compared with non-impoverished households, impoverished households face insufficient per capita land area, lack of productive fixed assets, unreasonable crop structure and relatively inadequate non-agricultural employment. In other words, the economic capital possession of these households is insufficient. Moreover, compared with Han households, ethnic minority households possess insufficient economic capital.

4. Social resources of rural impoverished households in ethnic minority regions

Table 3.10 shows that among surveyed households in the surveyed ethnic minority regions, 14.4% are households of CPC members or China Youth League (CYL) members, and 9.7% are households of officials. Compared with non-impoverished households, these two figures for impoverished households are both lower. From this we can see that rural impoverished households in the surveyed regions face shortages in social resources.

2.4 Causes of Rural Poverty in Ethnic Minority Regions

The aforementioned description and analysis on main socioeconomic features of surveyed rural impoverished households demonstrate that rural impoverished households have apparent differences from non-impoverished households in most cases. And according to the review on related theories in the former parts, these differences are relevant to the occurrence of poverty, as human capital, economic resource possession, structural status in political, social and economic terms and the degree of social exclusion all influence the socioeconomic development of any household. Therefore, we identify these indicators that describe the socioeconomic features of rural impoverished households as independent variables, in order to conduct the influencing factors analysis on the possible risks that put surveyed households into poverty.

Based on the former parts and theory review in Chapter One, we construct a binary dependent variables Probit model as the poverty determination model to analyze factors causing rural poverty in surveyed regions. All variables of the aforementioned capital are included in this model, the form of which is:

$$\mathrm{P}\,(\mathrm{poverty} = 1|x) \;=\; \mathrm{G}\,(\beta_0 + \beta_\mathrm{c}\mathrm{X}_\mathrm{c} + \beta_\mathrm{h}\mathrm{X}_\mathrm{h} + \beta_\mathrm{e}\mathrm{X}_\mathrm{e} + \beta_\mathrm{s}\mathrm{X}_\mathrm{s})$$

In this equation, "poverty" represents poverty, with 1 meaning impoverished household and 0 meaning non-impoverished household. *X* represents farmer household feature vector; X_h represents human capital possessed by households (and the model for using the capital), including six variables: age of household head,

Table 3.10 Social resources of surveyed households

		Proportion of households of CPC members or CYL members (%)	Proportion of households of non-CPC members or non-CYL members (%)	Proportion of households of township or village officials (%)	Proportion of households of non-township or village officials
General	General	14.4	85.56	9.7	90.26
	Impoverished households	12.6	87.40	7.3	92.66
	Non-impoverished households	14.8	85.19	10.2	89.77
	Han households	14.8	85.22	8.8	91.22
	Ethnic minority households	14.1	85.86	10.2	89.84
Southwest	Three southwestern provinces and regions	14.0	85.98	9.4	90.55
	Impoverished households	11.9	88.06	7.1	92.91
	Non-impoverished households	14.7	85.34	10.2	89.83
	Han households	14.23	85.77	8.4	91.62
	Ethnic minority households	13.83	86.17	9.7	90.33
Northwest	Four northwestern provinces and regions	14.8	85.21	10.0	90.03
	Impoverished households	13.7	86.26	7.8	92.24
	Non-impoverished households	14.9	85.07	10.3	89.74
	Han households	15.0	85.01	8.9	91.08
	Ethnic minority households	14.5	85.46	10.8	89.19

physical condition of household head, longest years of formal education of household members, number of household members, the proportion of per laborer non-agricultural working hours to total household working hours and the ratio of non-working age population to working-age population; X_e represents economic capital possessed by households, including four variables: per capita actually operated land, original value of per capita productive fixed assets, per capita household financial asset balance at the year-end and per capita area of farmland returned to forestry; and X_s represents social capital possessed by households, including two variables:

whether the household has CPC members or CYL members and whether the household has officials. Moreover, X_c is a controlled variable, including the ethnic identity of the head of household and the natural, economic and social features of the locality where the surveyed household lives in.

Table 3.11 shows the output of this model, and Table 3.12 shows the marginal effect estimated by the model. This model is overall significant. Based on Tables 3.11 and 3.12, we can have the following findings.

First, when other conditions are fixed, compared with the Han surveyed households, the probability of ethnic minority surveyed households falling into poverty is 6.51% higher, and this result is statistically significant ($p \leq 0.01$); compared with surveyed households in the four northwestern provinces and regions, the probability of those in the three southwestern provinces and regions falling into poverty is 3.39% higher, and this result is statistically significant ($p \leq 0.01$).

Second, the influences of human capital situation on probability of poverty of surveyed households conform with our experience in terms of direction, but vary in terms of significance. When other conditions are fixed, for every additional member in a rural household, the probability of the household falling into poverty increases by 1.89%, and this result is statistically significant ($p \leq 0.01$); for every additional year of the age the household head grows, the probability of the household falling into poverty increases by 0.19%, and this result is statistically significant ($p \leq 0.01$); for every additional year of the longest formal education of household members, the probability of the household falling into poverty increases by 0.05%, but this result is not statistically significant ($p > 0.1$); for every additional 1% in the ratio of non-working age population to working-age population, the probability of the household falling into poverty increases by 0.19%, and this result is statistically significant ($p \leq 0.01$). Compared with households whose heads do not have disabilities, the probability of households with physical disabilities falling into poverty increases by 5.52%, but this result is not statistically significant ($p > 0.1$).

Third, the influences of social capital possession on probability of poverty of surveyed households conform with our experience in terms of direction, but vary in terms of significance. In particular, compared with non-official households, the probability of households of officials falling into poverty decreases by 4.78%, and this result is statistically significant ($p \leq 0.01$); compared with non-CPC member households, the probability of households of CPC members falling into poverty decreases by 0.55%, but this result is not statistically significant ($p > 0.1$). It should be pointed out that households of CPC members and official households overlap to a certain degree. The overlap rate is 33.5%, which is basically acceptable and will not cause too serious collinearity.

Table 3.11 Poverty determinants of households in surveyed regions: Probit model estimation results (coefficients)

Variables	Coefficients	Standard deviation	Z	p>z
Northwest (1 = Northwest, and Southwest is the reference)	−0.18328	0.05361	−3.42000	0.00100
Distance from the village to the nearest county	0.00305	0.00093	3.29000	0.00100
Whether the village is located in suburban area (1 = yes)	−0.14029	0.09404	−1.49000	0.13600
Per capita net income of farmers in the village	−0.00004	0.00002	−2.78000	0.00500
In how many years among the recent five the village suffered from natural disasters	−0.05479	0.01292	−4.24000	0.00000
Relief rate of basic living allowances of the village	−0.00809	0.00227	−3.57000	0.00000
Coverage rate of new rural cooperative medical system (NCMS) of the village	−0.00386	0.00181	−2.13000	0.03300
Number of members	0.10314	0.02253	4.58000	0.00000
Age of household head	0.01057	0.00228	4.64000	0.00000
Ethnic minority household (1 = Han ethnicity household)	−0.37349	0.05460	−6.84000	0.00000
Household of CPC members (1 = CPC members)	−0.03067	0.07507	−0.41000	0.68300
Household of officials (1 = officials)	−0.30588	0.09293	−3.29000	0.00100
Physical condition of household head (1 = With disability and work, study and life affected)	0.25932	0.20313	1.28000	0.20200
Longest years of formal education of household members	0.00292	0.00891	0.33000	0.74300
The ratio of non-working age population to working-age population	0.01053	0.00168	6.26000	0.00000

(continued)

Table 3.11 (continued)

Variables	Coefficients	Standard deviation	Z	p>z
Per capita household financial asset balance (yuan)	−0.00005	0.00001	−5.45000	0.00000
Original value of per capita productive fixed assets (yuan)	−0.00001	0.00001	−2.49000	0.01300
Per capita actually operated land (mu)	−0.00039	0.00071	−0.55000	0.58200
Per capita area of farmland returned to forestry (mu)	−0.00672	0.00618	−1.09000	0.27700
The proportion of per laborer non-agricultural working hours to total household working hours	−1.19353	0.35482	−3.36000	0.00100
_cons	−0.94425	0.26887	−3.51000	0.00000
	Observed value = 5189 chi2(20) = 641.83Prob > chi2 = 0.0000Pseudo R^2 = 0.1426			

Fourth, the influences of economic capital possession on probability of poverty of surveyed households also conform with our experience in terms of direction, but vary in terms of significance. When other conditions are fixed, for every additional 10,000 yuan in per capita household financial asset balance, the probability of the household falling into poverty decreases by 9.01%, and this result is statistically significant ($p \leq 0.01$); for every additional 10,000 yuan in original value of per capita productive fixed assets, the probability of the household falling into poverty decreases by 2.67%, and this result is statistically significant ($0.05 \geq p > 0.01$); for every one percentage point increase in the proportion of per laborer non-agricultural working hours to total household working hours, the probability of the household falling into poverty decreases by 21.83%, and this result is statistically significant ($p \leq 0.01$). Moreover, for every additional *mu* in per capita actually operated land, the probability of the household falling into poverty decreases by 0.007%; and for every additional *mu* in per capita area of farmland returned to forestry, the probability of the household falling into poverty decreases by 0.12%. However, these two results are only applicable for the surveyed rural households, not statistically inferential ($p > 0.1$).

Fifth, all the controlled variables in the model have certain influences on the occurrence of poverty of the surveyed households, but the influence of each variable varies in terms of significance. In particular, when other conditions are fixed, for every additional kilometer in the village's distance from the nearest county, the probability of the household falling into poverty decreases by 0.56%, and this result is statistically significant ($p \leq 0.01$); compared with households living in suburban

Table 3.12 Poverty determinants of households in surveyed regions: probit model estimation results (marginal effect)

Variables	Coefficients	Standard deviation	Z	p>z
Northwest (1 = Northwest, and Southwest is the reference)	−0.03390	0.01016	−3.34000	0.00100
Distance from the village to the nearest county	0.00056	0.00017	3.30000	0.00100
Whether the village is located in suburban area (1 = yes)	−0.02382	0.01477	−1.61000	0.10700
Per capita net income of farmers in the village	−0.00001	0.00000	−2.78000	0.00500
In how many years among the recent five the village suffered from natural disasters	−0.01002	0.00239	−4.20000	0.00000
Relief rate of basic living allowances of the village	−0.00148	0.00042	−3.56000	0.00000
Coverage rate of new rural cooperative medical system (NCMS) of the village	−0.00071	0.00033	−2.12000	0.03400
Number of members	0.01887	0.00418	4.51000	0.00000
Age of household head	0.00193	0.00042	4.60000	0.00000
Ethnic minority household (1 = Han ethnicity household)	−0.06508	0.00915	−7.11000	0.00000
Household of CPC members (1 = CPC members)	−0.00553	0.01336	−0.41000	0.67900
Household of officials (1 = officials)	−0.04776	0.01223	−3.91000	0.00000
Physical condition of household head (1 = With disability and work, study and life affected)	0.05517	0.04944	1.12000	0.26400
Longest years of formal education of household members	0.00053	0.00163	0.33000	0.74300
The ratio of non-working age population to working-age population	0.00193	0.00031	6.21000	0.00000

(continued)

Table 3.12 (continued)

Variables	Coefficients	Standard deviation	Z	p>z
Per capita household financial asset balance (yuan)	−0.00001	0.00000	−5.73000	0.00000
Original value of per capita productive fixed assets (yuan)	0.00000	0.00000	−2.50000	0.01200
Per capita actually operated land (mu)	−0.00007	0.00013	−0.55000	0.58100
Per capita area of farmland returned to forestry (mu)	−0.00123	0.00111	−1.11000	0.26800
The proportion of per laborer non-agricultural working hours to total household working hours	−0.21834	0.06485	−3.37000	0.00100

Note Marginal effect (dF/dx) indicates the change of one unit of the independent variables or the change relative to the references

areas, the probability of those living in non-suburban areas falling into poverty is 2.38% higher, but this result is not statistically significant ($p > 0.1$); for every additional natural disaster in the recent five years, the probability of the household falling into poverty increases by 1.0%, and this result is statistically significant ($p \leq 0.01$); for every additional yuan in the per capita net income of the village, the probability of the household falling into poverty decreases by 0.001%, and this result is statistically significant ($p \leq 0.01$); for every additional percentage point in the relief rate of basic living allowances of the village,[21] the probability of the household falling into poverty decreases by 0.15%, and this result is statistically significant ($p \leq 0.01$); and for every additional percentage point in coverage rate of new rural cooperative medical system (NCMS) of the village, the probability of the household falling into poverty decreases by 0.07%, and this result is statistically significant ($0.05 \geq p > 0.01$).

2.5 Conclusions

In a nutshell, several main conclusions can be drawn.

First, based on the data of NBS, poverty alleviation in the eight ethnic minority provinces and regions shows a positive trend, but compared with the situation of the whole country, the current situation in these provinces and regions is still very severe.

[21] In this part, the relief rate of basic living allowances of the village = number of people entitled to basic living allowances / total population of the village * 100%; coverage rate of NCMS of the village = number of people covered by NCMS / total population of the village * 100%.

Second, based on CHES data, generally speaking, within the surveyed ethnic minority regions, rural households of different ethnicity or in different areas have differences in poverty headcount ratio, poverty gap and square poverty gap, and the provinces, regions and ethnic groups with greater poverty broadness also face greater poverty depth and intensity. In particular, among the seven surveyed provinces and regions, the three southwestern provinces and regions suffer more severe poverty than the four northwestern provinces and regions. Compared with other provinces and regions, Hunan and Guangxi suffer more severe rural poverty, while the problems in Inner Mongolia, Guizhou and Qinghai are relatively slight; compared with other ethnic groups, the surveyed households of Tujia, Uyghur and Salar people are more impoverished, while the poverty in surveyed households of Kazak, Mongol, Han and Tibetan people is slighter. In addition, the degree of rural poverty in the surveyed regions is sensitive to the changes in poverty lines, with all the three types of poverty indices increasing with the raised poverty line.

Third, ethnic minority households and impoverished households have something in common in terms of economic, natural and geographical conditions. The reason why ethnic minority households are relatively poorer than Han households lies in the fact that ethnic minority households mostly live in areas with adverse environment and underdeveloped economy and society. In other words, the ethnical differences in poverty distribution can largely be attributed to the differences in local conditions.

Fourth, impoverished households have more members, more children and a heavier burden, and the household head usually elder and less educated has poor health. From the perspective of demographic situation, ethnic minority households and impoverished households have something in common. In other words, the reason why ethnic minority households are poorer than Han households lies in such a demographic condition that ethnic minority households mostly have more members, more children, a heavier burden, and the household head usually elder and less educated has poor health.

Fifth, compared with non-impoverished households, impoverished households lack economic capital, which is demonstrated in insufficient per capita land area, shortage in productive fixed assets, unreasonable crop structure and relatively inadequate non-agricultural employment. In addition, compared with Han households, ethnic minority households possess insufficient economic capital.

Sixth, impoverished households in the surveyed rural areas suffer shortages in social resources.

Comparing the main poverty features and poverty determinants, we can find that these factors are both signs and causes of poverty. In summary, diverse factors influence the rural poverty in the surveyed ethnic minority regions, such as the natural geographical, social, cultural, family, policy and institutional factors. Among them, some factors in the living environment are hard to change in a short time, while some other factors can be improved through the efforts of external actors as well as the rural impoverished households themselves. Therefore, in anti-poverty campaigns, targeted and appropriate countermeasures shall be taken. For example, fragile ecosystem and insufficient public services are not only the main causes of temporary poverty in the surveyed regions, but also a main reason why it is hard to lift rural households in chronical poverty out of poverty. On this account, the government can put voluntary ecological migration high on the agenda of poverty alleviation policies. Additionally, in poverty alleviation through development, efforts should be made to improve local ecological environment and infrastructure development in combination with disaster prevention and relief so that the production and living conditions of impoverished villagers can be fundamentally improved, and risks that lead to poverty can be minimized. In this way, impoverished villagers can enter a sound track of poverty alleviation.

Chapter 4
Rural Poverty Alleviation and Development in Ethnic Minority Concentrated Areas—A Survey from a Macro Perspective

Since the policy of reform and opening up was introduced, especially in the twenty-first century, ethnic minority concentrated areas, like other rural areas in China, under the unified instructions of the central government, have taken a raft of measures for poverty alleviation and development and alleviated poverty by constantly improving and implementing the strategies of poverty alleviation. From a macroscopic perspective, this chapter focuses on practices of poverty alleviation in ethnic minority concentrated areas since the 11th Five-Year Plan period, so as to provide intellectual support for improving poverty alleviation policies in ethnic minority concentrated areas, achieving more scientific and effective poverty alleviation, and making up for weaknesses in building a moderately prosperous society in all respects.

1 The Practice of Poverty Alleviation and Development in Ethnic Minority Concentrated Areas

Since the beginning of the 11th Five-year Plan period, the poverty alleviation work in ethnic minority concentrated areas, which consists of special poverty alleviation, poverty elimination through industrial development and social participation in poverty alleviation and development, has become clear over time. First, in the aspect of special poverty alleviation, in ethnic minority concentrated areas, we carry out the poverty alleviation strategy with overall village-based poverty alleviation being the mainstay which is supplemented by poverty elimination through industrial development and poor laborer training. As a result, the infrastructures in poor rural areas have been improved, the comprehensive quality of the poor populations has been increased, and the ability of poverty elimination has been further enhanced. Second, in the aspects of poverty elimination through industrial development and social participation in poverty alleviation and development, ethnic minority concentrated areas have benefited more from governments at all levels, different industries,

X. Liu, *Complex Pictures of Poverty and Multiple Paths of Poverty Alleviation in Ethnic Areas of China*, https://doi.org/10.1007/978-981-97-4133-5_4

developed regions in eastern China and social institutions, a series of poverty alleviation projects have been implemented, and the work of poverty alleviation and development has delivered remarkable results.

1.1 Overall Village-Based Poverty Elimination

In the twenty-first century, the CPC Central Committee and the State Council released the *Guideline for China's Rural Poverty Alleviation and Development* (2001–2010), which states that "the Chinese government will give priority to poverty alleviation and development in ethnic minority concentrated areas in central and western regions, old revolutionary base areas, border areas and poor areas where the poor populations live in concentrated communities", and makes "strengthen basic cropland farming, infrastructure construction, environmental repair and restoration and construction of public service facilities based on poor townships and villages" the main content of and approach to poverty alleviation. In May 2008, the State Council clearly pointed out that "overall village-based poverty alleviation" is an important measure for poverty alleviation and development in the new era. Since then, the Chinese government has begun to launch the "overall village-based poverty alleviation" campaign and subsequently promoted it in the whole country including ethnic minority concentrated areas. At the end of 2011, the central government issued the *Guideline for China's Rural Poverty Alleviation and Development* (2011–2020), emphasizing that "overall village-based poverty alleviation" is an important part of China's efforts for special poverty alleviation and that China is beginning to carry out relevant work in an all-round way in poor rural areas, particularly ethnic minority concentrated areas.

For example, between 2011 and 2015, the overall village-based poverty elimination program has been carried out at over 2,000 poor villages in Xinjiang, effectively supporting 2.1 million poor people and meeting the basic needs of 1.74 million poor people.[1] During the 12th Five-Year Plan period, the government of Qinghai province carried out 368 projects for overall village-based poverty elimination and completed 1,972 projects for overall village-based poverty elimination.[2] Between 2014 and 2017, the government of Inner Mongolia carried out projects in and assigned officials to 2,834 poor villages, assisting poor villages and households in making plans and working out measures for poverty alleviation. In 2014 and 2015, it made an investment of 2.6 billion yuan in targeted poverty alleviation in poor villages in light of local conditions and achieved good results.[3]

---

[1] The Finance Department of Xinjiang Uygur Autonomous Region: Xinjiang's Poverty Alleviation Program Delivers Results through Fiscal Support, China State Finance, Issue 18, 2015.

[2] One Million Poor People Get Rid of Poverty in Qinghai in the 12th Five-Year Plan Period and 110 Thousand People Lifted out of Poverty in 2016, http:// news.ifeng.com/a/20160123/47200104_0.shtml; last access date: March 9, 2017.

[3] Fu Lijuan: Inner Mongolia Makes Remarkable Achievements in Poverty Alleviation through Development in the 12th Five-year Plan Period by Reducing 1.78 Million Poor People, February

1.2 Poverty Elimination Through Industrial Development

Poverty elimination through industrial development is an important part of China's special poverty alleviation and the main approach to increasing the self-development ability of the poor population and helping them overcome poverty and achieving prosperity. Through years of poverty elimination through industrial development, the rural industrial structure in ethnic minority concentrated areas has been improved, the industrial level of agriculture and animal husbandry has been enhanced, and the ability of poverty elimination of poor rural population has been further enhanced.

For example, in Guizhou Province, the poverty elimination through industrial development has progressed steadily. Since the 12th Five-year Plan period, Guizhou has invested a total of 6.65 billion yuan in the project of poverty elimination through industrial development, carried out more than 40,000 village-based industrial support projects, realized a total output value of 81.3 billion yuan, and formed a poverty alleviation pattern involving various industries.[4] Yunnan Province has been taking poverty elimination through industrial development as an important measure for accelerating poverty alleviation and development. Between 2011 and 2014, it spent a total of 924 million yuan in poverty alleviation, carried out 1,170 projects for poverty elimination with a total investment of 3.987 billion yuan, focused on supporting the development of traditional advantageous industries of vegetable, fruit, tobacco, tea, sugar, mulberry, gum, tobacco, and husbandry in poor counties and villages, energetically supported emerging and specialty industries of medicine, health food, flower, and coffee, etc., and launched 69 breeding projects, involving 3,881 poor village committees of 123 counties, assisting 542 thousand rural households (including 328 thousand poor households) in getting rid of poverty, and achieving an income increase of 2,552 yuan for each household.[5]

1.3 Poor Laborer Training

Poor laborer training is an important government-led program for poverty alleviation and development, and "the Dewdrop Project" is its main project. All ethnic minority provinces and autonomous regions, in accordance with their respective conditions, have carried out various poor laborer training projects in a targeted way, making certain contributions to poverty alleviation of poor farmers and herders in ethnic minority concentrated areas.

24, 2016, http://nm.people.com.cn/n2/2016/0224/c196689-27803017.html; last access date: March 9, 2017.

[4] Liu Zengbing: Guizhou as China's Main Battlefield Against Poverty -- A Summary of Poverty Alleviation and Development in Guizhou, Guizhou Daily, October 18, 2015.

[5] Hu Xiaorong, Zhuang Junhua: Grow Rich by Spurring Local Industrial Growth, Yunnan Daily, May 11, 2015.

For example, the government of Guangxi has been attaching great importance to poor laborer training and has trained poor laborers via multiple channels so as to enhance their employability. Between 2011 and the first half of 2013, Guangxi conducted practical technical training for 539,220 farmers and assisted 68,242 children from poor rural families in receiving vocational education.[6] In addition, during the 12th Five-Year Plan period, Guangxi invested 270 million yuan in implementing the Dewdrop Project, granted 213 million yuan to subsidize 58,800 students from poor families to receive academic education, implemented the pilot coordination program for vocational education through pairing assistance (Guangdong and Guangxi) and assisted a total of 803 poor students in studying in corresponding schools in the Guangdong, and arranged over 1,200 students to work as interns in Guangdong.[7] In 2006, Qinghai began to implement the "Dewdrop Project", and carried out academic and skills trainings in various forms to achieve the goal of promoting employment and increasing income. During the "11th Five-Year Plan" period, 23,000 poor laborers took part in the trainings organized by the government and basically attained the goals of employment and poverty elimination.[8] During the 12th Five-Year Plan period, Qinghai intensified its efforts to conduct trainings for transferring poor labor force. In 2014, Qinghai allocated 15 million yuan to carry out short-term skills training for 10,000 poor laborers, involving over 30 professions.[9]

1.4 Relocation of Poor Populations from Inhospitable Areas

It means relocating poor populations from inhospitable areas to other areas and assisting them in shaking off poverty and becoming rich over time by improving the working and living conditions of the areas they resettle, adjusting the economic structure and expanding the channels for income increase. Since the adoption of the 11th Five-year Plan, relevant authorities have released *The Opinions of the NDRC on Implementing the Pilot Project of Relocation of Poor Populations from Inhospitable Areas*, the *Notice of the NDRC on Issuing the 11th Five-Year Plan on Relocating*

[6] Guangxi Releases its 12th "Five-Year Plan" Interim Assessment Report on Development through Poverty Alleviation, Guangxi Daily, December 23, 2013.

[7] The Yearbook of China's Poverty Alleviation and Development (2015) compiled by The Yearbook of China's Poverty Alleviation and Development Editorial Board, The Unity Press, 2015; Guangxi Releases its 12th "Five-Year Plan" Interim Assessment Report on Development through Poverty Alleviation, Guangxi Daily, December 23, 2013; Poverty Alleviation Office of Guangxi Zhuang Autonomous Region: An Overview of the Poverty Alleviation and Development of Guangxi since the 12th Five-year Plan Period, www.xinhuanet.com, March 18, 2016, http://www.gx.xinhuanet.com/ topic/2015gxfp/2016-03/18/c_1118378734.htm; last access date: March 9, 2017.

[8] Qinghai Provincial Development and Reform Commission: *Qinghai's Program of Poverty Alleviation and Development in the 12th Five-year Plan Period*, http://xxgk.qh.gov.cn/fgw; last access date: March 9, 2017.

[9] The Yearbook of China's Poverty Alleviation and Development compiled by the Editorial Board of The Yearbook of China's Poverty Alleviation and Development (2012, 2014, 2015), The Unity Press, 2012, 2014, 2015.

Poor Populations from Inhospitable Areas, the 11th Five-Year Plan on Relocating Poor Populations from Inhospitable Areas, and *The 12th Five-Year Plan on Relocating Poor Populations from Inhospitable Areas*. In the principle of "carrying out trials before expansion", the relocation project has expanded its scope from Inner Mongolia, Guizhou, Yunnan and Ningxia at the very beginning to 17 provinces, municipalities and autonomous regions mainly covering the ethnic minority concentrated areas in western China. As of 2015, the central government had made an investment of 36.3 billion yuan in relocating more than 6.8 million poor people from inhospitable areas.[10] As of the start of the trial project of relocation of poor populations from inhospitable areas in the 10th Five-Year Plan period, the project has been successively implemented in all ethnic minority provinces and autonomous regions.

For example, Ningxia has begun to implement a project named "Diaozhuang relocation" since 1983, namely relocating some farmers from southern mountain areas to the northern plain areas for the purposes of relieving the population pressure in southern mountain areas and lifting poor farmers out of poverty. Between 1983 and 2000, Ningxia built 24 bases for "Diaozhuang relocation" in the Yellow River irrigation areas, tilled the land covering an area of 55,333 hectares, and relocated over 328,000 poor farmers (over 410 thousand persons if the 84 thousand persons covered by the projects for changing dry farmland into irrigable land are included).[11] During the 12th Five-Year Plan period, the NDRC allocated a total of 2.37 billion yuan as part of the central government budget for relocating 409,000 poor populations from inhospitable areas in Ningxia.[12]

In 1996, the relocation project was launched in Tibet for the purpose of poverty alleviation. Altogether 319 residents from the 45 poor households at Nixia Township of Dingri County took a lead in relocating themselves into the Changsuo Development Zone in the county. Between 2006 and 2008, the Tibetan government successively relocated 55 households froma remote village with inconvenient conditions to a place 12 km away from Changdu County.[13] In addition, the Tibetan government relocated the residents for the purpose of ecological protection. In 2001, the Tibetan government invested 8.3 million yuan in implementing the first batch of relocation projects for the protection of natural forests, resettling 948 poor farmers and herders from 144 households at six townships in Changdu Prefecture to four places of three

---

[10] NDRC Department of Policy Studies: *NDRC Makes Remarkable Achievements in Relocation of Poor Populations from Inhospitable Areas*, http://www.gov.cn/xinwen/2015-10/18/content_2948739.htm; last access date: March 9, 2017.

[11] Kong Weili: A Summary of Studies on the Relocation of Diaozhuang Village in Ningxia, Social Sciences in Ningxia, Issue 6, 2000.

[12] NDRC Department of Regional Economy: *NDRC Support Relocation of Poor Populations from Inhospitable Areas in Ningxia*, http://dqs.ndrc.gov.cn/gzdt/201503/t20150311_667078.html; last access date: March 9, 2017.

[13] Xu Jun: Parting and Attachment – A Survey on Relocated Villages in Xizang and Other Xizang Regions Through Poverty Alleviation, Journal of Tibet University (Social Science Edition), Issue 4, 2011; Dawa Tsering, Tsering, You Yuanyuan, Cangmula, Tenzin, Fang Xiaoling: A Brief Account of the Relationship between Relocation for Poverty Alleviation and Ecological Migration in Tibet, Tibetan Studies, Issue 5, 2014.

counties in Linzhi.[14] In addition, relocation measures have been taken in the major areas suffering Kashin-Beck disease in Lhasa, Rikaze and Changdu in Tibet. As of 2007, nearly 20,000 people of about 3,760 households had been relocated.[15]

1.5 Poverty Elimination Through Industrial Development

Since 2001 and especially since the "12th Five-year Plan" period, relevant departments actively performed their duties, gave full play to their advantages, released a raft of special policies on poor ethnic minority concentrated areas, and intensified their efforts for poverty elimination through industrial development.

The National Development and Reform Commission (NDRC) plays a leading role in poverty elimination through industrial development. During the 12th Five-Year Plan period, the NDRC gave priority to economic and social development in ethnic minority concentrated areas, strengthened and improved in due course the approaches to planning, policies, capital and comprehensive coordination, ensured that the people of all ethnic groups can share more fruits of development in a better way, and laid a solid foundation for poverty reduction in ethnic minority concentrated areas. During the 12th Five-Year Plan period, the NDRC took a lead in formulating the *12th Five-year Plan on the National Basic Public Services System*, emphasizing giving more support to ethnic minority concentrated areas. In addition, it took a lead in formulating the *12th Five-year Plan on Settlement of Herdsmen*, worked with relevant departments to develop for the first time regional policy documents and special plans on the development of the eight provinces and autonomous regions where ethnic minorities live in concentrated communities, introduced the *Plan on the Ningxia Inland Opening-up Pilot Economic Zone* and the *Plan on the Development of the Economic Belts on the Northern Slope of the Tianshan Mountains*, established key development and opening-up pilot economic zones in Dongxing (Guangxi), Ruili (Yunnan), Mengla (Mohan), Manzhouli (Inner Mongolia) and Erenhot (Inner Mongolia) and released implementation plans on the economic zones. The NDRC studied and drafted the *Opinions on Several Major Policies on and Measures for Supporting the Revitalization of Northeast China* and reported it to the State Council, which specified that the five leagues and cities in eastern Inner Mongolia and the three provinces in northeast China enjoy the same policies. In addition, during the 12th Five-Year Plan period, the NDRC arranged a total of 67.2 billion yuan (included in the central government budget) for ethnic minority concentrated areas and implemented a series of special social programs in education, healthcare, culture, tourism, and aged-care insurance, effectively improving the conditions of public services such as

---

[14] Dawa Tsering, Tsering, You Yuanyuan, Cangmula, Tenzin, Fang Xiaoling: A Brief Account of the Relationship between Relocation for Poverty Alleviation and Ecological Migration in Tibet, Tibetan Studies, Issue 5, 2014.

[15] Dawa Tsering, Tsering, You Yuanyuan, Cangmula, Tenzin, Fang Xiaoling: A Brief Account of the Relationship between Relocation for Poverty Alleviation and Ecological Migration in Xizang, Tibetan Studies, Issue 5, 2014.

access to education, medical services, and cultural entertainments in ethnic minority concentrated areas and laying a solid foundation for effectively reducing poverty in ethnic minority concentrated areas.[16]

The Ministry of Agriculture has been attaching great importance to rural economic development in ethnic minority concentrated areas and has made positive contributions to the agricultural and pastoral development, income increase of farmers and herders and poverty elimination in ethnic minority concentrated areas. During the 12th Five-Year Plan period, the Ministry of Agriculture, together with the NDRC and the Ministry of Finance, arranged a total of 110.68 billion yuan for various project investments in the five ethnic autonomous regions. Specifically, a total of 23.07 billion yuan was invested in capital construction, focusing on ecological and environmental protection projects for turning marginal farmland into forest or grassland, agricultural service system including community-level service system for spreading agricultural technology, as well as production and development projects related to grain and livestock and fowl breeding. A special fund of 87.61 billion yuan was used as subsidies for cultivating superior varieties and breeds, general subsidies for agricultural materials, and subsidies for grassland ecological conservation, training on transfer of rural laborers and training of new-type skilled farmers. In addition, since 2011, the central government of China has established a subsidy and award mechanism for grassland ecological conservation in the eight major pastoral areas in Ningxia, Inner Mongolia, Xinjiang, Tibet, Qinghai, Sichuan, and Yunnan to subsidize or reward grazing prohibition, balance between forage and livestock, production and performance assessment, not only protecting local grassland ecology, but also ensuring the supply of basic necessities for the local herders by giving them certain subsidies.[17]

The National Health Commission (hereinafter referred to as the "NHC"), in the principles of "focusing on general projects, giving priority to trial projects, and giving special support to projects for which no specific policy has been made", gives priority to ethnic minority concentrated areas and has made great efforts for poverty elimination through industrial development. For example, first, during the 12th Five-Year Plan period, the central government made a special investment of 29.11 billion yuan in supporting infrastructure construction of 27,620 health and family planning service institutions in ethnic minority concentrated areas, and the infrastructure and conditions of such institutions in ethnic minority concentrated areas were improved; second, in order to enhance the medical and health service capabilities in ethnic

[16] The Yearbook of China's Poverty Alleviation and Development compiled by the Editorial Board of The Yearbook of China's Poverty Alleviation and Development (2012, 2014, 2015), The Unity Press, 2012, 2014, 2015; New Practices of Services for Ethnic Minorities (4)—A Report from the National Development and Reform Commission, The official WeChat Account of the National Ethnic Affairs Commission of China, March 3, 2016.

[17] The Yearbook of China's Poverty Alleviation and Development compiled by the Editorial Board of The Yearbook of China's Poverty Alleviation and Development (2012, 2014, 2015), The Unity Press, 2012, 2014, 2015; New Practices of Services for Ethnic Minorities (5)—A Report from the National Development and Reform Commission, The official WeChat Account of the National Ethnic Affairs Commission of China, March 4, 2016.

minority concentrated areas, the NHC has opened ethnic minority classes at medical colleges and universities in five provinces, municipalities and autonomous regions including Beijing and Shanghai, organized special medical qualification examinations for Uygur, Mongolian, Tibetan and Dai physicians, and set the cutoff line separately for physician qualification examinations in Tibet and Qinghai, greatly increasing the quantity and medical practice level of ethnic minority physicians. Third, in order to strengthen disease prevention and control in ethnic minority concentrated areas and prevent people from falling into poverty due to illness, the NHC supported prevention and control of major infectious diseases and endemic diseases in ethnic minority concentrated areas, and carried out the national immunization programs. Fourth, the NHC offered public health services in ethnic minority concentrated areas in an all-around way. In 2015, in ethnic minority concentrated areas, the per-capita budgetary subsidy for basic public health services was raised to 40 yuan, and 11 types of basic public health services were fully implemented.[18]

In addition, in China many other industrial sectors have carried out poverty elimination programs through industrial development in ethnic minority concentrated areas and achieved certain results. We will not list them here.

1.6 Social Participation in Poverty Alleviation and Development

Pooling the strength of the whole society has been one of the important principles of China's poverty alleviation work. Since the 1980s, China has preliminarily developed a system for social participation in poverty alleviation and development, which is guided by assistance for targeted poor areas, collaboration on poverty alleviation between the eastern and western regions, and poverty alleviation by relying on the PLA army and armed police forces, and the poverty alleviation is extensively participated in by private enterprises, social organizations and individuals. Specifically, Guangxi, Ningxia, Inner Mongolia, Qinghai, Guizhou and Yunnan are important battlefields of China's efforts for rural poverty alleviation and development and important places for social participation in poverty alleviation and development, and fruitful results have been made in social participation in poverty alleviation and development in these provinces and autonomous regions.

For example, through the implementation of the 12th Five-year Plan, Guangxi has carried out programs of social participation in poverty alleviation and development at different levels and via different channels, making remarkable achievements. Regarding assistance for targeted poor areas, during the 12th Five-year Plan period, a total of 204 units directly under the central government or directly under the government of Guangxi Zhuang Autonomous Region engaged in assistance for targeted poor areas. At the end of 2014, each key county of Guangxi covered by the national/autonomous regional programs of poverty alleviation and development was

[18] Ditto.

supported by at least three units directly under the central government or directly under the government of Guangxi Zhuang Autonomous Region. Between 2011 and 2013, over 4.7 billion yuan has been invested for assistance in poverty alleviation. In addition, the army stationed in Guangxi also took active part in assistance for targeted poor areas, making an investment of nearly 60 million yuan in helping 136 villages. In the aspect of collaboration on poverty alleviation between the eastern and western regions, Guangdong provided Guangxi a special fund of 20 million yuan each year in the 11th Five-year Plan period and 35 million yuan each year in the 12th Five-Year Plan period. As of the end of 2014, Guangdong provided Guangxi with funds and goods for free equivalent to 47.5712 million yuan, and assisted the latter in holding 13 training sessions for 885 persons. In addition, good results were made in other social participation in poverty alleviation and development programs. During the 12th Five-Year Plan period, the World Bank and the Department for International Development invested 14.37 million yuan in the "Poor Rural Community Development Project", directly benefiting over 40,000 rural households in Guangxi who had participated in the project.[19]

Both Xinjiang and Tibet are regions with special ecological, political and economic conditions, which determine not only the particularity of their development goals and approaches, but also the particularity of their social participation in poverty alleviation and development. The social participation in poverty alleviation and development in Xinjiang and Tibet consists of governmental assistance for targeted poor areas, non-governmental poverty alleviation, as well as programs for aiding Xinjiang and Tibet in poverty alleviation. Next, we will focus on poverty alleviation in Xinjiang and Tibet.

As Xinjiang has a special position, the Chinese government and the people of all ethnic groups in China have already reached a consensus that "supporting Xinjiang's development is to safeguard the motherland. A prosperous Xinjiang ensures stability and prosperity in China's northwest borders and benefits the entire China and the Chinese nation". Hence, we must make supporting Xinjiang's development a national strategy that must be steadily adhered to. "Supporting Xinjiang's development" has increased the level of economic and social development of Xinjiang; moreover, it facilitates poverty reduction in poor areas and poor populations in Xinjiang. Particularly, since 2010, the central government of China has started a new round of pairing assistance to Xinjiang, adjusting the previous instructions in many aspects. Specifically, 19 provinces and municipalities offered the 12 prefectures of Xinjiang and 12 divisions of the Xinjiang Production and Construction Corps assistance through pairing programs, focusing on basic-level communities and southern Xinjiang. Nine provinces and cities including Beijing, Guangdong, Shenzhen, Tianjin, Jiangsu,

[19] The Yearbook of China's Poverty Alleviation and Development compiled by the Editorial Board of The Yearbook of China's Poverty Alleviation and Development (2012, 2014, 2015), The Unity Press, 2012, 2014, 2015; Wei Jichuan: Guangxi Deepens Social Poverty Alleviation and Makes New Ground in "Great Poverty Alleviation", the portal website of the People's Republic of China, http://www.gov.cn/gzdt/2012-02/07/content_2060102.htm; Tang Zhuo: Guangxi Makes New Breakthroughs in Educational and Social Poverty Alleviation, www.mzb.com.cn, December 12, 2014, http://www.mzb.com.cn/html/report/141230169-1.htm.

Shanghai and Shandong which have great economic strengths were assigned to support the three prefectures in southern Xinjiang suffering deeper poverty through pairing programs. Moreover, priority has been given to major construction projects in and investment plans for the three prefectures in southern Xinjiang. Obviously, one of the important tasks for the central government's new round of pairing programs for aiding Xinjiang is to lift the autonomous region out of poverty. According to statistics, between 2010 and 2014, 19 relevant provinces and municipalities, the central government, enterprises and public institutions earmarked aid funds totaling 47 billion yuan, and implemented 4,139 projects for aiding Xinjiang. As of the end of 2014, through the new round of pairing programs for aiding Xinjiang, 2,636 projects were carried out to bring in nearly 30,000 officials and talents and 776,200 persons were trained, which enhanced the talent development of Xinjiang. By means of the programs for assisting Xinjiang, a number of labor-intensive industrial companies made investments in Xinjiang, spurring local economic development and creating lots of jobs for local residents. In addition, Guangdong intensifies its efforts to support Xinjiang and encourages laborers in Xinjiang to work in coastal developed areas including Guangdong. For example, during the 12th Five-Year Plan period, Guangdong assisted a local agency for export of labor services in transferring over 100,000 local residents to work in other places in Xinjiang and over 16,000 local residents to work outside Xinjiang, of whom more than 3,000 people were transferred to work in Guangdong.[20]

Since the peaceful liberation of Tibet in 1951, the central government has taken a raft of support measures in Tibet. Notably, since 1980, the CPC Central Committee has held six forums on the work of Tibet, formed the regional development strategy of "national aid for Tibet" by mainly relying on the support from the central government and assistance through pairing programs, and worked out over time a series of measures for fiscal subsidies, tax preference, aiding project construction, financial investment preferences, and education aid, etc. Especially, at the third symposium on the Tibetan work held in 1994, the Chinese government decided to establish a system for aiding Tibet through pairing programs in the forms of "zoning, pairing, and periodic rotation". Between 2001 and 2008, the central government's fiscal subsidies for Tibet amounted to 104.6 billion yuan, and the other aids for Tibet (including funds for assistance through pairing programs and special funds) amounted to 120 billion yuan. The total aid for Tibet during the period is almost the total aiding funds for Tibet from the peaceful liberation of Tibet to the end of the twentieth century.[21] During the 12th Five-Year Plan period, the Tibetan government made the best use of

[20] Yu Yang: 'In a Concerted Effort' (A Stride in Xinjiang over the Past 60 Years) – A Record of the New Round of Work for Aiding Xinjiang Through Pairing Programs, The People's Daily, September 12, 2015; Aids for Xinjiang Through Pairing Programs Deliver Tangible Results (A Stride in Xinjiang over the Past 60 Years), The People's Daily, September 12, 2015.

[21] Wang Zhiwei, Ruan Pingnan: The Evolution Process of the Development Model of "Aiding Xizang", Regional Economy, Issue 12, 2012; Pan Jiuyan, Zhou Hongfang: "Aiding Xizang: Path of Reform and Policy Response", Journal of CPC Sichuan Committee Provincial Party School, Issue 2, 2010; Zou Debin: The Thoughts on Social Poverty Alleviation in Xizang in the New Era, Xin Xizang, Issue 12, 2014.

the pairing programs and vigorously carried out poverty alleviation. As a result, 80% of the funds for assistance to Tibet were spent in agricultural and pastoral areas, and special funds for aiding Tibet were earmarked for poverty alleviation and development in some regions. At present, "aid for Tibet for poverty alleviation" has become an important part of social participation in poverty alleviation and development in Xizang.[22]

2 Effects and Achievements of Poverty Alleviation and Development in Ethnic Minority Concentrated Areas

Considering the conditions and characteristics of the poverty in ethnic minority concentrated areas, under the unified instructions of the central government and local governments and under the support of all walks of life, the ethnic minority concentrated areas targeted for promoting economic and social development in poor areas and for lifting poor people out of poverty, implemented various poverty alleviation projects and made certain achievements.

2.1 The Poor Population Reduces Rapidly and Poverty Relief Accelerates in Ethnic Minority Concentrated Areas

From the above we can see that, due to the large poor population in various ethnic minority concentrated areas, there is a serious problem of poverty. Thanks to the continuous government support to ethnic minority concentrated areas, particularly since the CPC's 18th National Congress, the central government has significantly increased its support for ethnic minority concentrated areas and achieved notable results.

First, between 2000 and 2010, in accordance with the poverty line of the year, the rural population in the eight provinces and autonomous regions where ethnic minorities live in concentrated communities dropped from 31.44 million to 10.34 million (see Fig. 4.1), down by 21.1 million. The poverty headcount ratio decreased from 23% to 8.7% (see Fig. 4.2), down by 14.3% points; the difference between the poverty headcount ratio and the national average level dropped from 12.8% points to 5.9% points.[23]

Second, between 2011 and 2017, in accordance with the new poverty line (2,300 yuan, the price in 2010), the rural population in the eight provinces and autonomous

---

[22] Wu Haibo: *Tibet Goes All Out to Create a New Integrated Paradigm for Poverty Alleviation*, www.huanqiu.com, January 7, 2016, http://china.huanqiu.com/hot/2016-01/8338631.html; last access date: March 9, 2017.

[23] *The Poverty Monitoring Report of Rural China·2011* compiled by the Department of Household Survey of the National Bureau of Statistics of China, China Statistics Press, 2012, p. 61.

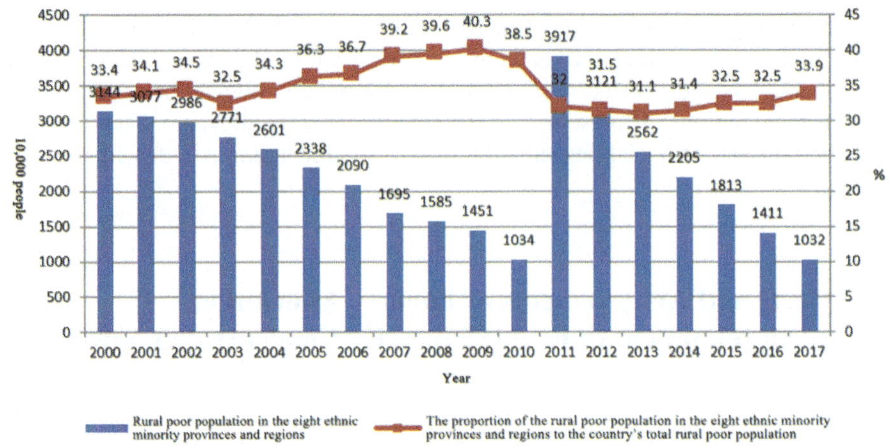

Fig. 4.1 A comparison between the rural poor population of ethnic minority concentrated areas and that of the whole country. *Source of data* sorted and calculated on the basis of the materials below: 2000–2008 data are based on relevant data in *2011 Poverty Monitoring Report of Rural China*. 2009–2015 data are based on the Economic Development Department of the National Ethnic Affairs Commission of the People's Republic of China: "The National Ethnic Affairs Commission Releases the Rural Poverty Monitoring Results in Ethnic Minority Areas in 2014", http://www.seac.gov.cn/art/2015/4/15/art_31_225897.html; "The National Ethnic Affairs Commission of the People's Republic of China releases the information on rural poverty in ethnic minority concentrated areas in 2015", the official website of the National Ethnic Affairs Commission of the People's Republic of China, April 11, 2016, http://www.seac.gov.cn/art/2016/4/11/art_31_251389.html

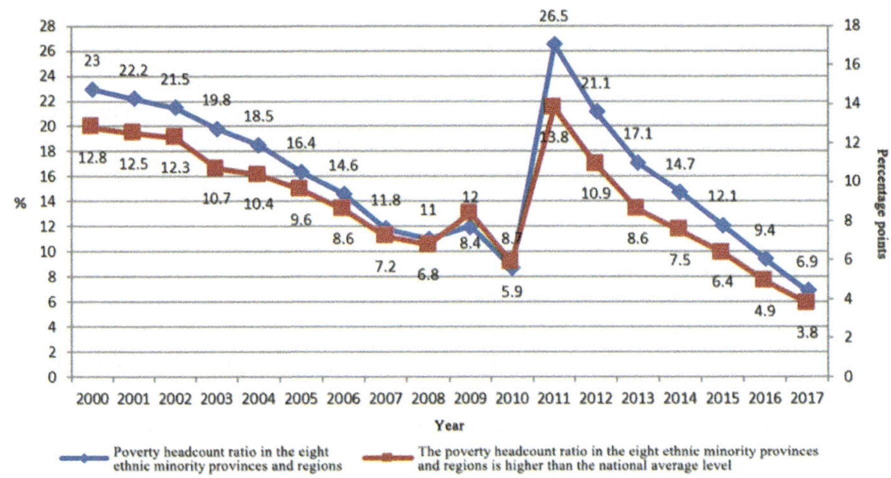

Fig. 4.2 A comparison between the rural poverty headcount ratio of ethnic minority concentrated areas and that of the whole country. *Source of data* same with that of Fig. 4.1

regions where ethnic minorities live in concentrated communities dropped from 39.17 million to 10.32 million over time, a decline of 28.85 million; the poverty headcount ratio dropped from 26.5% to 6.9%, the difference between the poverty headcount ratio and the national average level declined from 13.8% points to 3.8% points.

2.2 *The Working and Living Conditions and Social Programs in Poor Ethnic Minority Concentrated Areas*[24] *Have Improved Significantly*

Thanks to the implementation of the above poverty alleviation policies, the working and living conditions of poor ethnic minority concentrated areas have been significantly improved, the production capacity has been greatly enhanced, and the poverty alleviation efforts have delivered results in the following aspects.

First, the infrastructure in poor ethnic minority concentrated areas has been steadily improved. As is seen from infrastructure conditions, in 2017, in the poor areas in the eight provinces and autonomous regions where ethnic minorities live in concentrated communities, nearly all passageways and trunk roads were hardened (see Table 4.1), the communication infrastructure conditions improved continuously, villages' access to telephone and cable TV signals improved significantly. In the year, nearly all the residents in poor areas in the eight provinces and autonomous regions where ethnic minorities live in concentrated communities have access to telephone, and most rural residents living in natural villages can receive cable TV signals. Although the public transport in rural areas is not very convenient yet, it has improved to a certain extent compared with that in the previous year. For example, in 2017, the proportion of farming households that have convenient access to public bus in natural villages of poor rural areas in Guangxi, Guizhou, Yunnan, Qinghai and Ningxia was respectively 2.1% points, 7.5% points, 1.8% points, 5.2% points and 1.4% points higher than that in 2016.

Second, the cultural, health and education in poor areas keep improving. As is seen from the convenience of access to education, the educational service in poor rural ethnic minority concentrated areas continues to improve. In 2017, in the eight provinces and autonomous regions where ethnic minorities live in concentrated communities, more than 75% of the rural households of natural villages had convenient access to kindergarten or preschool education (see Table 4.2), 74% of the rural households of natural villages had convenient access to primary school education; both of the above two numbers were higher than those in 2016. As is seen from sanitation, in 2017, the natural villages where more than 44% of the rural households were located could conduct centralized waste disposal, and the natural villages where

[24] Poor areas include contiguous poor areas and national key counties for poverty alleviation beyond the contiguous poor areas. Poor ethnic minority concentrated areas include the contiguous poor areas in the eight provinces and autonomous regions where ethnic minorities live in concentrated communities and national key counties for poverty alleviation beyond the contiguous areas.

Table 4.1 Infrastructure status in poor ethnic minority concentrated areas in 2016 and 2017 Unit: %

	Proportion of farming households in natural villages with highway		Proportion of farming households in natural villages with telephone access		Proportion of farming households in natural villages with cable television signal		Proportion of farming households in natural villages with hardened trunk road		Proportion of farming households in natural villages with convenient access to public bus	
	2016	2017	2016	2017	2016	2017	2016	2017	2016	2017
Total	99.8	99.9	99.9	99. 8	94.2	96.9	96	97.6	63.9	67.5
Inner Mongolia	100	100	100	100	95.7	99.6	93.8	94.8	85.8	85.1
Guangxi	100	99.6	100	99.6	89.1	88.7	96.6	98.2	47	49.1
Guizhou	100	100	100	100	93	97	96.6	97.2	59	66.5
Yunnan	100	100	99.9	100	95.1	97.1	88.3	92.6	47.6	49.4
Tibet	100	100	100	99	81.8	77	97.4	100	55.3	51
Qinghai	97.3	97.3	97.1	97.1	80.2	89.5	96	96.9	71.6	76.8
Ningxia	100	100	100	100	92.3	96	100	100	85.4	86.8
Xinjiang	100	100	100	100	85.1	94	93.3	100	76.1	74.7

Source of data Poverty monitoring report of rural China (2017), poverty monitoring report of rural China (2018)

more than 73% of the rural households were located had medical stations (clinics); both of the above two numbers were higher than those in 2016. Such data show that the health and educational conditions in poor ethnic minority concentrated areas are relatively poor, but are improving over time.

Third, the living facilities of farmers in poor areas have been improved. In 2017, in the eight provinces and autonomous regions where ethnic minorities live in concentrated communities, 52% of the farmers had access to tap water (see Table 4.3), over 80% of the farming households had no difficulty in access to drinking water, over 71% of the farming households owned their private toilets, higher than those proportions in 2016. In addition, less than 70% of the rural households used firewood for cooking in 2017, lower than the figure in 2016. All of these show that the living condition of the farmers in poor ethnic minority concentrated areas is relatively poor, but it is steadily improving.

Fourth, so far, almost all residents in ethnic minority concentrated areas have been covered by the basic old-age insurance system, the basic medical insurance system and the major disease insurance scheme for non-working urban residents and the rural population. With the insurance programs' coverage expanding, the poor people have a growing sense of fulfilment.

Table 4.2 Health and educational conditions of poor areas in 2016 and 2017 Unit: %

	Proportion of farming households in natural villages capable of centralized waste disposal		Proportion of farming households in natural villages with medical stations (clinics)		Proportion of farming households in natural villages with convenient access to kindergarten education		Proportion of farming households in natural villages with convenient access to primary school education	
	2016	2017	2016	2017	2016	2017	2016	2017
Total	50.9	61.4	91.4	92.2	79.7	84.7	84.9	88.0
Inner Mongolia	53.4	57.1	95.4	97.7	70.1	75.6	71.8	74.8
Guangxi	80.7	85.4	80.3	81.5	84.5	86.5	91.3	92.5
Guizhou	48.3	57.5	95.2	97.1	78.1	87.6	88.6	93.4
Yunnan	37.2	44.9	84.8	84.9	73.7	80.1	83.3	86.5
Tibet	53.1	62.7	91.3	73.0	83.4	90.2	94.7	95.1
Qinghai	42.7	60.1	94.7	94.8	85.6	86.9	88.2	91.8
Ningxia	34.7	45.8	93.7	96.0	77.6	87.8	89.1	90.3
Xinjiang	39.0	66.3	93.3	94.8	95.0	97.5	94.6	96.6

Source of data The poverty monitoring report of rural China (2017), the poverty monitoring report of rural China (2018)

Table 4.3 Changes of housing and home facilities of rural households in the poor areas between 2014 and 2017 Unit: %

	Proportion of farming households with piped water supply		Proportion of farming households without difficulty in drinking water supply		Proportion of farming households with private toilets		Proportion of farming households with firewood for cooking	
	2014	2017	2014	2017	2014	2017	2014	2017
Total	55.9	70.1	82.3	89.2	93.1	94.5	57.8	49.7
Inner Mongolia	35.2	52.5	91.6	93.5	91.4	91.0	77.5	70
Guangxi	76.5	85.9	87.3	90.3	95.3	98.1	67.9	55.2
Guizhou	67.9	83.1	73.7	90.3	92.2	95.3	35.7	21.1
Yunnan	71.2	77.3	72.6	80.3	79.8	82.6	54.5	48.1
Tibet	50.0	60.7	64.8	81.0	69.4	71.2	68.2	54.7
Qinghai	77.0	86.7	84.9	92.7	93.0	92.5	37.5	19.8
Ningxia	58.3	72.3	88.7	92.2	97.8	98.7	31.0	14.4
Xinjiang	89.3	87.2	91.8	90.1	97.1	98.8	56.7	44.9

Source of data Yearbook of China's poverty alleviation and development (2015), the poverty monitoring report of rural China (2018)

3 Difficulties and Challenges of Poverty Alleviation and Development in Ethnic Minority Concentrated Areas

Since the 1980s, under the unified arrangement of the CPC Central Committee, large-scale poverty alleviation and development work has been launched in ethnic minority concentrated areas in an organized and planned way, and great achievement has been made. Nevertheless, China has to face various difficulties and challenges in poverty alleviation and development in ethnic minority concentrated areas.

3.1 At Present, the Poor Population in China's Ethnic Minority Concentrated Areas is Large and Widely Scattered, and the Poverty Varies Within the Poor Population

In 2017, China still had 10.32 million people living under the poverty line in ethnic minority concentrated areas, with a poverty headcount ratio of 6.9%, 3.8% higher than the national average level. Specifically, in 2017, seven provinces, municipalities or autonomous regions had a poor population of two million; among them three are in the eight provinces and autonomous regions where ethnic minorities live in concentrated communities, namely Guangxi, Guizhou and Yunnan (see Table 4.4); five provinces, municipalities or autonomous regions had a poverty headcount ratio of 7% or above; among them four are provinces and autonomous regions where ethnic minorities live in concentrated communities. Specifically, the poverty headcount ratio of Xinjiang was 9.9%, 3.2 times that of the average level of China. As is seen from within ethnic minority concentrated areas, the poverty status varies evidently. For example, in 2017, the poverty headcount ratio in rural areas in Xinjiang was 3.7 times that in Inner Mongolia.

3.2 The Implementation Effects of Poverty Alleviation Policies in Ethnic Minority Concentrated Areas Need to be Improved

We have made an analysis on the "survey data in ethnic minority concentrated areas" for 2014, and the results show that rural residents in such areas are not so satisfied with poverty alleviation and development. Specifically, amongst all rural respondents, only 60.8% are satisfied with the overall situation of poverty alleviation and

Table 4.4 Rural poor population and poverty headcount ratio across China and in the eight provinces and autonomous regions where ethnic minorities live in concentrated communities between 2010 and 2017 Unit: 10,000 persons, %

Year		Whole country	Eight provinces and autonomous regions where ethnic minorities live in concentrated communities	Inner Mongolia	Guangxi	Guizhou	Yunnan	Tibet	Qinghai	Ningxia	Xinjiang
2010	Poor population	16,567	5040	258	1012	1521	1468	117	118	77	469
	Poverty headcount ratio	17.2	34.1	19.7	24.3	45.1	40	49.2	31.5	18.3	44.6
2011	Poor population	12,238	3917	160	950	1149	1014	106	108	77	353
	Poverty headcount ratio	12.7	26.5	12.2	22.6	33.4	27.3	43.9	28.5	18.3	32.9
2012	Poor population	9899	3121	139	755	923	804	85	82	60	273
	Poverty headcount ratio	10.2	20.8	10.6	18	26.8	21.7	35.2	21.6	14.2	25.4
2013	Poor population	8249	2562	114	634	745	661	72	63	51	222
	Poverty headcount ratio	8.5	17.1	8.5	14.9	21.3	17.8	28.8	16.4	12.5	19.8
2014	Poor population	7012	2205	98	540	623	574	61	52	45	212
	Poverty headcount ratio	7.2	14.7	7.3	12.6	18	15.5	23.7	13.4	10.8	18.6
2015	Poor population	5575	1813	76	452	507	471	48	42	37	180
	Poverty headcount ratio	5.7	12.1	5.6	10.5	14.7	12.7	18.6	10.9	8.9	15.8
2016	Poor population	4335	1411	53	341	402	373	34	31	30	147

(continued)

Table 4.4 (continued)

Year		Whole country	Eight provinces and autonomous regions where ethnic minorities live in concentrated communities	Inner Mongolia	Guangxi	Guizhou	Yunnan	Tibet	Qinghai	Ningxia	Xinjiang
	Poverty headcount ratio	4.5	9.4	3.9	7.9	11.6	10.1	13.2	8.1	7.1	12.8
2017	Poor population	3046	1032	37	246	295	279	20	23	19	113
	Poverty headcount ratio	3.1	6.9	2.7	5.7	8.5	7.5	7.9	6	4.5	9.9

Source of data Poverty monitoring report of Rural China (2017), the official website of the National Ethnic Affairs Commission of the People's Republic of China, August 17, 2018, http://whxcs.seac.gov.cn/seac/xxgk/201808/1101635.shtml

development, which is barely satisfactory.[25] Therefore, as is seen from at least the subjective assessment of rural residents in ethnic minority concentrated areas, the performance of rural poverty alleviation and development in ethnic minority concentrated areas needs to be improved. Currently, some rural poor populations in ethnic minority concentrated areas cannot or can hardly benefit from poverty alleviation policies, so about 40% of the people are dissatisfied with the implementation effects of poverty alleviation policies.

3.3 The Trend of the Increasing Ratio of the Poor Population in Ethnic Minority Concentrated Areas has Not Been Completely Reversed

Between 2000 and 2009, the proportion of the rural poor population in the eight provinces and autonomous regions where ethnic minorities live in concentrated communities in China's total rural poor population increased from 33.4% to 40.3%, showing a clear trend of increasing ratio of rural poor population in ethnic minority concentrated areas. The proportion declined from 32% in 2011 to 31.5% in 2012 and 31.1% in 2013, but increased to 31.4% in 2014 and 33.9% in 2017. As thus, the increasing tendency of the ratio of rural poor population in ethnic minority concentrated areas was reversed in the first two years, but it began to increase in the following years.

4 Policy Suggestions

Since the 18th National Congress of the CPC, the central government has proposed a lot of new ideas, new concepts and new strategies for targeted poverty alleviation over time. General Secretary Jinping Xi has pointed out: "targeted poverty alleviation is an important approach to solving such problems as unclear population size, inaccurate target and poor effect in the work of poverty alleviation and development. In the actual work, we shall take targeted and dynamic measures to identify and support poor people, ensuring that poverty alleviation reaches those who truly need it and delivers genuine outcomes for poor villages and poor households."[26] In light of the current development situation and poverty characteristics of rural ethnic

[25] Liu Xiaomin: An study on the performance evaluation of rural poverty and development in ethnic minority concentrated areas from the perspective of rural households' satisfaction: An analysis on the survey data of ethnic minority concentrated areas in 2014, Ethno-National Studies, Issue 2, 2016.

[26] Liu Yongfu: Fight the battle against poverty and finish building a moderately prosperous society in all respectsEarenestly study and implement the guiding principles of Jinping Xi's important speeches on poverty alleviation and development, People's Daily, April 9, 2014.

minority concentrated areas as well as the problems existing in poverty alleviation and development, we should adhere to the strategy of targeted poverty alleviation in the future and make sure that measures are taken in light of local conditions.

(I) Grasp the opportunities to accelerate economic development in ethnic minority concentrated areas. Economic development is a fundamental way to reduce and eliminate poverty and the most important driving force for poverty elimination in ethnic minority concentrated areas. The 13th Five-Year Plan period is a crucial period for China to achieve its goal of finishing building a moderately prosperous society in all respects. To achieve the great goal, the central government has adopted a raft of policies and measures to improve the layout of development across regions and promote economic development in ethnic minority concentrated areas, for examples, by formulating and implementing the 13th Five-year Plan on the large-scale development of the western region, and by supporting the development of ethnic minority concentrated areas, border areas and poor areas. It can be said that the 13th Five-Year Plan period is an important period of strategic opportunities for the economic and social development in ethnic minority concentrated areas. Therefore, we must grasp the opportunities to accelerate the economic development in ethnic minority concentrated areas and help poor areas and poor people get rid of poverty.

(II) Conscientiously take relevant measures for poverty alleviation. On October 16, 2015, General Secretary Jinping Xi presented for the first time a combination of measures for poverty eradication in the *2015 Global Poverty Reduction and Development Forum*. Soon after, the measures were written into the *Decision of the CPC Central Committee and the State Council on Winning the Battle against Poverty* and examined and approved at the meeting of the Political Bureau of the CPC Central Committee. In poor ethnic minority concentrated areas, the measures shall be implemented in a targeted way in accordance with the types and causes of poverty of disadvantaged groups. First, we shall introduce special policies on poverty elimination through spurring local industrial growth, guide and support poor households with laborer, develop advantageous industries (including advantageous planting and breeding industries and traditional handicraft industry) in light of local conditions, and achieve poverty elimination by relying on our own efforts; second, for those poor people living in regions where the ecological environment is vulnerable and natural disasters frequently occur, we shall speed up the implementation of the relocation projects for poverty alleviation, and ensure that they are willing to be relocated, and can live a steady life and get out of poverty after the relocation; third, we shall intensify our efforts for ecological protection and restoration in poor ethnic minority concentrated areas, increase transfer payment in key ecological functional zones in poor ethnic minority concentrated areas, and expand the scope of policy implementation in ethnic minority concentrated areas. For example, we shall further give priority to major state-level ecological projects for turning vulnerable farmland into forests and grasslands and stopping grazing to let grasslands recover and funding instructions tilt toward poor ethnic minority concentrated areas, increase the participation of and benefit to the poor population, and achieve the goal of ecological compensation and poverty elimination; fourth, we shall energetically implement poverty alleviation projects through education, so as to ensure that all children from poor families can have fair access to good education and stop poverty from being passed on to the next generation; fifth, we shall improve the subsistence allowances system in rural areas, and formulate policies to meet the basic needs of poor people who have totally or partially lost their ability to work.

(III) Give top priority to improving the ecological environment and strengthening infrastructure construction in poor ethnic minority concentrated areas. Only when the ecological environment and infrastructures in poor ethnic minority concentrated areas have been improved, can we improve the working and living environment of poor people in poor ethnic minority concentrated areas, thereby increasing their income level and effectively eliminating poverty. In addition, frequent natural disasters constitute an important cause for the vulnerability of the poor population in ethnic minority concentrated areas. Hence, one the one hand, we shall do a good job of "relocating poor people from inhospitable areas" of ethnic minority concentrated areas, and guide poor population living in areas where natural disasters occur frequently to settle in urban areas and engage in other industries. On the other hand, the current agricultural production of individual households is weak and they can hardly avoid the risk of natural disasters, so we shall guide those poor people who engage in agricultural production to join specialty farmer cooperatives to increase their capabilities against natural disasters and minimize the impacts of natural disasters.

(IV) Adhere to the strategy of targeted poverty alleviation and intensify efforts to ensure that poverty alleviation reaches those who truly need it and deliver genuine outcomes.[27] China has shifted its poverty alleviation policy from focusing on poor counties to focusing on poor villages and the policy has achieved better effects. Nevertheless, even in the overall village-based poverty alleviation program, if we do not tilt the poverty alleviation policies toward the neediest people in the implementation process of the policies, the disadvantaged groups will benefit less, which will lead to poor effects of poverty alleviation. Hence, we should implement the strategy of targeted poverty alleviation and launch more poverty alleviation projects for poor households and population.

The 18th National Congress of the CPC proposed that China shall finish building a moderately prosperous society in all respects in 2020. Ethnic minority areas are weak areas for building a moderately prosperous society in all respects, and there are huge pressures and arduous tasks of assisting the poor population in rural ethnic minority concentrated areas. At present, the central government and local governments at all

[27] Liu Yongfu: Fight the battle against poverty and finish building a moderately prosperous society in all respects: Earnestly study and implement the guiding principles of Jinping Xi's important speeches on poverty alleviation and development, The People's Daily, April 9, 2014.

levels attach great importance to poverty elimination in ethnic minority concentrated areas, mobilize all forces that can be mobilized, and make unprecedented efforts to support poverty elimination in ethnic minority concentrated areas. It is expected that China's poverty reduction program for ethnic minority concentrated areas will attain its goal by 2020.

Chapter 5
Poverty Alleviation in Rual Ethnic Minority Areas: A Micro Perspective

Ethnic minority concentrated areas are underdeveloped areas in China and the main battleground for poverty alleviation in the country. The Chinese government has always tilted to ethnic minority concentrated areas in terms of poverty alleviation policies and project funding. From 2006 to 2013, the poverty alleviation funds allocated by the central government to the eight provinces and autonomous regions for ethnic minority groups increased from 5.15 billion yuan to 16.6 billion yuan, with a cumulative input of 75.84 billion yuan in the eight years, accounting for 40.6% of the total national poverty alleviation funds in the same period.[1] Thanks to the strong support of governments at all levels and all sectors of society as well as the hard work of officials and the masses of people in ethnic minority concentrated areas, the rural economy in ethnic minority concentrated areas has developed in an all-round way, and the problems of subsistence, food and clothing for rural residents have been basically solved. The number of people living in poverty has decreased significantly. According to the poverty standard of that year, the poverty-stricken population in the eight ethnic minority provinces and autonomous regions decreased from 31.44 million in 2000 to 22.05 million in 2014. However, the situation of poverty alleviation in ethnic minority concentrated areas is still grim. At the end of 2014, the rural poor population in the eight ethnic minority provinces and autonomous regions accounted for 31.4% of the country's total rural poor population, nearly doubling the proportion of their rural population to the country's total rural population. The incidence of rural poverty in the eight ethnic minority provinces and autonomous regions was 14.7%, 7.5% points higher than the national incidence of rural poverty.[2]

[1] Ethnic Policy Theory Research Office of the National Ethnic Affairs Commission: Reader about the Guiding Essence of the Central Ethnic Work Conference, website of the Ethnic Affairs Commission of the People's Republic of China, June 1, 2015. http://www.seac.gov.cn/art/2015/6/1/art_143_228926_51.html.

[2] National Bureau of Statistics: China Statistical Yearbook 2015; Department of Economic Development of the National Ethnic Affairs Commission: Released by the National Ethnic Affairs Commission: 2014 Monitoring Results of Rural Poverty in Ethnic Minority Concentrated Areas, http: //

X. Liu, *Complex Pictures of Poverty and Multiple Paths of Poverty Alleviation in Ethnic Areas of China*, https://doi.org/10.1007/978-981-97-4133-5_5

The poverty alleviation of the rural poor population has become the biggest challenge for the ethnic minority concentrated areas to build a well-off society in an all-round way, which also affects and restricts the realization of the grand goal of building a well-off society in an all-round way by 2020. Therefore, proceeding from the goal of building a moderately prosperous society in all respects, the Fifth Plenary Session of the 18th Central Committee of the Communist Party of China made it clear that by 2020, all rural poor people and all poverty-stricken counties should be out of poverty under the current Chinese standards. In addition, that problem of overall regional poverty should be solved.

1 Research Questions and Literature Review

In order to lift all the rural poor out of poverty by 2020 according to the current standards, the central government held a poverty alleviation work conference in November 2015. The conference requested many provinces and autonomous regions, including the eight ethnic minority provinces and autonomous regions, to make pledges and sign letters of responsibility for poverty alleviation. In February 2016, the General Office of the CPC Central Committee and the General Office of the State Council issued the *Measures for Evaluating the Effectiveness of Poverty Alleviation and Development Work of Provincial Party Committees and Governments (the Measures),* which aims to assess the effectiveness of the poverty alleviation and development work of the Party committees and governments of the 22 central and western provinces, autonomous regions and municipalities directly under the Central Government, including the eight ethnic minority provinces and autonomous regions. *The Measures* promulgates the contents about the poverty alleviation and development work assessment, and specifies some soft indicators related to people's comment and feedback in addition to the hard indicators for poverty alleviation such as the number of poverty-stricken people and the income of the poor people. *The Measures* also emphasizes that the data for the assessment indicators will include the official data from the Poverty Alleviation and Development Information System and the National Rural Poverty Monitoring System, as well as the third-party assessment. The people's satisfaction as indicated by the third-party evaluation not only means that the poverty eradication data are more realistic and reliable, but also allows the poor groups to have a say in the poverty reduction evaluation.[3]

It should be said that by including the satisfaction of the masses in the assessment indicators, the *Measures* can, effectively avoid getting rid of poverty by numbers in numeral terms and nominal poverty eradication. Moreover, we can analyze the degree of satisfaction of the poor groups with the poverty alleviation policies, find out

www.seac.gov.cn/art/2015/4/15/art_31_225897.html, last accessed on March 9, 2017.The data in this chapter are based on relevant statistical data from the literature.

[3] Xinhua News Agency: "Poverty Alleviation Assessment in 22 Provinces Cited from Third Party", *Beijing Morning News*, February 17, 2016.

the main factors influencing the satisfaction, adjust the poverty alleviation measures in time, and better implement the targeted poverty alleviation, so as to improve effectiveness of related policies. It is noteworthy that the satisfaction is more than simple statistical survey data as it holds rich connotations. Only by grasping these connotations thoroughly and comprehensively, can the poverty alleviation evaluation function of the satisfaction survey be brought into better play. This chapter just represents an attempt of such research. Based on the data of the survey on the degree of people's satisfaction with rural poverty alleviation and development in ethnic minority concentrated areas, this chapter examines the degree of the target groups' satisfaction with different poverty alleviation and development projects, analyzes their influencing factors, and builds the theoretical framework for satisfaction research, so as to enhance the refinement and precision of the analysis upon the degree of satisfaction with poverty alleviation and development in one dimension.

Effectiveness is also known as performance. The term performance originated from human resources management, and then came to be used in public service and other aspects. Performance is defined by OECD as the effectiveness of the implementation of an activity related to the objective, which includes not only the efficiency, economy and effectiveness of the activity, but also includes the degree of compliance of the implementer of the activity with the intended process of the activity and the degree of public satisfaction with the activity.[4]

The performance evaluation of poverty alleviation based on farming household satisfaction originates from the Customer Satisfaction Index (CSI). In 1985, the CSI was first put forward by American scholars, and then it was widely used in developed countries and introduced into the government performance evaluation of these countries. In recent years, the CSI has been more and more widely used in the performance evaluation of public goods supply in China, and many scholars have introduced this theory into the study of government performance evaluation.[5] Some scholars began to use the CSI to evaluate the performance of government poverty alleviation.

Based on a series of poverty alleviation projects implemented in poverty-stricken areas of Yunnan Province, Hongmei Liu evaluates the degree of satisfaction with poverty alleviation projects of farming households, and conducts weight analysis on the index factors constituting the satisfaction. The results show that farmers have the highest requirements for the transparency of and engagement in poverty alleviation projects. In addition, the impact of the project on the improvement of infrastructure in poor areas and on local religious and cultural practices is greater

[4] Jack Diamond:Performance measurement and evaluation.Oecd Working Papers, 1994.

[5] Xu Youhao and Wu Yanbing, "The Application of Customer Satisfaction in Government Performance Evaluation", *Journal of Tianjin University (Social Science Edition)*, No. 4, 2004; Zeng Li, Government Performance Evaluation Based on Public Satisfaction Orientation, *Academic Forum*, No. 6, 2006; Li Yanling, Zeng Fusheng: "Analysis of Farmers' Satisfaction Degree with the Supply of Rural Public Goods and the Influencing Factors", *Journal of Quantitative & Technological Economics*, No. 8, 2008.

than its economic and environmental impact.[6] Based on the investigation into Fujian Benefit-delivering Project (the relocation for poverty alleviation project), Chunxia Zhang evaluated the implementation effect of the Benefit-delivering Project from the perspective of farmers' satisfaction and willingness for relocation. The study found that the comprehensive evaluation score about farmers' satisfaction with the projects was 2.594, which was at the average level. In the survey, 44.25% of the respondents found that the project had an average effect; another 23.72% were dissatisfied or very dissatisfied with the projects. Obviously, there is a lot of room to be improved in the benefit-delivering project to improve the farming household's economic conditions and improve the public policies.[7]

Based on a survey of 208 rural residents in Songzi City, Hubei Province, Hongjie Wang, Haifeng Feng, and Dongyue Li studied the degree of satisfaction of rural residents in poor areas with the policy of poverty alleviation through agricultural industrialization. The results show that there is a significant positive correlation between the two factors (the years of schooling and the effect of the policy of poverty alleviation through agricultural industrialization on addressing income inequality) and the degree of satisfaction of the poverty-stricken people in rural areas of Songzi City with the policy of poverty alleviation through agricultural industrialization.[8] In addition, the three scholars, based on a survey of 241 rural residents in Songzi City, Hubei Province, who enjoyed the support of the Rain and Dew Plan transfer training policy, studied the degree of satisfaction of the rural population in poverty-stricken areas with the poverty alleviation policy of transferring training of the Rain and Dew Plan. The results show that there is a significant positive correlation between the two factors (the income level of local rural residents and the improvement of income inequality by the "Rain and Dew Plan" poverty alleviation policy of transferring training) and the degree of satisfaction of the rural poor in Songzi with the policy.[9]

Based on a survey of 399 rural households in Gansu Province, Xiaolin Yang made an empirical study on the degree of satisfaction of rural households participating in the pilot project of mutual aid fund in poor villages. He found out all these things including the income changes of the farming households after joining the co-operatives, whether they understand the mutual fund regulations, the fund occupation rate, the tedium of loan granting, whether the identification and decision-making of

[6] Liu Hongmei, "Analysis of the Factors Influencing Farmers' Satisfaction with Poverty Alleviation Projects in Yunnan", *Journal of Kunming University of Science and Technology (Social Science Edition)*, No. 5, 2010.

[7] Zhang Chunxia, "Research on the Satisfaction Degree with and Relocation Intention of the Farmers in Fujian Welfare Project: A Perspective of Farmers", Ph. D. Thesis of Fujian Agriculture and Forestry University, April 2013.

[8] Wang Hongjie, Feng Haifeng, and Li Dongyue: "Analysis of Satisfaction Degree of the Rural Population in Poverty-stricken Areas with Policy of Poverty Alleviation through Agricultural Industrialization: Based on a Survey of 208 Rural Residents in Songzi City, Hubei Province", *Laoqu Jianshe*, Issue 8, 2015.

[9] Wang Hongjie, Feng Haifeng, Li Dongyue: "Analysis of the Satisfaction Degree of Rural Population in Poverty-stricken Areas with the Policy of Transferred Training for Poverty Alleviation under the Rain and Dew Plan: Based on a Survey of 241 Rural Residents in Songzi City, Hubei Province", *Economic Forum* No. 3, 2015.

the poor households are democratic, whether the financial affairs are transparent, and the ability of the members of the board of directors and the board of supervisors have a significant positive impact on the degree of satisfaction of the farmers while the economic characteristics of the farmers have a significant negative impact on their degree of satisfaction. Specifically, the lower the income level of the farmers, the more satisfied they are with the pilot project, but the factors such as the age and the education level of the head of household and the per capita income of the farming household have no significant influence.[10]

According to the existing research, aside from the effect of the development-oriented poverty alleviation policy itself, the personal characteristics, family circumstances, economic, social, cultural backgrounds and other factors of the object of poverty alleviation affect the degree of people's satisfaction with the related projects. These findings shed light on the rich and complex connotations of the degree of satisfaction of the targeted groups of poverty alleviation with the performance of the poverty alleviation and development projects. Of course, we have also noticed that different factors exert different effect on farmers' satisfaction with poverty alleviation; some directly affect farmers' satisfaction with poverty alleviation, and some play a role through intermediate variables. Many existing researches generally take these factors as the factors that directly affect the degree of people's satisfaction with poverty alleviation, and make no difference between the direct and indirect factors that affect the degree of people's satisfaction with poverty alleviation. Therefore, it is difficult to conduct in-depth study upon the process or mechanism of different factors influencing people's satisfaction with poverty alleviation. Based on the findings of the existing researches on the factors influencing the degree of satisfaction of the targeted groups of poverty alleviation and development projects in association with the preliminary theoretical and methodological consideration, this chapter sets a theoretical framework and model for in-depth analysis upon the factors influencing people's satisfaction and the related mechanism. Firstly, we will identify the direct and indirect factors that affect the satisfaction according to relevant researches, and then construct a path analysis model by combining the optimal scale analysis and path analysis. We will use the questionnaire survey data of the research group of the Chinese Academy of Social Sciences regarding "Comprehensive Survey on the Economic and Social Development of China's Ethnic Minority Regions in the Early 21st Century (2014)" and use this analysis model to study the satisfaction of farming households in ethnic minority concentrated areas with the performance of related poverty alleviation and development projects. For one thing, this research attempts to evaluate the performance of the rural poverty alleviation and development policies in ethnic minority concentrated areas from the perspective of people's satisfaction. For another, it is a preliminary test of our analysis theory, method and model.

---

[10] Yang Xialin, "An Empirical Analysis of Farmers' Satisfaction Degree with the Pilot Project of Mutual Aid Funding in Poverty-stricken Villages: Based on a Survey of 399 Farming Households in Gansu Province", *Rural Finance Research,* No. 4, 2014.

2 Research Strategy and Data Sources

2.1 Research Strategy

The government-led development-oriented poverty alleviation program mainly drives the poverty-stricken areas and the poverty-stricken people out of poverty through the implementation of poverty-alleviation projects. Poverty alleviation projects mainly include special poverty alleviation projects and comprehensive development-oriented poverty alleviation projects. Special poverty alleviation projects mainly include village-wide promotion, industrial development, relocation, work relief, poverty alleviation through financial means, skills training and employment guidance and other poverty alleviation projects. Comprehensive development-oriented poverty alleviation projects involve government-led, multi-sector and multi-industry coordination. A variety of intervention measures are adopted to develop infrastructure, advance industrial development, and promote science and technology, culture and education, social security and employment on the basis of solving the problems of people in poverty-stricken areas in terms of food, clothing, housing and transportation, with a view of enhancing regional development and poverty alleviation.[11]

According to the information we learned from our field research in the ethnic minority concentrated areas, the poverty alleviation and development policies implemented by in the vast ethnic minority concentrated areas mainly cover 15 types under six major categories.

(1) Relocation. The main purpose is to solve the long-standing problem that rural residents in the areas with poor ecological environment find it hard to get rid of poverty through local development and self-development by relocating them to the places more suitable for human survival and development.
(2) Poverty alleviation through education. The main purpose is to substantially improve the education level and quality of the rural poor in ethnic minority concentrated areas and to enhance their ability to participate in the market and obtain better development opportunities. It concerns exemptions of fees for books and miscellaneous items and subsidy for living expenses for rural poor students, financial assistance for children's schooling and literacy education, and poverty alleviation by developing education.
(3) Poverty alleviation through training. The main purpose is to improve the skills and technical level of the labor force of poor peasant households through technical training, enhance their competitiveness and entrepreneurship in the labor market, create favorable conditions for the popularization of relevant technologies, and as thus help poor rural families get out of poverty. Specifically, it includes the programs for poverty alleviation training, and technology promotion and training.

[11] Office of Household Survey, National Bureau of Statistics, *China Rural Poverty Monitoring Report 2011*, China Statistics Press, 2012.

(4) Poverty alleviation through industrial development. The main purpose is to help poor areas and poor farmers to develop local industrial projects, to develop the economy, and thus to achieve poverty eradication. The projects include the production projects for poverty alleviation, and the planting, breeding, forestry poverty alleviation funding, conversion of farmland to forest, subsidy projects for grass restoration, and basic farmland construction projects.
(5) Poverty alleviation through infrastructure construction. The main purpose is to improve the infrastructure of poor areas and provide basic conditions for their economic and social development. Specifically, it includes road construction, reconstruction and expansion projects, power facilities construction projects, and the Extending Radio and TV Broadcasting Coverage to Every Village Project (radio and television, roads, and communication networks).
(6) Poverty alleviation through healthcare. It aims to promote medical and health care at the grass-roots level and in poor rural areas in China, narrow the health gap between urban and rural residents, and improve the quality of life of vulnerable groups by launching a series of public welfare service projects. It aims to demonstrate the social equity and justice of "health for all" and gradually eliminate the poverty caused by illness and the relapse to poverty due to illness. Specifically, it includes sanitary facilities construction projects and water diversion projects for people and livestock.

As noted above, the primary analytical method in this chapter is about path analysis. In essence, the main purpose of the research on the evaluation of the satisfaction with poverty alleviation is to understand the satisfaction of different groups of people with the poverty alleviation and development work and the causes behind the differences in their satisfaction. In the final analysis, the different groups of people are defined on the basis of their demographic and social characteristics, which become the main independent variables to be involved into the analysis and they are called the initial variables in the path analysis. The overall satisfaction with the poverty alleviation and development work of the related entity (the interviewee) is the dependent variable under our study. Such overall evaluation is generally based on the overall impression of the evaluators on the poverty alleviation and development work, but at the same time, it is influenced by their evaluation (or impression) on specific projects. The interviewee's satisfaction with each major project justifiably becomes the so-called intermediate variable. All these show that a path analysis approach is appropriate.

With this method, we must first identify the relevant independent variables (initial variables), and determine the relationship between different variables according to the logic of theory and practice. Based on existing studies and preliminary observations by using quantitative data, we found that the regions in which the evaluators stayed, their age, sex, and health status, education level, ethnicity, political status and professional status as well as their family size and per capita income constitute the initial variables for reporting their overall satisfaction with the poverty alleviation and development efforts. At the same time, these initial variables will also

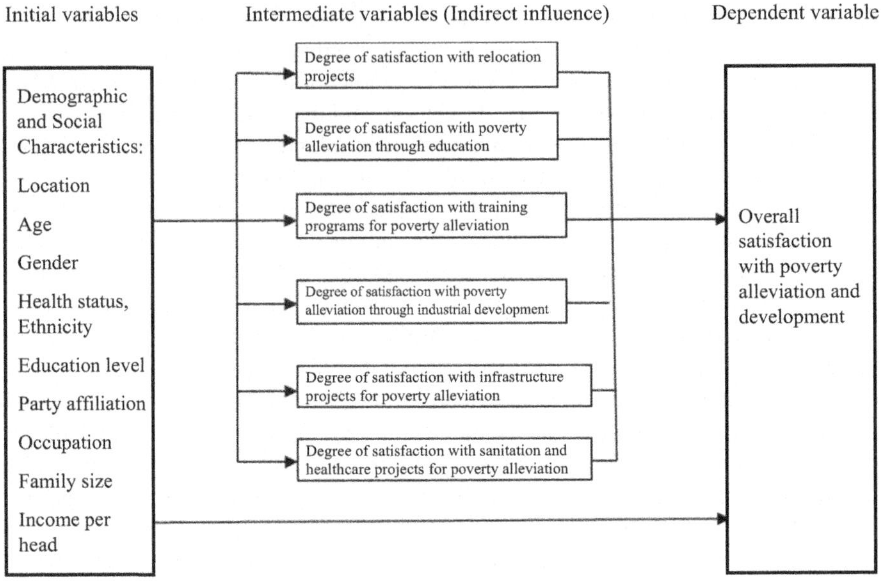

Fig. 5.1 Analytical framework

indirectly influence their overall satisfaction through their influence on the satisfaction with various poverty alleviation and development projects, and the latter are the above intermediate variables. Inspired by related research,[12] we take the satisfaction of rural residents from ethnic minority concentrated areas with the relocation, the poverty alleviation through education, poverty alleviation through training, poverty alleviation through industrial development, poverty alleviation through infrastructure construction, and poverty alleviation through sanitation and healthcare improvement as the intermediate variable. We construct the overall analysis framework as shown in Fig. 5.1.

In this chapter, the dependent variable is originally a classified variable, and the measurement scale in the actual survey involves two levels: dissatisfaction and satisfaction, with an additional option of "hard to say". In the actual analysis, the sample with the answer of "hard to say" is discarded, and then the answers are directly assigned with value according to the requirements of the optimal scale regression model: 1 is assigned to "dissatisfied" and 2 is assigned to "satisfied". In the survey, the measurement of the intermediate variables adopts the five-level scale, namely, very dissatisfied, dissatisfied, just so so, satisfied and very satisfied. We assign values to the five-level scale from 1 to 5, namely, the value 1 for "very dissatisfied" and 5 for "very satisfied". Regarding the measurement of the six intermediate variables, except

[12] Wang Yanzhong and Jiang Cuiping, "Analysis of the Factors Affecting Rural Residents' Satisfaction Degree with Medical Service", *China Rural Survey,* No. 4, 2010; Xu Lilai, Yan Zhen, Cui Shenghui: "Path Analysis of Factors Affecting the Output of Urban Domestic Waste: A Case Study of Xiamen City", *Acta Scientiae Circumstantiae,* No. 4, 2013.

for the satisfaction with the resettlement project, the rest are measured by the comprehensive scores of the satisfaction with a series of secondary projects. Specifically, the evaluation of the poverty alleviation through education consists of the evaluation upon the compulsory education policy of "two exemptions and one subsidy," upon the project of subsidizing children's schooling and literacy education, and upon the project of education-based poverty alleviation. The evaluation of the training-based poverty alleviation consists of the evaluation upon the training for poverty alleviation, upon technology popularization and upon the training project. The evaluation upon the projects of poverty alleviation through industrial development consists of evaluation upon the production projects for poverty alleviation, planting industry, breeding industry, forestry poverty alleviation fund, subsidy project of returning farmland to forest and grass, and basic farmland construction project. The evaluation of infrastructure construction for poverty alleviation consists of the evaluation of road construction and extension projects, of power facilities construction projects, and of the Extending Radio and TV Broadcasting Coverage to Every Village Project (radio and television, roads, and communication networks). The evaluation of healthcare for poverty alleviation consists of the evaluation of the sanitary facilities construction project and the water diversion project for human and livestock. The initial variables are mainly the personal, social, demographic and family characteristics of the interviewees, covering the age, sex, ethnicity, educational level, political status, occupation, family size and family income level of the respondents (who fall into either group of poverty or non-poverty which are respectively assigned the value 1 and 2); the areas where the families are located are assigned with a value ranging from 1 to 3 (western surveyed counties with 1, central surveyed counties with 2 and eastern surveyed counties with 3).

Given that some of the dependent variables, initial variables and intermediate variable in this chapter are classification variables (such as occupation) and disorderly multi-category variables (such as ethnicity), this chapter uses an optimal scaling regression model for analysis upon the research question. The optimal scaling regression analysis is specially used to conduct quantitative analysis upon classification variables in statistical modeling, and the basic logic behind is based on the model framework to be fitted in, to find the influence of each level of the classification variables on the dependent variables, to use a certain non-linear transformation method for repeated iteration, and thus to conduct the best quantitative scoring for each category of the original classification variables; then quantitative analysis is used in place of the original variables for regression analysis and an optimal equation is sought.[13]

[13] Zhang Wentong, Zhong Yunfei, *Selected Practical Cases of IBM SPSS Data Analysis and Mining*, Tsinghua University Press, 2013; Lu Zimin, "Optimal Scaling Regression Analysis upon the Factors Affecting Job Satisfaction of Service Personnel of Pension Institutions in Zhejiang Province", *Chinese Economist*, Issue 2, 2015.

2.2 *Data Sources*

The microdata used in this chapter are from the Comprehensive Survey on Economic and Social Development of China's Ethnic Minority Regions in the Early 21st Century, a special project entrusted by the National Social Science Fund and a major innovation project of the Chinese Academy of Social Sciences. Questionnaire surveys were conducted in 2014 in both urban and rural areas of 18 cities and counties across 10 provinces and autonomous regions, including Inner Mongolia, Jilin, Zhejiang, Hubei, Guangxi, Sichuan, Tibet, Qinghai, Ningxia and Xinjiang (the "2014 survey on ethnic minority concentrated areas"). The survey was conducted by the Institute of Ethnology and Anthropology of the Chinese Academy of Social Sciences in cooperation with Xinjiang Normal University and the Minzu University of China. A professional investigation team mainly composed of graduates and undergraduates majoring in ethnology and sociology was set up to conduct household survey among urban and rural residents, and the respondents were selected by stratified random sampling. In the 18 cities and counties involved in the survey, urban and rural communities were selected according to their different economic development (high, medium and low level) and ethnic minority population distribution in urban and rural areas. The urban–rural division of the investigated households was determined according to the local urbanization rate, and specific samples were selected by random equidistant sampling of the households at the selected community or administrative village. A total of 400–500 households were involved in the questionnaire survey which concerned economic development, social undertakings, ethnic culture, ethnic policies, ethnic relations, social security and social harmony, and a total of 7,341 households of urban and rural areas were interviewed. This chapter only adopts the samples of rural households. Since this survey does not adopt random sampling among all ethnic minority districts and county of the country, the research result can not represent the general situation of the country, but it hopes to shed light on poverty alleviation and development in ethnic minority concentrated areas to a certain extent.

3 Statistical Analysis of Factors Influencing Evaluation of Poverty Alleviation and Development Projects

3.1 *Descriptive Statistical Analysis*

1. **Evaluation of overall satisfaction of rural residents with the implementation of poverty alleviation policies**

According to the results of the survey, rural residents in ethnic minority concentrated areas are not satisfied with the overall effect of the poverty alleviation policies they are involved in. Specifically, of the 4,316 respondents, 60.8% indicated "Satisfied", 10.6% indicated "Dissatisfied", and 28.6% "Unclear." In other words, 60% of the interviewees clearly expressed satisfaction with the overall results of the poverty alleviation policies or activities they had participated in while about 40% of the interviewees were dissatisfied or unclear.

2. **Statistical description of the initial variables**

Table 5.1 represents a statistical description of the initial variables. As can be seen from Table 5.1, of the 5,018 respondents with an agricultural household registration including the residents who once held an agricultural household registration, 84.7% lived in the surveyed counties in the western region and most of them were middle-aged people, in the age group of 30–59; the number of men was 12% points higher than that of men; the number of people from minority ethnic groups was 53% points higher than that of Han people; more than 10% were unhealthy; 14% were members of the Communist Party of China; nearly 60% of the respondents had an education at the primary school level or the junior high school level; nearly half of the respondents were mainly engaged in agricultural production; and nearly 70% of the respondents had four or more members in their family. Based on their reported income levels at the time of the survey and the rural poverty line for the year, all households surveyed were divided into poor and non-poor households, with poor households accounting for slightly more than one-fifth of the total.

3. **Statistical description of the intermediate variables**

As mentioned above, in ethnic minority concentrated areas, we have found in our survey that there are roughly 15 types of poverty alleviation and development projects which can be put under six categories. We first describe the respondents' satisfaction with the performance of 15 types of projects (see Table 5.2).

Generally speaking, the respondents are highly satisfied with the implementation of all the projects. Among the 15 types of projects, the lowest average score is 3.65 (subsidy projects for returning farmland to forests and grasslands). Considering that the highest score (or full score) is 5, 3.65 is equivalent to 73% of the full score, that is, the satisfaction score of the subsidy project of returning farmland to forest and grassland is 73 points on a 100-point system. The highest average score is 4.22 for the "Two Exemptions and One Subsidy" policy; likewise, the score can be converted into 84.4, which can be said to be quite good. Among all the 15 types of projects ranked by the average score of satisfaction, the top five concern the implementation of the "Two Exemptions and One Subsidy" policy, the Extending Radio and TV Broadcasting Coverage to Every Village Project (radio and television, road, communication network), the project of poverty alleviation through education, school enrolment, literacy programs, and road construction, repair and expansion projects; the projects in the bottom five concern technology promotion and training, drinking water for people and livestock, poverty alleviation training, resettlement and subsidies for returning farmland to forests and grasslands. Two trends showed in Table 5.2 deserve special attention. First, the satisfaction rating of projects delivering universal benefit is relatively high, such as the first-ranked "Two Exemptions and One Subsidy" policy and the second-ranked "Extending Radio and TV Broadcasting

Table 5.1 Statistical description of initial variables

Variable		Assigned value	Frequency	Percentage (%)
Regions	Surveyed counties in Western China	1	4251	84.7
	Surveyed counties in Central China	2	431	8.6
	Surveyed counties in Eastern China	3	336	6.7
Age groups	16–29 years	1	750	15.0
	30–39 years	2	1034	20.7
	40–49 years	3	1322	26.5
	50–59 years	4	1007	20.2
	At 60 and above	5	884	17.7
Gender	Female	1	2199	43.9
	Male	2	2805	56.1
Ethnicity	Ethnic minorities	1	3855	76.8
	Han Chinese	2	1163	23.2
Health status	Unhealthy	1	579	11.6
	General	2	1318	26.5
	Healthy	3	3084	61.9
Party affiliation	Non-member of the CPC	1	4293	85.9
	Member of the CPC	2	704	14.1
Education level	No schooling	1	1207	24.1
	Elementary to junior high school	2	2980	59.5
	High school	3	544	10.9
	University and above	4	277	5.5
Work status	Housework, etc.	1	711	15.5
	Just farming	2	2172	47.3
	Part-time work	3	911	19.8
	Just non-agricultural work	4	801	17.4
Family size	1-person	1	141	2.9
	2-person	2	537	10.9
	3-person	3	865	17.6
	Of 4 or more members	4	3379	68.7
Income profile	Poor households	1	822	20.7
	Non-poor households	2	3153	79.3

Note In this table, as the values of some variables are missing, the sum of samples for all the variables may not be equal and may not be equal to the number of valid samples (5018). This problem exists in all the following tables. The chapter keeps a record of the sample where values are missing and includes those samples into the optimal scaling regression model

Table 5.2 Evaluation distribution of project implementation performance satisfaction degree unit:%, score

Projects	Very dissatisfied	Dissatisfied	Just so so	Satisfied	Very satisfied	Average score	Score ranking	Number of samples
Resettlement project	0.9	9.1	24.6	49.5	16.0	3.71	13	1225
"Two exemptions and one subsidy" policy	0.1	3.1	5.6	56.3	34.8	4.22	1	3500
Funding for school enrolment and literacy programmes for children	0.7	6.0	15.0	59.6	18.8	3.90	4	1637
Poverty alleviation through education	0.6	6.9	9.7	58.0	25.0	4.00	3	2007
Poverty alleviation through training	1.0	9.9	23.7	47.6	17.8	3.71	13	1218
Technological promotion and training program	0.8	8.8	21.1	55.0	14.4	3.73	11	1515
Poverty alleviation production projects	0.8	8.9	16.4	57.4	16.5	3.80	9	1879
Poverty alleviation fund for planting, breeding and forestry	0.8	10.1	18.6	55.2	15.4	3.74	10	1308
Construction project of basic farmland	0.7	9.4	10.7	61.4	17.8	3.86	7	1774

(continued)

Table 5.2 (continued)

Projects	Very dissatisfied	Dissatisfied	Just so so	Satisfied	Very satisfied	Average score	Score ranking	Number of samples
Subsidy project of returning farmland to forest and grassland	2.3	13.1	16.3	54.7	13.7	3.65	15	1868
Road construction, reconstruction and expansion	1.2	11.9	4.9	60.0	22.0	3.90	4	3393
Power facility construction project	1.8	12.0	5.1	63.7	17.5	3.83	8	2718
Extending radio and tv broadcasting coverage to every village project	0.5	6.9	4.1	59.3	29.3	4.10	2	3248
Construction project of sanitation facilities	1.5	10.9	6.3	62.2	19.2	3.87	6	2328
Drinking water project for humans and livestock	4.3	13.1	6.5	57.7	18.4	3.73	11	2613

Coverage to Every Village Project". The average score of satisfaction in both items is more than 4 points (or more than 80 points in the centesimal system). In addition, the projects of children's education support and literacy education, road construction, reconstruction and expansion also deliver great universal benefit. Therefore, these items also get high scores. For one thing, these projects do help the poor directly (for example, by offering jobs to the labor force of poor rural households). For another, these projects, once implemented, benefit almost everyone in the region where the projects are located, which indicates they have multiple strong positive externalities. Second, with the poverty alleviation and development projects that rank relatively low by the average score of satisfaction, the respondents who express strong dissatisfaction or dissatisfaction account for a relatively high proportion. For example, more than 10% of the respondents are dissatisfied or very dissatisfied with the implementation of the projects that ranked below the 10th place. Up to 17.4% of the respondents are dissatisfied with the human and livestock drinking water projects, and the projects about which over 20% of the respondents feel just so so are also ranked in the bottom five.

In applying the analytical framework presented above, we mentioned six categories of poverty alleviation projects as the so-called intermediate variables. Except for the relocation project upon which our survey data includes a direct evaluation of satisfaction, the rest have no direct evaluation data. In the process of sorting out variable data, we adopt the method of merging similar items. Specifically, we merge the projects or items belonging to the other five categories into a corresponding major item or a new variable, of which the value is the average of the satisfaction scores of all related projects. As can be seen from Table 5.2, the number of respondents reporting satisfaction differs from project to project, which means the same respondent reports satisfaction with some projects but not with others where relevant values are missing. How to deal with the missing values is a very complex issue. In order to ensure that enough samples are entered into the statistical analysis model, the chapter adopts a simple approach: For each sample, only the scores of the projects or programs with satisfaction scores are considered when constructing a new variable under the assumption that the average of related scores shall fill up the missing value. The results of a simple statistical description of the newly created variable or the so-called intermediate variable are presented in Table 5.3.

In general, after comprehensive treatment, there is not much difference in the respondents' evaluation of the performance of the six major types of project or programs, with the highest comprehensive score being just 6.7% higher than the lowest comprehensive score. In the centesimal system, the scores range from 74 to 80, almost at a quite good level. From the perspective of ranking, the greater the universal benefit the project delivers, the higher its ranking is.

Table 5.3 Statistical description of intermediate variables

	Min	Max	Comprehensive average	The comprehensive score in the centesimal system	Comprehensive ranking
Resettlement	1	5	3.71	74.2	6
Poverty alleviation through education	1	5	3.84	76.8	2
Poverty alleviation through training	1	5	3.75	75.0	5
Poverty alleviation through industrial development	1	5	3.76	75.2	4
Infrastructure construction for poverty alleviation	1	5	3.96	79.2	1
Sanitation and healthcare for poverty alleviation	1	5	3.81	76.2	3

3.2 *Regression Analysis of Overall Satisfaction with Rural Poverty Alleviation and Development Projects Based on Intermediate Variables*

According to the research strategy, this paper first conducts regression analysis on the evaluation results about the overall satisfaction with the poverty alleviation and development projects based on the intermediate variables, and the interpretation degree of the model is 22.7% (see Table 5.4), a good fitting degree. The results show that the poverty alleviation projects of education, infrastructure construction and healthcare fail to pass the significance test.[14] This may be due to the fact that poverty alleviation projects in education, infrastructure construction and health care all deliver universal benefit, benefiting not only poor households but also rural residents in poor areas. These projects involve a high degree of participation and record a high degree of satisfaction, but they exert less than significant impact upon people's general evaluation of the poverty alleviation projects. However, the evaluation of the satisfaction with the resettlement project, the evaluation of the satisfaction with the poverty-alleviation training project and the evaluation of the satisfaction with the poverty-alleviation project through industrial development have passed the significance test. Among them, the evaluation of the satisfaction with the poverty-alleviation training project has the greatest influence, with the standard regression coefficient standing at 0.316, which is followed by the evaluation of the satisfaction with the project of poverty alleviation through industrial development of which the standard regression coefficient is 0.164, and the last is the evaluation of satisfaction with the resettlement project with the standardized regression coefficient of 0.039. Therefore, in the following path analysis, the evaluation of the projects of poverty alleviation through education, infrastructure construction, and healthcare shall not be included in the regression model.

3.3 *Multiple Regression Analysis of the Influence of Initial Variables on Intermediate Variables and Dependent Variables*

As mentioned above, this paper conducts the optimal scale regression analysis. Table 5.5 reports a multiple regression analysis of the effects of the initial variables

[14] That the impact of the projects of poverty alleviation through infrastructure construction, education and healthcare on the overall evaluation of the satisfaction with poverty alleviation and development fail to pass the significance test does not mean these project are not important, but just show that they have no statistically significant impact on the overall evaluation of the satisfaction with the poverty alleviation projects. This may be due to the fact that those projects are all inclusive in nature, benefiting not only poor households but also rural residents in poor areas. Therefore, they involve a high degree of participation and record a high degree of satisfaction, exerting less than significant impact upon the overall evaluation of the satisfaction with the poverty alleviation projects.

Table 5.4 Multiple regression analysis of the intermediate variables' influence on the satisfaction with poverty alleviation and development

	Non-standard co-efficient	Standard co-efficient
Resettlement	0.019*	0.039*
Poverty alleviation through education	0.005	0.010
Poverty alleviation through training	0.158***	0.316***
Poverty alleviation through industrial development	0.097***	0.164***
Infrastructure construction for poverty alleviation	0.038	0.062
Healthcare for poverty alleviation	0.003	0.006
Constant	0.817***	
F	20384	
R^2	0.20	

Note * * *, * *, * denote significance levels of 0.001, 0.01, and 0.05, respectively.

on the intermediate and dependent variables. It can be seen that the four regression models all show good "goodness of fit". The degree of interpretation of the initial variables to several intermediate variables is above 13%, and the degree of interpretation of the initial variables to the dependent variable is 15.5%, obviously lower than that of the intermediate variables to the dependent variables. This shows that there are some defects in using the initial variables to explain the dependent variables directly. The initial variable mainly influences the dependent variable through the intermediate variable. Therefore, the foregoing overall analysis framework is reasonable.

According to the results in Table 5.5, the regional factors have statistically significant influence on the four models, but the influence on the overall satisfaction evaluation of the relocation project, the project of poverty alleviation through industrial development and the poverty alleviation and development project is negative. That is to say, with the advancement of the regional economic and social development, the respondents tend to show declining satisfaction with these aspects; the evaluation of the training project for poverty alleviation is positive. The higher the economic and social development level is, the greater satisfaction the respondents (both the poor and non-poor) in the related region show to such programs. In other words, locals prefer to learn fishing than to get the fish.

However, in regions with a relatively low level of economic and social development, migration and poverty alleviation through industrial development are more significant. In addition, the influence of regional factors on the overall satisfaction with poverty alleviation projects is also negative, which shows that the poverty alleviation projects play a more significant role in the regions with a relatively low economic and social development level. The age factor has no statistically significant effect on the degree of satisfaction with the resettlement project, but has statistically significant effect on the other three items about satisfaction. However, the

Table 5.5 Multiple regression analysis of the influence of initial variables on intermediate variables and dependent variables (standardized regression coefficients)

	Intermediate variables			Dependent variables
	Satisfaction degree with resettlement for poverty alleviation	Satisfaction degree with training programs for poverty alleviation	Satisfaction degree with industrial development for poverty alleviation	Overall satisfaction with poverty alleviation and development
Region	−0.132***	0.161***	−0.122***	−0.049***
Age	0.069	−0.073***	−0.055***	0.097***
Gender	−0.047	0.034***	0.055	−0.023
Ethnicity	−0.094***	−0.004	0.039	−0.068***
Health status	0.064	0.044***	−0.007	0.046***
Party affiliation	0.016***	0.081***	−0.057***	0.048***
Education level	−0.082***	0.065***	0.114***	0.053***
Occupation	−0.077***	0.047***	−0.067***	0.031***
Family size	−0.144***	−0.116***	−0.141***	−0.119***
Household income	−0.087***	−0.106***	−0.144***	−0.075***
F	15.224	15.266	18.856	11.113
R^2	0.176	0.176	0.194	0.155

Note * * *, * *, * denote significance levels of 0.001, 0.01, and 0.05, respectively

age factor has negative influence upon anti-poverty training programs and industrial anti-poverty programs has been negative, and it is understandable since young people are more likely to benefit from anti-poverty training and industrial development than elderly people. The gender factor only has a positive effect on the degree of satisfaction with the training programs for poverty alleviation; in other words, the male respondents are more satisfied with these programs than the female ones. Ethnic factors have a negative impact on migration and overall satisfaction evaluation; that is to say, compared with ethnic minorities, the Han respondents report a relatively low level of satisfaction with these two aspects. The reason may be that most of the Han respondents come from the areas with good ecological and environmental conditions and high economic and social development level. The health factor also has statistically significant positive effects on both anti-poverty training and overall satisfaction evaluation, which may mean that the implementation of existing poverty alleviation projects or programs has more positive implications for people in good health. The political aspect factor has statistically significant influence in the four models, and except for the negative influence on the satisfaction evaluation of the industrial poverty alleviation project, the influence on the other three aspects is positive. The CPC members are more proactive, but whether they are motivated by the benefits to gain from the anti-poverty projects or by the political consideration that they as the CPC members should be are more supportive of the state's anti-poverty policies deserves further study. The education level has statistically significant influence on the four aspects, but the influence on the satisfaction with the resettlement project is negative. As for the projects being implemented, it is obvious that relocation is less significant for the respondents with a high education level than for those with a low education level. At the same time, the poverty alleviation training programs and industrial poverty alleviation programs mean more to people with a high education level who benefit more. The occupation status has statistically significant influence upon the four aspects; the influence on the overall satisfaction with the resettlement project, the project of poverty alleviation through industrial development and the poverty alleviation and development project is negative because the resettlement projects and the projects of poverty alleviation through industrial development are often concentrated in the agricultural industry which has not much relevance with the respondents who work part-time and who engage in non-agricultural work. But the anti-poverty training often also includes skills related to non-farming employment and thus has a positive effect on both part-time and non-farming workers. The effect of family size on the satisfaction with the four aspects is significantly negative, which indicates that the existing poverty alleviation projects can not well meet the needs of the farmers with large family size. However, judging from the impact of the per capita income of the families, if the surveyed peasant households are truly poor households, they will show greater satisfaction. It also indicates that, on the whole, the existing rural poverty alleviation and development projects in ethnic minority concentrated areas have played a good role in poverty alleviation.

3.4 Path Analysis Upon the Influencing Factors on Overall Satisfaction Evaluation of Poverty Alleviation and Development

Here, we conduct path analysis to see the impact of the initial variables and intermediate variables on the overall satisfaction with poverty alleviation development. Table 5.6 reports the process by which the independent variable affects the dependent variable. The indirect influence = the standardized regression coefficient of the independent variable to each intermediate variable × the standardized regression coefficient of the intermediate variable to the dependent variable, and the total influence = the indirect influence + the direct influence. That is, the results of Table 5.6 are based on Tables 5.4 and 5.5. In addition, the standardized regression coefficients with a significance level greater than 5% in Table 5.5 are not included in Table 5.6.

The results of path analysis show that the initial variable that has the greatest overall impact on the evaluation of people's satisfaction with poverty alleviation and

Table 5.6 Path analysis of factors in overall satisfaction with poverty alleviation and development based on initial and intermediate variables

	Indirect influence			Direct influence	Total influence
	Satisfaction degree with resettlement project	Satisfaction degree with technological promotion and training for poverty alleviation	Satisfaction degree with poverty alleviation through industrial development		
Region	−0.0051	0.0509	−0.0200	−0.0490	−0.0233
Age	–	−0.0231	−0.0090	0.0970	0.0649
Gender	–	0.0107	–	–	0.0107
Ethnicity	−0.0037	–	–	−0.0680	−0.0717
Health status	–	0.0139	–	0.0460	0.0599
Party affiliation	0.0006	0.0256	−0.0093	0.0480	0.0649
Education level	0.0059	0.0205	0.0187	0.0530	0.0981
Occupation	−0.0026	0.0149	−0.0110	0.0310	0.0323
Family size	−0.0203	−0.0367	−0.0231	−0.1190	−0.1991
Household income status	−0.0161	−0.0335	−0.0236	−0.0750	−0.1482

development (according to the absolute value of the path coefficient) is the family size, followed by the family income status, and then the education level. The overall impact of gender, region and occupation is relatively small. This is explained further below.

The regional factors as the initial variables and the satisfaction with the three types of projects have negative overall impact on people's overall satisfaction with poverty alleviation and development projects. Among them, the direct influence of the regional factor has made the biggest contribution; in its indirect influence, the influence produced by the evaluation of the degree of satisfaction with the anti-poverty training project is the only positive influence. Generally speaking, the resettlement project and the project of poverty alleviation through industrial development benefit the rural households (including poor households, the same below) all the more in the surveyed counties in the western region while the anti-poverty training project is more popular among rural households in the surveyed counties in the eastern region.

The age factor has no significant influence on people's overall satisfaction with anti-poverty development through affecting the respondents' degree of satisfaction with the resettlement project, but it has notable negative indirect impact upon people's overall satisfaction through affecting the evaluation of the other two types of projects. The significant positive direct effect of this factor on people's overall satisfaction is much larger. In other words, on the whole elderly respondents are more satisfied with the poverty alleviation and development work. In order to further enhance the degree of satisfaction with poverty alleviation and development work of the rural residents in ethnic minority concentrated areas, it is necessary to increase the accessibility and assistance of anti-poverty training projects and projects of poverty alleviation through industrial development to elderly people, and especially the poor people.

The gender factor has no obvious direct influence on people's overall satisfaction with poverty alleviation and development, and only has some indirect influence through affecting their satisfaction with the anti-poverty training project. Therefore, to eliminate the influence of gender factor, the key is to increase the benefit of the anti-poverty training project to women and thus to further enhance the overall satisfaction of rural residents in ethnic minority concentrated areas with the poverty alleviation and development project.

Ethnic factors not only have an indirect impact on the overall satisfaction with poverty alleviation and development through affecting the resettlement project, but also have a direct impact on the latter, with the direct impact being far greater than the indirect impact. Both the direct and indirect impact is negative. That is to say, the overall satisfaction of the rural minority groups in the ethnic minority concentrated areas with the poverty alleviation project is obviously higher than that of the Han residents. In general, in the rural ethnic minority concentrated areas, ethnic minority residents are poorer than Han residents.[15] Therefore, some poverty alleviation projects tilt to ethnic minority people who benefit more and show a relatively high degree of satisfaction. Such ethnic differences may be difficult to eliminate and we do not need to eliminate such differences since all in all the poverty alleviation project aims to help the poor.

The factors of health status have direct significant positive influence on the respondents' overall satisfaction with poverty alleviation and development, and have indirect significant positive influence only through affecting the evaluation of the anti-poverty training project. That is to say, the average satisfaction of the respondents in good health is higher than that of those in poor health. The key to eliminating this disparity is to give more consideration to the needs of people with relatively poor health and to provide them with accessible assistance.

The factor of political status has indirect influence on the respondents' overall satisfaction through affecting the evaluation of the three types of projects, and itself also exerts direct influence. Its indirect influence exerted through affecting the respondents' evaluation of the project of poverty alleviation through industrial development is negative, but its direct and indirect influence on aspects is positive, thus on the whole its influence is positive. Generally speaking, the evaluation of the CPC members is more positive, which is notably reflected in its direct impact and the indirect impact exerted through affecting the evaluation of the anti-poverty training project. The reasons behind, as mentioned above, are yet to be further studied.

---

[15] Ding Sai, "Empirical Analysis of Income Differences between Rural Han and Ethnic Minorities," Chinese Labor Economics, No. 4, 2006; Liu Xiaomin: "A Comparative Study of Rural Poverty in Ethnic Areas from the Perspective of Ethnic Groups - Taking Guangxi, Guizhou and Hunan as Examples," Ethnic Studies, No. 4, 2013.

The factor of education level has significant direct and indirect positive effects on the respondents' evaluation of the poverty alleviation and development work. This shows that the higher the education level of the respondents, the greater the impact on the overall satisfaction evaluation of the poverty alleviation and development work. It can be said that in the implementation of various poverty alleviation projects, those with a high education level may be in a more advantageous position, or they may have a better understanding about poverty alleviation.

The direct and indirect effects of family size on the overall satisfaction of the respondents with the poverty alleviation work are significant and negative. In general, therefore, the larger the household of the respondents, the lower their overall degree of satisfaction with poverty reduction. Considering that poverty-stricken rural households in ethnic minority concentrated areas tend to have a large family and have a greater demand for poverty-relief assistance, when the poverty-relief assistance is certain, the per capita gains of a large household are likely to be lower than the expected level. In addition, large rural households often face the pressure of a relatively high labor force dependency coefficient, and some poverty alleviation projects targeting the working-age population provide less effective help to such households than to the households with a low family dependency coefficient.

The direct influence of the occupation factor and its indirect influence exerted through affecting the evaluation of the anti-poverty training project are significant and positive. Its indirect influence exerted through affecting the evaluation of the resettlement project and the project of poverty alleviation through industrial development is significant but negative. On the whole, its effect is positive. It shows once again that the projects of resettlement and poverty alleviation through industrial development benefit the respondents all the more who do housework and are engaged in farming while the anti-poverty training project and the project of poverty alleviation through industrial development deliver greater benefit to the respondents who work part-time or engage in non-agricultural work. Such difference may be very difficult to eliminate in the actual work. To do a good job in the poverty alleviation work targeting different groups of people helps to enhance their overall satisfaction with the poverty alleviation work.

The direct and indirect effects of family income status on the respondents' overall satisfaction with poverty alleviation work are significantly negative. That is to say, the overall satisfaction of non-poor rural households in ethnic minority concentrated areas is generally lower than that of poor rural households. This is understandable. However, the survey data failed to make clear whether the respondents actually participated in the poverty alleviation projects and whether the non-poor respondents had shaken off poverty thanks to the poverty alleviation projects. It is therefore difficult to further analyse in depth the specific causes of these direct and indirect effects.

4 Conclusions and Suggestions

Based on the data on rural households from the 2014 Survey of Ethnic Minority Regions, this paper conducts quantitative analysis on the influencing factors of the overall satisfaction with the current poverty alleviation and development work of rural residents in ethnic areas by using the path analysis method. This study represents an academic response to the concept of targeted poverty alleviation put forward by the central government and the requirement of the *Measures for Evaluating the Effectiveness of Poverty Alleviation and Development Work of Provincial Party Committees and Governments* for incorporating "the degree of satisfaction" as a "soft indicator" into the evaluation indicator system.

Generally speaking, rural residents in ethnic areas are not so satisfied with the poverty alleviation; in other words, the performance of poverty alleviation needs to be improved. Regarding the evaluation of the specific poverty alleviation projects, it is rare to see the projects with an average score of over 80 points in the centesimal system since and most of them are scored more than 70. However, after the related projects are merged into six major categories, none of the categories gets an average score of 80 points in the centesimal system. As for the overall satisfaction with the poverty alleviation and development work, only 60.8% of all the respondents indicate "satisfied", which is at a pass level. The path analysis model is used to examine the influencing factors of the overall satisfaction with the poverty alleviation work. The results show that all the "initial variables" included in the analysis model, namely, the main demographic and social characteristics of the respondents, all have a significant direct impact on the overall satisfaction with the poverty alleviation work, and have an indirect impact on the overall satisfaction with poverty alleviation work through all or some of the six major categories of poverty alleviation projects. In terms of the sum of the direct and indirect effects, the initial variable with the largest absolute value is the family size, followed by the household per capita income, and then the education level of the respondents. These results conform to our daily observations and provide a good explanation for the ways and mechanisms by which these factors influence the respondents' overall satisfaction with poverty alleviation.

Some of the research results have clear policy implications. General Secretary Jinping Xi proposed the "targeted poverty alleviation" strategy during his inspection tour in Xiangxi, Hunan Province, in November 2013. "Poverty alleviation should be based on facts and local conditions," he said. "We must not just shout slogans or aim too high for targeted poverty alleviation".[16] General Secretary Jinping Xi also pointed out that "in order to carry out poverty alleviation and development, we need to work together as a whole, have common requirements and measures, and at the same time, highlight priorities and strengthen assistance to the especially poor

[16] *Jinping Xi Investigates into Poverty Alleviation in Western Hunan*, Xinhuanet, November 3, 2013, http://news.xinhuanet.com/politics/2013-11/03/c_11798426.htm.

villages and families".[17] Therefore, "targeted poverty alleviation is an important way to end the confusion about the basic situation and the goal as well as poor effect in poverty alleviation and development. In practical work, we should carry out precise identification, targeted support and dynamic management of poor villages and households to help the really poor and truly help the poor".[18] To better implement the guiding essence of General Secretary Jinping Xi's instructions on targeted poverty alleviation and further enhance the public's satisfaction with poverty alleviation work, it is necessary to conduct more precise design of poverty alleviation projects and improve their performance by bearing in mind the needs of different groups of people and their demographic and social characteristics.

(1) We should do a better job in basic poverty alleviation projects (including infrastructure construction, education and healthcare) that both directly help poverty alleviation and deliver benefit to the general population. The respondents show a high degree of satisfaction with these projects and the degree of satisfaction differs little among the respondents such that it does not have a statistically significant impact on the respondents' overall satisfaction with poverty reduction. It is worth mentioning that on April 20, 2016, the State Council held an executive meeting to deploy poverty alleviation work through transport infrastructure construction. On April 27, the State Council held an executive meeting to determine measures to accelerate the development of education in the central and western parts of China. At present, the central and local authorities are jointly promoting the improvement of public services in poor areas, including infrastructure, education and health, so as to enhance the ability of poor areas to lift themselves out of poverty, with a view to tamping the foundation for lifting all poor people out of poverty and making all related counties take off the "poverty" cap by 2020 as well as addressing the general poverty of the region.
(2) We should design poverty alleviation projects that are more accessible and helpful to elderly poor people, to enable the poor elderly to gain more practical benefits from such projects and to get out of poverty. As thus, it helps to eliminate the effects of age differences on the overall evaluation of poverty reduction work.
(3) Poverty alleviation projects should be designed and implemented with a gender perspective. Some of the existing poverty alleviation projects may be inaccessible to poor rural women in ethnic minority concentrated areas or are not so effective in helping them get out of poverty. Solving this problem will help to eliminate the gender gap in the overall evaluation of the poverty alleviation work and thus enhance people's overall satisfaction.

[17] "Jinping Xi, during his inspection tour in Hunan, stressed: Deepening reform and opening up, advancing innovation-driven development, and realizing the annual economic and social development goals", CCTV, November 5, 2013, http://news.cntv.cn/2013/11/05/ARTI1383649079486805.shtml,lastvisitedonMarch9,2017.

[18] Liu Yongfu, "Winning the Poverty Alleviation Campaign for Building a Moderately Prosperous Society in All Respects: Studying and Implementing the Essence of Comrade Jinping Xi's Important Speech on Poverty Alleviation and Development", *People's Daily*, April 9, 2014.

(4) The design and implementation of poverty alleviation projects should consider more about the target group with a low education level. For them, the projects that require a high level of knowledge, skill and understanding are obviously inaccessible to them. Their main advantages lie in their physical strength and their endurance of hardships. Poverty alleviation projects or projects should be designed and implemented to bring their strengths into play, so as to have an immediate effect in helping them out of poverty.

(5) In the design and implementation of poverty alleviation projects, more attention should be paid to the target groups with health problems. It is important not only to help them improve their health, but also enable them to participate in the projects as far as they can, so ensure they directly benefit poverty alleviation efforts. It can reduce influence of the difference in health status on the overall evaluation of poverty alleviation work.

(6) When designing and implementing poverty alleviation projects, sufficient attention should be paid to large rural households. Such households often have a relatively high dependency ratio, and some poverty alleviation projects designed primarily with the working-age population in rural areas in mind may put such poor households at a disadvantage, delivering less benefit than either what the authorities intended or what these households themselves expected. This can negatively impact the overall assessment by these large household of the effectiveness of poverty alleviation work.

Chapter 6
Anti-poverty Effects of Rural Subsistence Allowance System in Ethnic Minority Concentrated Areas

Since 2007, the Chinese government has comprehensively implemented the rural subsistence allowance system, which provides financial assistance to the rural poore whose per capita household income falls below the legal minimum in order to help them meet their basic needs. Intended as a safety net for poor households in rural areas, the system is designed to mitigate rural poverty and improve social justice. In this study, we mainly focus on whether in ethnic minority concentrated areas in the China's western region, where poverty is especially severe, this assistance program which targets extremely low-income rural households has produced the internted outcome. In short, what have the anti-poverty effects of rural subsistence allowance programs been in these areas? How can it promote social justice in these areas? How to further improve it for better anti-poverty effects and social justice? According to the 18th CPC National Congress, China should complete the building of a moderately prosperous society in all respects by the end of 2020. To achieve this goal, whether poverty alleviation in rural ethnic minority concentrated areas will achieve the best results in the last five years is of vital importance. Therefore, studying and answering these questions play a significant role in theory and practice.

1 Literature Review

According to A.C. Pigou, the British economist, government interference in income distribution through policies should, provided it would not hamper the growth of national incom, be strengthened to increase the income of poor people and narrow the gap between the rich and the poor. He believed, by extension, that it is the best form of interference is progressive income tax and inheritance tax, so money collected from the rich can be transferred to low-income earners in the form of

A substantial section of this chapter was first published in *Ethno-National Studies,* No. 2, 2015.

X. Liu, *Complex Pictures of Poverty and Multiple Paths of Poverty Alleviation in Ethnic Areas of China*, https://doi.org/10.1007/978-981-97-4133-5_6

increased unemployment benefits and social assistance. Meanwhile, the government should also increase necessary cash assistance for workers, provide them with various social service facilities, and universal pension system or offer universal allowances in accordance with the standard of minimum income.[1] Acceptance of this theory has led many countries in the world to adopt progressive income taxes and provide assistance to low-income households. For example, in 2001, the average proportion of expenditure on social security in GDP in Organization for Economic Co-operation and Development (OECD) countries reached 13.23%. A large share of the expenditure goes toward guaranteed income, i.e., allowances meant to supplement the income of low-income households.[2]

DeFina and Thanawala conducted a research on poverty-alleviation effects of public assistance in 17 OECD countries with LIS data. In addition to poverty rate, poverty gap and other indicators, they also analyzed with the index of income inequality among the poor. The result shows that after the implementation of public assistance for low-income earners, the poverty headcount ratio dropped by 61% on average in these countries; specifically, it dropped 29.5% in the United States, 56.1% in Canada and 85.6% in Sweden. Moreover, the social assistance system targeting low-income earners not only reduced poverty, it also had macroscopic distributive effects, especially the horizontal redistribution of income.[3]

Chinese scholars have also paid attention to anti-poverty effects of the subsistence allowance system in rural China and the improvement of social justice. Results of their researches mainly concern four aspects. First, the rural subsistence allowance system covers the poor households to the maximum extent and achieves excellent effects, alleviating poverty to some extent, improving internal income distribution in rural areas and narrowing the income gap between groups affected by poverty and other groups.[4] Second, there are obvious disparity and hierarchy in the operational performance of the system among provinces and regions. Although the overall performance of the system is improved, certain efforts still need to be made to achieve the

---

[1] *The Economics of Welfare* (trans: Jin Di). Beijing: Huaxia Publishing House.

[2] World Bank: *Social Safety Nets in OECD Countries*. http://siteresources.worldbank.org/safetynetsandtransfers/Resources/281945-1124119303499/SSNPrimer-Note25.pdf.

[3] DeFina, R. H., & Thanawala, K. (2002). International evidence on the impact of transfers and taxes on alternative poverty indexes. *Luxembourg Income Study Working Paper Series* No. 325;

Allegrezza S., Heinrich, G., & Jesuit, D. (2004). Poverty and income inequality in Luxembourg and the Grande Région in comparative perspective. *Socio-Economic Review*, (2): pp. 263–283;

Hölsch, K. & Kraus, M. (2006). European schemes of social assistance: an empirical analysis of set-ups and distributive impacts. *International Journal of Social Welfare*, (5): pp. 50–62.

[4] Tong Wanheng. (2005). A survey and reflection on the system of minimum living guarantee (SMLG) of rural residents in Fujian Province. *Issues in Agricultural Economy*, (1); Xie Dongmei. (2010). Research on distributive effectiveness and targeting efficiency of the rural minimum living standard security system. Beijing: China Agriculture Press; Dai Weidong. (2010). Financial expenditure analysis of the rural subsistence allowance system: A comparison of negative income tax law and differential subsidy law, *Henan Social Sciences*, (5); Household survey department of national bureau of statistics. (2012). *Poverty Monitoring Report of Rural China 2011*, China Statistics Press.

goal of covering all poor households.[5] Third, aim bias and aim omission still exist in the implementation of the system. Moreover, with the rather low standard of poverty line and even lower standard of subsistence allowance, the overall income of the rural poor people including the subsistence allowance is still at a low level. This causes the problems that only a small part of the poor receive the relief, low-income households in need of relief are excluded, the needs of poor people are not met effectively, and effects of poverty alleviation are limited. Especially in western rural areas severely affected by poverty, some local governments, without enough financial resources, can only implement the rural subsistence allowance system by means of mass-based control. As a result, not all rural poor people eligible for subsistence allowance are covered. In one word, the implementation of the system faces problems of low standard of subsistence allowance, little subsidy for the per capita compensation, and limited coverage.[6] Fourth, the system incurs a high financing cost of the government, but fails to achieve the desired effects, or even causes negative incentive effects, that is, welfare dependence.[7]

To sum up, scholars at home and aboard have conducted theoretical and practical researches on poverty alleviation effects of subsistence allowance system, reaching different conclusions due to different locations and time they focused on. As is known to all, Chinese government has made great efforts in supporting ethnic minority concentrated areas in the west since the start of the large-scale development of the western region. The government-led subsistence allowance system may have different effects on poverty alleviation and promotion of social justice among different regions. With limited data, there is not enough quantitative analysis and researches on the effects of the system in poverty alleviation and promotion of social equality in these areas in the existing documents. On this account we try to make up the gap in this chapter, through the large sample data of the survey of rural households captured in 2012 based on the cooperation between the Institute of Ethnology and Anthropology of Chinese Academy of Social Sciences, and the School of Economics of Minzu University of China. By doing so, we assess the implementation of the rural subsistence allowance system in ethnic minority concentrated areas, and what the government could do to further improve the system.

---

[5] He Hui, & Deng Dasong. (2010). Performance evaluation of the rural subsistence allowance system in rural China", *Jiangxi Social Sciences*, (11).

[6] Li Xiaoyun, Dong Qiang, & Liu Qiming. (2006). The minimal life guarantee (MLG) policy: Implementation and targeting in rural areas. *Problems of Agricultural Economy,* (11); Wang Zengwen. (2009). Empirical analysis of the effect of the rural subsistence allowance system on poverty alleviation, *Guizhou Social Sciences,* (12); Niu Qin. (2011). Discussion on problems and policy responses related to the minimum living standard security system in west rural areas of China, *Journal of Anhui Agricultural Sciences*, (10); Wang Lihua, & Meng Xiang Hong. (2012). Arrangement of social assistance system from the perspective of anti-poverty. *Gansu Social Sciences*, (2).

[7] Wang Zengwen. (2009) Empirical analysis of the effect of the rural minimum living guarantee system on poverty alleviation, *Guizhou Social Sciences,* (12); Li Shengji, Lu Kangyin, & Zhu Jinxia. (2014). An analysis of the poverty reduction effectiveness of rural subsistence allowance system. *Taxation and Economy*, (3).

2 Data Sources and Analytical Strategies

In 2012, the Institute of Ethnology and Anthropology of Chinese Academy of Social Sciences, and the School of Economics of Minzu University of China worked together to conduct the Chinese Household Ethnicity Survey (CHES). The survey covers urban and rural communities and residents in seven provinces and regions, including Xinjiang, Inner Mongolia, Xiang, Xingu, Qinghai, Guizhou and Hunan. Through random sampling in the urban and rural areas, it laid stress on the households of major ethnic groups in each region, and considered the difference among ethnic and non-ethnic regions, natural geography, and social and economic development. For the survey on the income of rural households in 2011, we select 7,257 households from 81 counties and 757 administrative villages in seven provinces and regions, with a total of 31,671 people. According to the international norms, we add the estimated value of the rent of the per ca pita housing ownership to the per ca pita net income of rural households defined by National Bureau of Statistics.[8]

Some terms and analysis strategies in this chapter are defined as follows.

1. Poverty line

Poverty has economic, social, political, cultural, and many other dimensions. From income and income distribution equality, this study provides qualitative assessment of the poverty condition of rural groups affected by poverty and its changing trend, and the changes of the condition and distribution after the implementation of the system in rural areas. This paper adopts the poverty line of 2,300 yuan newly adopted by the Chinese government in 2011.

2. Measuring poverty

We measure poverty based on the income standard mainly with the FGT index. See more in Chap. 3.

3. Measuring income inequality measurement

We use Gini coefficient to measure the overall inequality and use Theil index and its segmentation to analyze the composition of equality. See more in Chap. 3.

[8] This questionnaire covers seven provinces and regions, including Inner Mongolia, Ningxia, Xinjiang, Qinghai, Guangxi, Guizhou, and Hunan. The first five are all located in the western ethnic minority concentrated areas. The survey in Hunan covers Xiangxi Tujia-Miao autonomous prefecture, Shaoyang City, Yongzhou City and Huaihua City, most of which are ethnic minority concentrated areas. For convenience, the seven surveyed provinces and regions in this paper are referred to as "the surveyed ethnic minority concentrated areas" for short. Inner Mongolia, Ningxia, Xinjiang and Qinghai are referred to as "one province and three autonomous regions in northwestern China". Guangxi, Hunan and Guizhou are referred to as "two provinces and one autonomous region in southwestern China" (although Hunan belongs to the central and southern part of China rather than the southwestern part). According to the per capita net income of rural households defined by the research group, we make some revision on the data in this research. For details of CHES database and data processing methods, please see Li Keqiang, Long Yuanwei, & Liu Xiaoming (2014). *Chinese Household Ethnicity Survey 2013*. Social Sciences Academic Press. In addition, all the data without notes in this paper come from CHES.

4. Decomposition of redistribution effect

We decompose the redistribution effect of the rural subsistence allowance system by means of APK re-ranking measure in this chapter.

Atkinson, Plotnick and Kakwani once proposed the decomposition of redistribution effect with Kakwani index respectively, by means of APK re-ranking measure.[9] This method separates the reordering effect caused by changes of individual sequencing and gets the "purified" vertical effect. The equations of the APK re-ranking measure are:

$$REAPK = VK - RAPK\ VK = K = CT - GXRAPK = GN - CN$$

VK represents the vertical effect, and *t* represents average tax rate. *K* represents Kakwani index, the difference between the concentration coefficient of tax[10] and Gini coefficient (Kakwani, 1977). *K* represents progressive tax when it is less than 0, proportional tax when equal to 0, and regressive tax when more than 0. *RAPK* represents the reordering effect, namely, the difference between Gini coefficient (GN) and concentration coefficient (CN).

3 Profile of Surveyed Rural Areas

The proportions of those from Hunan, Guangxi, Guizhou, Ningxia, Qinghai, Xinjiang, and Inner Mongolia to the population of surveyed households are 14.26%, 15.17%, 17.32%, 13.34%, 15.37%, 13.00%, and 11.53%, respectively (See Table 6.1). The surveyed households are ethnically mixed, of which 11,494 people are Han and 19,530 are from ethnic minority groups, among which, the ethnic groups of Miao, Hui, Dong, Uyghur, Zhuang, Tibetan, Mongolian, Tujia, Yao, Kazak and Sala predominate.

From the perspective of the population burden in a household, the total dependency ratio of rural households in the surveyed ethnic minority concentrated areas is 34.72%, slightly higher than the national average of 34.41% in the same year.[11] There is insignificant difference between those in southwestern and northwestern China. In terms of provinces and regions, the total dependency ratio in Ningxia is

[9] Atkinson. A.B. (1980). *Horizontal Equity and the Distribution of the Tax Burden.* Washington D.C.: Brookings Institution; Plotnick. R. (1981). A measure of horizontal inequity, *The review of Economics and Statistics,* 63 (2), 283–288; Kakwani. N. C. (1984). On the measurement of tax progressivity and redistributive effect of taxes with applications to horizontal and vertical equity. *Advances in Econometrics.* 3: pp.149–168.

[10] When decomposing with APK re-ranking measure, we can regard the subsistence allowance as the negative income tax.

[11] By the end of 2011, the population aged 65 and above had reached 122.88 million, accounting for 9.1% of the national population. Working people aged 15-64 accounted for 74.4% and children aged less than 14 accounted for 16.5%. National Bureau of Statistics. (2012). *China's Total Population and Structural Changes in 2011*, National Bureau of Statistics website.

Table 6.1 Basic characteristics of rural households in surveyed ethnic minority concentrated areas Unit: Household, Population, %, yuan

Region	Total samples				Subsistence allowance samples			
	No. of households	Population	Total dependency ratio	Per capita net income of rural families	No. of households	Population	Per capita net income of rural families	Per capita subsistence allowance income
Surveyed ethnic minority concentrated areas	7257	31,671	34.72	6059.40	1367	2820	4313.8	338.23
Two provinces and one autonomous region in southwestern China	3237	14,809	34.32	4636.92	724	1618	3938.65	269.46
Hunan	1007	4516	32.73	3361.81	116	263	3091.83	321.81
Guangxi	1030	4806	30.84	5831.27	150	348	3385.99	291.50
Guizhou	1200	5487	38.91	4640.81	458	1007	4252.95	253.61
One province and three autonomous regions in northwestern China	4020	16,862	35.08	7313.25	643	1202	4730.63	414.33
Ningxia	970	4224	41.30	6718.17	213	257	4769.68	161.41
Qinghai	1000	4867	38.68	6028.07	193	522	5237.79	579.71
Xinjiang	1000	4118	36.89	9075.93	184	360	3657.47	519.29
Inner Mongolia	1050	3653	22.74	7729.82	53	63	6535.34	569.35
Han	2955	11,494	29.38	7676.40	362	752	5481.09	391.44
Ethnic minorities[a]	4175	19,530	37.80	5147.98	969	1980	3948.96	321.64

(continued)

Table 6.1 (continued)

Region	Total samples				Subsistence allowance samples			
	No. of households	Population	Total dependency ratio	Per capita net income of rural families	No. of households	Population	Per capita net income of rural families	Per capita subsistence allowance income
Mongolian	205	860	25.57	8777.92	8	8	6288.21	358.33
Hui	611	2926	48.96	6245.38	161	253	4458.24	273.93
Tibetan	304	1483	36.82	6079.32	58	149	5053.89	547.06
Uyghur	509	2326	41.46	4781.90	127	269	2821.18	500.62
Miao	964	4534	39.68	3948.68	302	639	3851.41	234.73
Zhuang	390	1741	29.58	5116.00	50	139	3357.34	314.71
Dong	530	2436	32.17	4328.57	122	227	4178.61	277.26
Yao	153	722	30.55	5146.24	31	64	4006.40	240.14
Tujia	162	774	32.75	3633.44	27	62	3934.08	356.51
Kazak	120	500	43.84	10,655.63	21	29	6502.90	425.87
Sala	68	448	65.81	4727.08	10	29	2994.49	505.91
Other ethnic groups	159	779	28.01	4230.46	52	111	3753.19	280.42

Note The "total dependency ratio" in the table refers to the proportion of the population "aged between 0 and 14" and "above 65" to the working-age population in a household. In the table, the "household" in the subsistence allowance samples refers to a household with subsistence allowance income or surveyed people entitled to subsistence allowance assistance; the "people" refers to those who are entitled to subsistence allowance assistance; the "per capita net income of rural families" refers to the per capita net income of the households with subsistence allowance income. In addition, some values are found missing when we collect the statistics of the database in this chapter. Due to the absence of different variables such as ethnicity, registered permanent residence, gender, age and educational background, the collected samples are inconsistent in some cases. However, it does not affect the analysis of the overall situation in the surveyed ethnic minority concentrated areas. There is no further explanation for the similar problems of data in the following tables in this chapter

[a]All the family data in this paper refer to ethnic minority families. A family with 50% or above members being ethnic minority people is an ethnic minority family, and if otherwise it is a Han family. An ethnic minority family with 50% or above members of a certain ethnic group is a family of this ethnic minority group. Liu Xiaomin. (2013). The comparative studies on the poverty problems of rural residents from the ethnic point of view: A case study of Guangxi, Guizhou and Hunan. *Ethno-National Studies*, (4)

the highest (41.30%) while that in Inner Mongolia is the lowest (22.74%). In terms of ethnic groups, the total dependency ratio in households with Sala ethnicity is the highest (65.81%) while that in Mongolian households is the lowest (25.57%). In general, the population burden of rural households in the surveyed ethnic minority concentrated areas is relatively heavier than the national average, especially those in Ningxia and of Sala ethnicity.

Table 6.1 shows that there is a significant difference among provinces, regions and ethnic groups in surveyed minority areas in terms of rural household income. The per capita net income of rural households living on subsistence allowances in Inner Mongolia and Qinghai is even higher than that of the overall samples in Hunan and Guizhou. The per capita net income of rural families covered by the subsistence allowances of Kazak and Mongolia is even higher than that of all samples of Hui, Tibetan, Yao, Zhuang, Uyghur, Sala, Dong, Miao and Tujia ethnic groups.

As seen from the coverage of the subsistence allowance system, the proportion of households with subsistence allowance in ethnic minority concentrated areas is 18.8%, and that in the three provinces and one region in the northwest is 16.0%, 2.8% points lower than the overall average; the proportion of surveyed households in the two provinces and one autonomous region in southwestern China is 22.4%, 3.5% points higher than the overall average and 6.4 percentage points higher than the average level of the areas in the northwest. In terms of provinces and regions, Guizhou tops in the proportion of surveyed households with subsistence allowance (38.2%), and Inner Mongolia registers the lowest rate of 5%. Speaking from ethnic groups, the proportion of surveyed households of Miao, Hui and Uyghur with subsistence allowance are relatively high at 31.3%, 26.4%, and 25.0% respectively, while those of Mongolian, Zhuang and Sala are relatively low at 3.9%, 12.8% and 14.7% respectively. Comparing the official data[12] of those rural households in each province and region, we can conclude that the ratio of rural households with subsistence allowance assistance in ethnic minority concentrated areas in Hunan, Guangxi, Guizhou, and Qinghai is higher than the national standard while that of Ningxia, Xinjiang and Inner Mongolia is lower than the national standard. Some researches show that the surveyed households tend to underreport or not report that they are under the subsistence allowance.[13]

---

[12] The subsistence allowance assistance rates for rural households in Hunan, Guangxi, Guizhou, Ningxia, Qinghai, Xinjiang and Inner Mongolia in 2011 were 7.57%, 13.31%, 26.45%, 22.15%, 15.14%, 19.89% and 22.06% respectively, which are calculated and collected in accordance with relevant data of China *Civil Affairs Statistical Yearbook in 2012 (Statistics of China Social Services)*. Ministry of Civil Affairs of the People's Republic of China. (2012). China Statistical Press.

[13] Gustafsson. B. & Deng. Q. H. (2007). Social assistance receipt and its importance for combating poverty in urban China. *IZA Discussion Paper*, No. 2758; Gao.Q. Garfinkel. I. & Zhai. F. (2009). Anti-poverty effectiveness of the minimum living standard assistance policy in urban China. *Review of Income and Wealth*, Vol. 55 (1): pp. 630–655; Wen Wen. (2013). A study on poverty reduction and redistribution effects of subsistence allowance system in urban China. Nankai University.

4 Poverty Reduction Effects of the Subsistence Allowance Program in Rural Areas

Table 6.2 shows the decline of the poverty index of rural households in the surveyed ethnic minority concentrated areas after they received the subsistence allowance assistance. Under the subsistence allowance system, the poverty headcount ratio of rural households in these areas has been decreased by 4.82%. The poverty gap index representing the depth of poverty has been reduced by 7.77%, and the squared poverty gap index representing the intensity of poverty has been cut by 11.54%. This indicates that the implementation of the system in ethnic minority concentrated areas has not only decreased the proportion of poor households among people who have subsistence allowance to some extent, but also largely cut down the depth of poverty of subsistence allowance recipients, especially those most in need.

Table 6.2 also shows that with the subsistence allowance added into the per capita net income of the surveyed households there is a difference among regions and ethnic groups in surveyed minority areas in terms of per capita net income of rural household. In terms of regions, the headcount ratio, poverty gap rate, and squared poverty gap of the surveyed rural households in the province and three autonomous regions in northwestern China are higher than those in the two provinces and autonomous region in the southwest, which are 2.51, 5.48 and 8.61 percentage points higher respectively. As for provinces and regions, the headcount ratio, poverty gap rate and squared poverty gap of the surveyed rural households in Qinghai, Guizhou and Xinjiang have significantly declined. The headcount ratio and poverty gap rate of the surveyed rural households in Qinghai decrease the most, by 12.18% and 16.47% respectively. The squared poverty gap in Guizhou drops the most, by 23.52%. Inner Mongolia and Hunan show a relatively small decrease in the three aspects. In detail, the poverty headcount ratio of those households in Inner Mongolia remains the same before and after adding the subsistence allowance income, and the poverty gap rate only decreases by 3.38%, the lowest among the three provinces and four autonomous regions. The squared poverty gap in Ningxia is cut down by 4.25%, the smallest level.

In terms of ethnic groups, the rural subsistence allowance system has the best poverty reduction effect on the surveyed rural households of Tibetan, Hui and Uyghur ethnic groups. It has greatly reduced the coverage, depth and intensity of poverty. In particular, the headcount rate of poor people in households of Sala and Kazak ethnic groups remains the same before and after the subsistence allowance assistance is included, but the depth and intensity of poverty have been significantly reduced (by 12.27–28.65%) after that. The poverty reduction effect of the system is relatively weak on households of Mongolian, Zhuang and Miao ethnic groups, as reflected in the limited scale, depth and intensity of poverty reduction.

In the table above, we evaluate the poverty reduction effects of the rural subsistence allowance system in western minority areas regionally and ethnically. Then, we investigate the households that benefit most from the system with their living condition improved significantly from a micro level.

Table 6.2 Decline of FGT index of the surveyed rural households after receiving the subsistence allowance assistance Unit: %

Region	Headcount ratio H*100	Poverty gap ratio PG*100	Squared poverty gap ratio SPG*100
Two provinces and one autonomous region in southwestern China	3.77	5.51	7.77
Hunan	1.26	2.83	4.65
Guangxi	2.94	5.80	9.00
Guizhou	11.25	16.15	23.52
One province and three autonomous regions in northwestern China	6.28	10.99	16.38
Ningxia	3.15	3.69	4.25
Qinghai	12.18	16.47	19.80
Xinjiang	7.35	13.73	20.54
Inner Mongolia	0.00	3.38	5.23
Three provinces and four autonomous regions in ethnic minority concentrated areas	4.82	7.77	11.54
Han	4.92	5.16	5.03
Mongolian	0.00	1.00	1.56
Hui	8.16	11.25	16.08
Tibetan	12.50	15.89	14.58
Uyghur	6.94	13.04	19.57
Miao	3.44	5.60	8.77
Zhuang	0.88	4.14	8.09
Dong	6.36	9.61	12.29
Yao	0.00	5.30	12.69
Tujia	4.05	3.37	4.25
Kazak	0.00	12.27	24.85
Sala	0.00	15.95	28.65
Other ethnic groups	7.27	8.00	7.38

As is shown in Table 6.3, first, the smaller the household, the greater the poverty alleviation effects of subsistence allowance assistance. In addition, the smaller the household is, the greater the depth and intensity of poverty for the poor households are decreased. There is no poor single-person household after the subsistence allowance is counted in. Therefore, the assistance has the best effects on poverty alleviation for single-person households (up to 100%). Second, the more children in a household there are, the less effects of the assistance will have on poverty alleviation. In particular, the assistance has no effect on poverty alleviation for households with four or more children, but has a great effect on reducing the poverty depth and intensity for households with three children. Third, the effect is relatively better for households where the head of the household is female, at a relatively old age, in less than good health, the township or village official, a member of the CPC, or unemployed, and their depth and intensity of their poverty is cut down greatly. In a word, the assistance has the best effect on poverty reduction for single-person households, and has relatively great effect for households without children, or the head of the household who is disabled, female, elderly, township or village official, unemployed, and a member or the CPC.

5 Income Redistribution Effects of the Rural Subsistence Allowance Program

Economic growth and income distribution are two essential factors affecting poverty. When the income distribution is relatively equal, economic growth can certainly reduce poverty. When the economy is growing, the higher the degree of income distribution equality is, the lower the headcount ratio will be.[14] By improving the income level of poor people in rural areas, rural subsistence allowance can reduce poverty, narrow the income gap among them, improve the income distribution of the whole society, and eventually realize social justice. Meanwhile, the increase of income equality further promotes anti-poverty in turn. In the next chapter, we use Gini coefficient and Theil index to measure the inequality of income distribution, and then analyze the effect of subsistence allowance on income redistribution in rural areas.

5.1 Narrowing the Income Gap

When implementing a policy, it is necessary to ensure equity so that individuals who have welfare parity before will enjoy the same afterwards. Furthermore, equity is subdivided into vertical equality and horizontal equality. Vertical equality means that people's income can be changed, rather than the ranking of their income before and after the policy takes effect. Horizontal equity requires that individuals with the same income be treated equally.[15] In practice, different redistribution policies have certain differences in specific functions. To investigate whether a certain policy is equitable vertically and horizontally, we need to decompose the effect of redistribution with certain means, so as to better understand the "core" of the policy. At present, people

[14] Liu Xiaomin. (2013). A comparative study on the poverty problems of rural residents from the ethnic point of view: taking Guangxi, Guizhou and Hunan as examples. *Ethno-National Studies*, (4).

[15] Feldstein. M. (1976). On the theory of tax reform. *Journal of Public Economics*. Vol. 6(1–2): pp. 77–104.

Table 6.3 Decline of FGT index of the surveyed rural households covered by subsistence allowance

Region	Headcount ratio H*100	Poverty gap ratio PG*100	Squared poverty gap ratio SPG*100
By household size			
Single-person household	100.00	100.00	100.00
Two-person household	13.04	17.17	27.39
Three-person household	4.28	10.80	19.22
Multi-person household	4.27	6.87	9.84
By gender of the head of the household			
Male	4.51	7.62	11.50
Female	10.41	9.00	9.90
By age of the head of the household			
Young-aged household	3.65	6.70	10.72
Middle-aged household	3.72	6.80	9.81
Old-aged household	7.89	10.62	15.85
By health condition of the head of the household			
Healthy	4.37	7.07	10.53
Disabled 1	7.69	12.43	17.45
Disabled 2	12.91	20.08	27.35
Number of children			
None	5.92	8.35	11.48
One	4.96	7.60	11.36
Two	3.89	7.21	11.71
Three	2.15	8.03	12.32
Four and above	0.00	2.81	4.95
Identity of the head of the household			
Township or village cadre	6.32	13.30	18.81
Not township or village cadre	4.66	7.32	11.03
Communist League or CPC member	7.98	13.27	20.73
Neither Communist League nor CPC member	4.38	6.95	9.99
By employment of the head of the household			
Employed	3.85	6.70	10.42
Unemployed	8.40	12.20	16.23

usually apply APK re-ranking measure, AJL decomposition and UL decomposition to decompose the effect of redistribution. Inspired by Wen Wen, we decompose the redistribution effect of rural subsistence allowance mainly with the APK re-ranking method in this chapter.[16]

Table 6.4 shows the income redistribution effect of rural subsistence allowance in the surveyed ethnic minority concentrated areas measured with the Gini coefficient. It is clearly that the Gini coefficients of the overall income inequality of rural households in these areas before and after receiving the subsistence allowance assistance are 0.4168 and 0.4123 respectively, and the income gap has been reduced by 1.1%. Therefore, the subsistence allowance assistance has a little effect on narrowing the income gap to some extent. After decomposing the Gini coefficients of total income, the vertical effect is 0.005. The concentration coefficient of the assistance is −0.2126. The negative coefficient indicates that assistance is mainly aimed at people with low income. Theoretically, the greater the absolute concentration coefficient is, the more assistance the households with low per capita net income gets.

In terms of provinces and regions, before the implementation of subsistence allowance assistance, the per capita net income gap of surveyed rural households in Xinjiang, Guangxi and Ningxia is relatively great, with the Gini coefficient above 0.4. The gap among the surveyed rural households in Guizhou is the smallest, with an income Gini coefficient of 0.2837. After the assistance, the income gap among these households in the three regions remains large while that in Guizhou remains the smallest. However, the income gap of these households has been greatly narrowed in Qinghai, Guizhou and Xinjiang, with the decrease of Gini coefficient by 1.95%, 1.94% and 1.34% respectively while the decrease of the coefficient of these households in Hunan, Guangxi, Ningxia and Inner Mongolia is less than 1%. In addition, the absolute values of concentration coefficients of these households with subsistence allowance assistance in Xinjiang, Guangxi and Inner Mongolia are relatively high, which are 0.5181, 0.3323 and 0.3154, respectively. It indicates that the rural subsistence allowance systems in these three regions are well implemented. The lower the income of the surveyed households is, the more subsistence allowance assistance they receive. After decomposing the income redistribution effects, we find that there are income re-ranking effects at different levels while income redistribution effects of subsistence allowance systems in each province and region are achieved. Guizhou, Qinghai and Hunan register relatively large ranking effect, and their loss accounts for 15.25%, 15.3% and 19.32% of the income redistribution effects.

Speaking from the perspective of ethnic groups, before the implementation of subsistence allowance assistance, the per capita net income gap of the surveyed rural households of Zhuang, Uyghur and Hui ethnic groups is large, with the income Gini coefficient higher than 0.4 while that of Dong, Miao and Tibetan ethnic groups is small, with the coefficient standing at 0.3273, 0.3339 and 0.355 respectively. After the assistance, the per capita net income gap of these households of different ethnic groups remains unchanged. But, the per capita income gap of Uyghur, Sala and

[16] Wen Wen. (2013). A study on poverty reduction and redistribution effects of subsistence allowance system in urban China. Nankai University, (5).

Table 6.4 Income redistribution effects of rural subsistence allowance measured by Gini coefficient in the surveyed rural areas

	$GINI_{pre}$	$GINI_{post}$	Concentration coefficient	RE	RE (%)	Vertical effect	Re-ranking effect	Loss of redistribution effect (%)
Surveyed ethnic minority concentrated areas	0.4168	0.4123	−0.2126	0.0045	1.09	0.0050	0.0005	9.87
Hunan	0.3677	0.3649	−0.1338	0.0027	0.74	0.0034	0.0007	19.32
Guangxi	0.4298	0.4267	−0.3323	0.0032	0.74	0.0034	0.0002	6.56
Guizhou	0.2837	0.2782	−0.0821	0.0055	1.94	0.0065	0.0010	15.25
Ningxia	0.4106	0.4084	−0.1056	0.0022	0.54	0.0025	0.0002	9.35
Qinghai	0.3434	0.3367	−0.1921	0.0067	1.95	0.0079	0.0012	15.3
Xinjiang	0.4793	0.4729	−0.5181	0.0064	1.34	0.0067	0.0003	4.42
Inner Mongolia	0.3424	0.3406	−0.3154	0.0019	0.54	0.0022	0.0003	15.59
Han	0.3955	0.3927	−0.2228	0.0028	0.71	0.0032	0.0004	12.37
Mongolian	0.3735	0.3728	−0.2095	0.0007	0.19	0.0008	0.0001	8.08
Hui	0.4256	0.4205	−0.1728	0.0051	1.2	0.0058	0.0007	11.32
Tibetan	0.355	0.3476	−0.2646	0.0073	2.07	0.0084	0.0011	12.63
Uyghur	0.4434	0.4275	−0.3856	0.0158	3.57	0.0171	0.0013	7.55
Miao	0.3339	0.33	0.0035	0.0038	1.15	0.0045	0.0006	13.97
Zhuang	0.4643	0.4618	−0.1622	0.0024	0.53	0.0027	0.0003	9.86
Dong	0.3273	0.3236	−0.0699	0.0036	1.1	0.0043	0.0007	15.47
Yao	0.3535	0.3502	−0.2462	0.0033	0.92	0.0035	0.0003	8
Tujia	0.3906	0.3862	−0.0477	0.0044	1.12	0.0062	0.0018	29.39
Kazak	0.3936	0.3928	−0.1882	0.0008	0.2	0.0008	0.0000	2.96
Sala	0.3889	0.3766	−0.4822	0.0122	3.14	0.0135	0.0013	9.41

Tibetan has been greatly narrowed, with the decrease of 3.57%, 3.14% and 2.07% respectively while that of the surveyed households of Mongolian, Kazak, Han, Yao and Zhuang is less than 1%. In addition, the absolute values of the concentration coefficients of Sala, Uyghur, and Yao are 0.4822, 0.3856, and 0.2462 respectively. These relatively great values partly show that the local governments have well targeted the households of Yao, Sala, and Uyghur. The lower the income of these households of Sala, Uyghur, and Yao, the more subsistence allowance assistance they get. After decomposing the income redistribution effects of the subsistence allowance system, we find that there are income re-ranking effects at different levels when income redistribution effects of the subsistence allowance system in ethnic minority households are realized. Households of Tujia, Sala, Uyghur and Tibetan see relatively large ordering effect, and their loss accounts for 29.39%, 9.41%, 7.55% and 12.63% of the income redistribution effects.

To sum up, subsistence allowance assistance has little effects on the income redistribution of ethnic minority concentrated areas in the surveyed provinces and regions, differing among regions (provinces) and ethnic groups.

5.2 *Income Redistribution Effects of Provinces and Ethnic Groups*

As China is a vast country, its economic and social development as well as the effects of many systems and policies differs greatly among different regions. Due to the different standards of subsistence allowances adopted in different regions and different ways in practice, the impact of the subsistence allowance system on the income distribution may differ among different regions and ethnic groups.

After decomposing the Theil index GE (0) and GE (1) of the overall income inequality of rural households in the surveyed ethnic minority concentrated areas within and among provinces and regions, we obtain results shown in Table 6.10. After the implementation of subsistence allowance assistance, the contribution rates of income inequality GE (0) and GE (1) within the provinces and regions are 85.25% and 85.98%, with a year-on-year decrease of 3.78% and 2.22% respectively. The Thiel index GE (0) and GE (1) of contribution rate of income inequality among provinces and regions is only 14.75% and 14.02%, which are respectively 1.33% and 1.38% lower than that before the assistance.

We decompose the Theil index GE (0) and GE (1) of overall income inequality in ethnic minority concentrated areas within and among ethnic groups (see Table 6.10). The result shows that after the implementation of subsistence allowance assistance, the contribution rates of the income inequality within ethnic groups to the overall inequality measured by the Theil index GE (0) and GE (1) are 87.02% and 87.58% respectively, with a year-on-year decrease of 3.57% and 2.03% respectively. The contribution rates of the income inequality among ethnic groups are 14.75% and 14.02% respectively, with a year-on-year decrease of 2.68% and 2.65% (Table 6.5).

Table 6.5 Thiel index decomposition of the income before and after receiving the subsistence allowance

		Before		After		Decline (%)	
		GE (0)	GE (1)	GE (0)	GE (1)	GE (0)	GE (1)
Regionally	Within regions	0.2724	0.2726	0.2621	0.2665	3.78	2.22
	Among regions	0.0460	0.0441	0.0454	0.0435	1.33	1.38
Ethnically	Within ethnic groups	0.2779	0.2772	0.2680	0.2715	3.57	2.03
	Among ethnic groups	0.0411	0.0396	0.0400	0.0385	2.68	2.65

In general, on the one hand, the rural subsistence allowance narrows the income gap within and among provinces and regions, and its effect on the former is greater than on the latter. Meanwhile, it also reduces the income gap within and among ethnic groups, and its effect on the former is slightly greater than on the latter. On the other hand, as the Theil index GE (0) is relatively sensitive to the income changes of common people while Theil index GE (1) to changes of those with high income, the decline of GE (0) is greater than that of GE (1) after the implementation of the subsistence allowance assistance. This shows that the assistance has a greater improving effect on income distribution for poor people than those with high income.

6 Brief Conclusion and Discussion

With the rural data in CHES 2011, this chapter analyzes poverty-alleviation effect and income redistribution effect of the rural subsistence allowance system on surveyed ethnic minority concentrated areas. The main conclusions can be drawn as below.

First, the implementation of the rural subsistence allowance system in ethnic minority concentrated areas can help people shake off poverty. It not only reduces the proportion of poor families in the subsistence allowance recipients at a certain level, but also drastically lowers their poverty depth, especially for those who living an extremely difficult life.

Second, the system has different effects upon different regions and ethnic groups. It exerts better effects upon the two provinces and one autonomous region in southwestern China than in one province and three autonomous regions in northwestern China. Compared to other provinces and regions, under the system, more poor families have been lifted out of poverty in Guizhou, Qinghai and Xinjiang than Inner Mongolia and Hunan. Compared to other ethnic groups, the poverty-alleviation effects of the system upon the ethnic groups of Tibetan, Hui and Uyghur are stronger than those upon Mongolians. Except for history, nature and environment factors, as well as different economic development in the last two decades, the rural subsistence allowance system may play the main role in easing poverty among the surveyed people in the above-mentioned provinces, regions and ethnic groups. Besides, thanks to the superfast development of Inner Mongolia in the last two decades, the poverty level in rural areas is relatively low, though the system has exerted less than great poverty-alleviation effect.

Third, certain differences in poverty headcount ratio and poverty-alleviation effects of the rural subsistence allowance system exist in different types of surveyed rural households. The headcount ratio of multi-child families, old-aged households, female-headed households, multi-person households, non-township/village official households and households with the disabled as the head of the household is higher than that of other types of households. The rural subsistence allowance system has different effect on poverty alleviation for different types of surveyed rural households. It has the best effect on single-person households, and has relatively great effect on households without children, or the head of the household who is disabled, female elder, a member of the CPC, or unemployed.

Fourth, the implementation of rural subsistence allowance system has improved the income distribution of rural households of all surveyed provinces and ethnic groups, but to a limited extent and with differences among these provinces and ethnic groups. Qinghai, Guizhou and Xinjiang, and ethnic groups of the Uyghur, Sala and Tibetan benefit the most from income distribution improvement while Hunan, Guangxi, Ningxia and Inner Mongolia, and ethnic groups of Mongolian, Kazak, Han, Yao and Zhuang benefit little. Besides, it has greater effects on income distribution of the poor group than the high-income group.

Fifth, the system narrows the income gap within and between provinces and regions, the gap narrows greater within the provinces than between provinces, and greater within ethnic groups than between ethnic groups.

Sixth, the subsistence allowance acquisition ratio of different kinds of surveyed rural households is almost similar to the poverty headcount ratio of these households, but there are differences to some extent. This is because that when implementing the system, the low-income residents in the surveyed ethnic minority concentrated areas were identified according to the two standards stipulated by the *Notice of the Ministry of Finance and the Ministry of Civil Affairs on the Relevant Issues about Strengthening the Administration of the Use of Rural Minimum Living Security Funds* issued by the State Council in 2007. But there are residents who received the unjustifiable allowance due to favor giving/returning or corruption by some cadres in some regions. This fact evoked our deep thoughts during the research into some cases in practice.

To sum up, the discovery in this chapter is similar to the first three in the four research conclusions proposed in previous chapters. In other words, these three existing conclusions are supported by empirical evidence in reality, and they are not mutually exclusive, which shows that the reality is complex. However, in this study, we have quantitatively analyzed some effects with more solid and comprehensive micro data covering more extensive areas. We also find that the rural subsistence allowance system has more evident effects on poverty alleviation and promoting social justice in ethnic minority concentrated areas. It may be related to the policy orientation that China pays more attention to anti-poverty and social justice in these areas.

Of course, this discovery is greatly different from the fourth conclusion mentioned in the above to some extent. We believe that under the rural subsistence allowance system, actual effects have been reached, but still need to be improved. In the future, we should notice the following issues when trying to further improve the system in practice. First, the central government should continue to grant more funds for rural subsistence allowance to ethnic minority concentrated areas, and try to cover all families in difficulty. It should increase and stabilize the insurance level, so as to enhance poverty-alleviation effects of the system and better promote social justice. Second, the government should strengthen the supervision on village organizations, or consider the transfer of the decision-making power regarding the qualification and treatment of the subsistence allowance recipients from villages and townships to the civil affairs department at the county level.[17] In this way, the residents who received the allowance due to favor giving/returning or corruption by some officials can be minimized. Also, the system can be more targeted and concentrate more on poor groups. Therefore, effects on poverty alleviation and income distribution improvement of the system can be well strengthened. Third, while implementing the system, the local government should provide some employment support, such as employment training, for subsistence allowance recipients who have the ability or conditions to work. Through work-relief programs and other measures, they can get into the labor market with improved employability, which effectively stabilizes poverty alleviation and stops the poor from falling into "poverty traps" due to "welfare dependence". Fourth, comprehensive assistance methods aiming at special poor groups such as children, elderly people, chronic patients, the disabled, and so forth should be implemented in villages of ethnic minority concentrated areas. For example, some farmers and herders have serious endemic diseases due to the harsh living environment in these areas. It is serious that most of them are reduced to or return to poverty because of illness. Therefore, we should provide all-round assistance for them, including both guarantee for basic living conditions and certain medical assistance. For the children of poor families, general subsistence allowance is not enough. We should ensure that they have access to school, and can finish compulsory, secondary, and even higher education like those from ordinary families. Thus, we can stop poverty from being

[17] Although the central and local governments have stipulated that family budget survey is the main way to identify assistance recipients, but measuring household income accurately still remains a tough issue in implementing the rural subsistence allowance system. Besides, due to the incompetence of civil administration at the grassroots level, these recipients are identified through democratic process by village committees, namely "community poverty ranking method" or "poor-family democratic selection method," rather than the family budget survey in most rural areas. As a result, village officials hold more power in the process of community democratic poverty ranking. Abuse of power by village officials to practice nepotism and favor giving/returning, or village organization manipulation by families and small groups are not rare. This directly leads to some residents receiving the allowance due to favor giving/returning or corruption by some officials. Zhang Xiulan, Xu Yuebin, & Wang Xiaobo. (2012). Subsistence allowance system and rural anti-poverty. *China Social Security System Development Report (2012)*. Social Sciences Academic Press (China), pp. 152–175.

passed on to the next generation. Of course, ideally, the social rural assistance system with rural subsistence allowance system as the core can change the existing way of only providing post-event assistance, and go further to play a more active role in anti-poverty practice.

Chapter 7
Targeted Measures for Multidimensional Poverty Alleviation in Ethnic Minority Concentrated Areas

With the economic and social development and the changing scenario of poverty reduction, the anti-poverty strategy in rural China has undergone three major changes since China began to implement the poverty alleviation and development strategy in the early 1980s. The first change happened in the mid-1980s when China adopted a strategy in rural areas that aimed to gradually establish a governance structure of development-oriented poverty alleviation with public governance as the core, and promote the economic and social development in poverty-stricken counties where the poor are concentrated. Before that, the strategy China carried out was to mainly increase the income of the poor via economic growth promoted through systemic reform with the support of appropriate relief.[1] The year 2000 witnessed the second change. With increasingly more rural poor people shaking off poverty, those still in poverty are scattered over an extensive area in compact communities. The areas where the poor concentrate have shrunk from former key counties of poverty alleviation to villages. In view of the new distribution of the rural poor, Chinese government issued the *Outline for Development-oriented Poverty Reduction for China's Rural Areas (2001–2010)* that year, and began to implement the "one body and two wings" poverty alleviation and development strategy. Here, one body refers to the village-based poverty reduction and two wings refer to the poverty reduction-oriented industrial development and labor training and transfer. The third change occurred in 2011 when China issued the *Outline for Development-oriented Poverty Reduction for China's Rural Areas (2011–2020)* (hereinafter referred to as the "New Outline"), and set a new rural poverty line (that is, the per capita net income of rural families was lower than 2,300 yuan estimated according to the price level in 2010). The deepening of poverty alleviation brought about another change to the distribution characteristics of the poor. According to the old poverty alleviation standard, the poor are scattered, while under the new standard, the poor are concentrated in contiguous impoverished

[1] Wang Chaoming (2008). Thirty years of development-oriented poverty alleviation in rural China: Policy practice and theoretical reflection. *Journal of Guizhou University of Finance and Economics*, (6).

X. Liu, *Complex Pictures of Poverty and Multiple Paths of Poverty Alleviation in Ethnic Areas of China*, https://doi.org/10.1007/978-981-97-4133-5_7

regions, in more complex and diverse situations. Given this, the "New Outline" clearly states that by 2020, the rural poor people are free from worries over food and clothing, and have access to compulsory education, basic medical services and safe housing (hereinafter referred to as "be free from two worries and have three accesses"), which shows that the poverty status and the goal of poverty alleviation in rural China have changed significantly. Absolute poverty has shifted to relative poverty, and the goal of poverty alleviation has shifted from one dimension to multiple dimensions (that is, from solving the problem of food and clothing to being free from two worries and gaining three accesses).[2]

The anti-poverty process in China over the past three decades indicates that the number of the rural poor in China has been reduced greatly and the life of the remaining people in poverty has been effectively improved. This result is brought about by the rapid development of national economy and society, and supported by the government-led development-oriented poverty reduction strategy and the social security system China constructed. Of course, we should notice that on the one hand, the gap in economic and social development has become wider over a long period of time across regions, urban and rural areas and social strata, while China sees a fast economic and social growth. This cripples economic and social growth's positive role in poverty reduction, which makes it marginally diminish.[3] On the other hand, deviations used to be detected in implementing the strategy. Many important poverty alleviation and development projects, including those based on the region (such as those of lifting poor counties out of poverty and village-based poverty reduction), and those based on the poor (such as those of poverty reduction-oriented industrial development, poverty reduction discount loans, technology-aid poverty reduction, and labor training and transfer), were commonly inaccessible to the poor and low-income groups. Therefore, different degrees of deviation occurred between the concrete results and expected goals of poverty alleviation. In many cases, it is usually the non-poor or less-poor in poor areas that have benefited from those projects, while the poor and those in extreme poverty in particular have hardly received any direct benefits. Thus, poverty alleviation and development has been less successful.[4] To handle the changing situation of rural poverty and deal with previous problems in poverty alleviation practice, the central government has incorporated poverty alleviation and development into the strategic layout of building a moderately prosperous society in all respects, and put forward a new strategy of taking targeted measures

---

[2] Du Zhixiong & Zhan Lin (2015). Difficulties and Solutions of Implementing the New Strategy of Targeted Poverty Alleviation. *China Development Observation*, (8).

[3] Zheng Changde. (2013). *Report on economic development in China minority region (2013)*. Beijing: China Economy Publishing House.

[4] Department of Household Surveys, National Bureau of Statistics of China. (2011). *Poverty monitoring report of rural China 2010*. Beijing: China Statistical Press; Shuai Chuanmin. (2010). *Research on poverty alleviation and development methods and efficiency in rural China*. Beijing: People's Publishing House; Liu Xiaomin. (2014). A study on the effect of poverty alleviation and development in the rock desert in Yunnan, Guangxi and Guizhou: A case study of Kaili in Southeast Guizhou Province. *Journal of Yunnan Agricultural University*, (8).

for poverty alleviation and eradication since the 18th National People's Congress of the Communist Party of China (CPC).

Accurate identification is the first step. Only when the poor are accurately identified, can they be targeted by all related policies and measures. Since 1978, China has adopted three poverty alleviation standards, namely, "Standard 1978", "Standard 2008" and "Standard 2010". They are defined by the income poverty line, and the income standards have been gradually increased with the development of national economy and society. The second step is to establish an delisting mechanism for the households who have been lifted out of poverty. In 2016, the General Offices of the CPC Central Committee and the State Council issued the *Opinions on Establishing a Delisting Mechanism*, clearly stating that the delisting from the poverty registrar is based on the household, with the main criterion assessing whether the annual per capita net income of the household stably exceeds the national poverty alleviation standard, and whether they are free from the two worries and have three accesses. Obviously the two aspects are included in the evaluation criterion put forward by the 18th National Congress of the CPC, that is, to lift all the rural poor out of poverty by 2020 under the current standard.[5] The formulation and implementation of China's targeted measures for poverty alleviation strategy at present and in the future should start from the multidimensional poverty in rural areas. As we all know, the income of the rural poor in ethnic minority concentrated areas is much less than that in Han and non-ethnic minority concentrated areas. Then, what about the multidimensional poverty in these areas? What are the characteristics? To lift all the rural poor in these areas out of poverty by 2020 under the current poverty standard, what should China pay more attention to? This paper is designed to answer these questions. Therefore, we built a suitable MPI system to have a general analysis upon the structure and characteristics of multidimensional poverty in these areas in rural China and put forward targeted measures for poverty alleviation accordingly.

1 Research Review and Subject

In theory, poverty can be summarized into two categories: the low-income poverty and multidimensional poverty. The latter is based on Amartya Sen's capability approach. Sen asserted that poverty is caused by a deprivation of basic capabilities, besides inadequate income and materials. The deprivation is reflected in many dimensions, such as premature death, malnutrition, chronic diseases, widespread illiteracy, and so forth. He reached a conclusion that people's basic capabilities can be improved through education and medical care.[6] In the *Human Development Report*

[5] Wang Xiaolin. (2016). Eliminating all forms of poverty: Connotation and policy orientation. *Sub National Fiscal Research*, (8).

[6] Sen, A. (1983). *Poverty and Famines*. Oxford: Oxford University Press. Chinese edition: Sen, A. (2011). *Poverty and Famines* (trans: Wang Yu and Wang Wenyu). Beijing: The Commercial Press; Sen, A. (2000). *Development as Freedom*. New York: Anchor. Chinese edition: Sen, A. (2012). *Development as Freedom* (trans: Ren Ze and Yu Zhen). Beijing: China Renmin University Press.

1997, the United Nations Development Program (UNDP) defines that poverty can mean more than a lack of what is necessary for material well-being. It can also mean the denial of opportunities and choices most basic to human development—to lead a long, healthy, creative life and to enjoy a decent standard of living, dignity, self-esteem and the respect of others.[7] Apparently, the "human poverty" defined here is also multidimensional, referring to both low income, and the deprivation of opportunities, rights, health, dignity, decent life and others. The definition involves various aspects of human development, such as quality of life, development opportunities and basic rights. It is richer in meaning and more comprehensive in reflecting the economic standards and living conditions of poor groups than that of the income poverty.

Based on Amartya Sen's theory, Sabina Alkire and James Foster proposed a method of multidimensional poverty measurement and decomposition, namely, the Alkire Foster (AF) method for calculating the multidimensional poverty index (MPI), to evaluate the multidimensional poverty.[8] The UNDP has adopted the results of the multidimensional measurement of global poverty measured and analyzed in the AF method by the two people, and published the overall situation in the *Human Development Report* since 2010. The global MPI includes three dimensions, namely, education, health and living standards. The AF method evidently measures poverty in a more integrated and scientific manner than an income-based measurement does. However, in practice, what relevant factors are included and how to determine the poverty thresholds of relevant factors remain open for discussion. Thus, it affects the operability of the AF method and its application.[9]

It is noteworthy that the Chinese academic community focuses more on multidimensional poverty. Some scholars have already begun to explore and establish indexes suitable to China's conditions, and have conducted empirical research accordingly. Xiaolin Wang and Sabina Alkire studied the multidimensional poverty of urban and rural households in China in the AF method with the China Health and Nutrition Survey (CHNS) data in 2006. Their indexes include eight poverty dimensions, i.e. health facilities, electricity consumption, housing, drinking water, assets, land, education and health insurance. The results showed that in China, nearly one fifth of urban and rural households suffered from poverty in any three of dimensions above, besides income. Moreover, it was severer than income poverty. Poverty in health insurance, health facilities and education contributed the most to the MPI.[10]

Based on the 2011 CHNS data and with the AF method and the Logit model, Hexia Feng, Xiaolin Wang and Qingjie Xia analyzed the connections and differences

[7] Jin Fengfeng. (2005). Alleviating Poverty through Development: Policy Choices for Alleviating Poverty in Relatively Well-off Rural Areas. Shanghai: SDC Joint Publishing Company.

[8] Alkire, S., & Foster, J. E. (2007). Counting and multidimensional poverty measurement. *OPHI Working Paper: 07*. Oxford: University of Oxford.

[9] Guo Jianyu & Wu Guobao. (2012). Measure- and weight-based measurement of multidimensional poverty: A case study of poverty-stricken counties in Shanxi Province. *Chinese Rural Economy*, (2).

[10] Wang Xiaolin & Alkire, S. (2009). Multidimensional poverty measurement in China: estimates and policy implications. *Chinese Rural Economy*, (12).

between income poverty and multidimensional poverty. They came to a conclusion that the two categories have 30.62% of similarity in their concepts, meaning that 69.38% of multidimensional poor households had been left out in income poverty. Therefore, they recommended the poverty standards where the two are complementary to illustrate how multidimensional and complicated the poverty is. By doing so, poverty alleviation can be carried out in a more effective way, and poor people can receive higher income and better education, and live a healthier life.[11]

Based on the 2000 and 2009 CHNS data, Yanyun Gao measured the dynamic changes of multidimensional poverty in China with the AF model. The research showed that poverty in both urban and rural areas in China had been alleviated, but rural poverty was severer than urban poverty. Therefore, they suggested that great attention should be paid to the future rural poverty alleviation in medical insurance, health facilities and urban housing.[12]

With the data from the rural poverty monitoring survey, Long Yang and Sangui Wang measured multidimensional poverty in poor rural areas and decomposed the MPI there. As is shown in their study, low-income peasant households suffered severer multidimensional poverty, and drinking water problem was severer than income augmentation for rural residents in these areas. Accordingly, they suggested relieving multidimensional poverty by way of more human capital investment, public health service amelioration and enhanced infrastructure construction (including the construction of medium- and small-sized water conservancy facilities) in rural areas in the new era.[13]

Jianyu Guo and Guobao Wu studied the multidimensional poverty in Shanxi Province by analyzing the household data of the poverty-stricken counties in the province with the UNDP's MPI measure. They found that region-specific poverty in different dimensions had different effects on the MPI. Therefore, region-specific poverty indexes and weights should be selected appropriately for a better-focused poverty relief and better effects of poverty relief policy in practice.[14]

The existing theoretical and empirical researches are very enlightening for us to study the multidimensional poverty in ethnic minority concentrated areas in rural China and put forward targeted policies. We believe that rural poverty in these areas is also multidimensional and it is more prominent than that in non-ethnic areas. In this paper, we conduct a multidimensional analysis of rural poverty in ethnic minority concentrated areas in China, with the data of the 2011 Chinese Household Ethnicity Survey (CHES2011). Considering the real situation, the dimension of asset poverty

[11] Feng Hexia, Wang Xiaolin and Xia Qingjie. (2015). A study on income poverty and multidimensional poverty. *Studies in Labor Economics*, (6).

[12] Gao Yanyun. (2012). The multidimensional poverty in urban and rural China: Measurement and comparison. *Statistical Research*, (11).

[13] Yang Long & Wang Sangui. (2015). The measurement and decomposition of multidimensional poverty of peasant households in poverty-stricken regions: An analysis of the relevant data from the poverty monitoring in rural China in 2010. *Population Journal*, (2).

[14] Guo Jianyu & Wu Guobao. (2012). Measure- and weight-based measurement of multidimensional poverty: A case study of poverty-stricken counties in Shanxi Province. *Chinese Rural Economy*, (2).

is added to cover the shortage of the MPI, like the non-monetary index, to study the rural poverty in western ethnic minority concentrated areas in China. Many studies have shown that the household assets of peasant households are of vital importance to their involvement in the market and the development of household economy. To sum up, based on the changing scenario and status quo of poverty in these areas in the new era, we establish an MPI system with four dimensions and sixteen indexes, which is more suitable for the study of multidimensional poverty there. With this system, we make an overall analysis of the multidimensional poverty there, and then decompose the dimensions of different provinces, ethnic groups and poverty level. In this way, we can further understand the structure and characteristics and put forward targeted policies accordingly.

2 Method of Analysis and Data Sources

Theoretically, the MPI measurement mainly includes fuzzy set approach (FS approach),[15] axiomatic approach,[16] input–output efficiency approach,[17] information theory-based approach,[18] "dual cut-off" method[19] and so forth. Among them, the "dual cut-off" method is for multidimensional poverty measurement (AF method) developed by Alkire and Foster in 2007 based on Amartya Sen's capability approach. With this method, they constructed the MPI to evaluate multidimensional poverty. At present, the relatively simple AF method has been widely used in domestic and international institutions and academic community. Therefore, we also use the AF method in this paper to measure the MPI of rural poverty in ethnic minority concentrated areas in China, and conduct a decomposition research.

2.1 Analysis Methods

To carry out the multidimensional poverty measurement, we first obtain the individual or household value of each dimension through household surveys, set a poverty standard, and identify whether each individual or household is poor. Then, we decompose the poverty into several dimensions and obtain their contributions to the poverty,

---

[15] Cheli, B., & Lemmi, A. (1995). A totally fuzzy and relative approach to multidimensional analysis of poverty. *Economic Notes*, (24), pp. 115–134.

[16] Bourguignon, F., & Chakravarty, S. R. (2003). The measurement of multidimensional poverty. *Journal of Economic Inequality*, 1(1), pp. 25–49.

[17] Ramos, X., & Silber, J. (2005). On the application of efficiency analysis to the study of the dimensions of human development. *Review of Income and Wealth*, 51(2): pp. 285–310.

[18] Lugo, A. M., & Maasoumi, E. (2009). Multidimensional poverty measures from an information theory perspective. *OPHI Working Paper* 10.

[19] Alkire, S., & Foster, J. (2011). Counting and multidimensional poverty measurement. *Journal of Public Economics*, 95 (7), pp. 476–487.

according to the multidimensional indexes.[20] In this way, we have two mathematical analysis models.

The first is the multidimensional poverty measurement model, and its equation is:

$$M_0(y, z) = \mu[g^0(k)] = HA \tag{1}$$

In Eq. (1), M_O represents the multidimensional poverty index, which consists of two parts: H (poverty headcount ratio) and A (average deprivation share), and $A=|c(k)|/(qd)$. In addition, y represents the value of the research subject in a certain poverty dimension; g0 represents a deprivation matrix, which will be assigned the value of 0 when there is no poverty problem in a certain dimension, and otherwise the value of 1; c represents the total number of poverty dimensions constructed by the researcher; q represents the total number of poor individuals under the poverty standard of a certain dimension; and d represents the total number of poverty dimensions.

The second is the multidimensional poverty grouping decomposition model. In this study, research subjects are divided into two groups, namely, Han ethnicity and ethnic minorities. When s represents the data matrix of ethnic minorities, h represents the data matrix of Han ethnicity, and z represents the critical point of a poverty dimension, the equation of the model is:

$$\mathrm{M(s, h, z)} = \frac{\mathrm{n(s)}}{\mathrm{n(s, h)}}\mathrm{M(s; z)} + \frac{\mathrm{n(h)}}{\mathrm{n(s, h)}}\mathrm{M(h; z)} \tag{2}$$

2.2 Data Sources

We use the survey data of rural households in the CHES2011 in this paper, including the income and expenditure of urban and rural households, employment or unemployment, rural labor mobility, education, time, social security, subjective will and others. Therefore, it is a large sample from which we can study the multidimensional poverty in western ethnic minority concentrated areas as a whole. In the rural household survey, 7,257 sample households (31,671 people) in 81 counties and 757 administrative villages were selected from seven ethnic minority provinces. We mainly investigate the multidimensional rural poverty in ethnic minority concentrated areas, taking the household as a unit. The estimated rent value of self-owned houses per capita is added to the per capita net income of rural households, based on the data of the National Bureau of Statistics. Some data is processed in the calculation of the per capita net income of rural households.[21]

[20] Wang Xiaolin. (2012). *The Measurement of Poverty: Theories and Methods*. Beijing: Social Sciences Academic Press (China).

[21] CCHES2011 questionnaires cover three provinces and four autonomous regions, including Qinghai, Inner Mongolia, Ningxia, Xinjiang, Guangxi, Guizhou and Hunan, of which the first

In addition, for exceptional values and missing values of poverty dimensions, relevant samples are deleted in the CHES2011.

2.3 Dimensional Indicators and Weight Setting of Multidimensional Poverty

Since 2010, the UNDP has adopted the AF method to reveal the overall situation of global multidimensional poverty in the annual *Human Development Report*. The global MPI consists of ten indicators in three dimensions, namely, education, health and living standards. Using the UNDP global multidimensional poverty dimension and indicator system as the framework and referring to the indicator system proposed by other domestic scholars,[22] this article establishes a multidimensional poverty measurement indicator system for the poor population in ethnic minority concentrated areas as shown in Table 7.1, in which the adjusted dimensions, indicator variables and deprivation thresholds are also reported. It also associates with the CHES2011 survey data, and takes China's poverty alleviation goals of rural poor

five are in western ethnic areas. We carried out rural surveys in some counties of Hunan province, including Suining County and Chengbu Miao Autonomous County in Shaoyang City; Jianghua Yao Autonomous County in Yongzhou City, Yuanling County, Chenxi County, Mayang Miao Autonomous County, Xinhuang Dong Autonomous County, Jingzhou Miao and Dong Autonomous County and Tongdao Dong Autonomous County in Huaihua City; Luxi County, Fenghuang County, Baojing County, Guzhang County and Yongshun County in Xiangxi Tujia and Miao Autonomous Prefecture, which are mostly areas inhabited by ethnic minority groups. Although the CHES2011 does not cover Xizang and Yunnan of the "eight provinces of ethnic minorities", these seven places are enough to represent the western ethnic minority regions. Therefore, in this paper, the seven surveyed places are referred to as "ethnic areas", and Inner Mongolia, Ningxia, Xinjiang and Qinghai are referred to as "four provincial areas in northwest China", and Guangxi, Hunan and Guizhou are referred to as "three provincial areas in southwest China" (although Hunan is located in the central south China rather than the southwest). For details of CHES2011 database and data processing methods, please refer to *Chinese Household Ethnicity Survey 2013* (Beijing: Social Sciences Academic Press) edited by Li Keqiang, Long Yuanwei and Liu Xiaomin in 2014. In addition, all the data in this paper are from CHES2011 database, if not specified otherwise.

[22] Wang Xiaolin, Sabina Alkire. (2009). Multidimensional poverty measurement in China: Estimates and policy implications, *Chinese Rural Economy*, (12); Feng Hexia, Wang Xiaolin, and Xia Qingjie. (2015). A study on income poverty and multidimensional poverty. *Studies in Labor Economics*, Volume 3, (6); Guo Jianyu & Wu Guobao. (2012). Measure- and weight-based measurement of multidimensional poverty: A case study of poverty-stricken counties in Shanxi Province, *Chinese Rural Economy*, (2); Yang Long & Wang San'gui. (2015). The measurement and decomposition of multidimensional poverty of peasant households in poverty-stricken regions: An analysis of relevant data from the poverty monitoring in rural China in 2010, *Population Journal*, (2); Zhang Quanhong & Zhou Qiang, (2014), "Multidimensional Poverty in China and Solution: 1989-2009", in *Journal of Quantitative & Technical Economics*, (6); Wang Yanhui, Qian Leyi, Duan Fuzhou, (2013), "Multidimensional Poverty Measurement and Spatial Distribution Pattern in the Country: A Case Study on Key Country from National Contiguous Special Poverty-stricken Areas", in *Scientia Geographica Sinica*, (12).

people free from two worries and having three accesses in the new era into consideration. Due to the lack of monetary indicators significant to the welfare of individuals and families in the ten poverty indicators of the three dimensions of the global MPI, we add the asset dimension in the analysis of this paper based on the existing three dimensions of education, health and living standards. When measuring multidimensional poverty, we assign equal weight to each dimension, and to each indicator within each dimension. Since the number of indicators within each dimension is different, the weights of indicators in different dimensions are different.

Besides, although the MPI in this paper does not include the income dimension, we will compare and analyze it and the income poverty index to provide the feasibility for further comprehensive identification and analysis of the poverty mechanism of the poor in ethnic minority concentrated areas.

3 Results of Multidimensional Poverty Measurement in Ethnic Minority Concentrated Areas

3.1 Multidimensional Poverty Measurement

We applied the CHES2011 rural data and the AF method widely used at home and abroad to estimate the multidimensional poverty research results in ethnic minority concentrated areas (see Table 7.2). When one dimension is considered, H is 41.04%, indicating that 41.04% of households are in poverty in terms of any of the four dimensions, with A being 36.27% and M_0 0.1489. When two dimensions are considered simultaneously, H is 15.78%, indicating that 15.78% of households are in poverty in any two of the four dimensions, with A being 45.44% and M_0 0.0717.

Besides, in ethnic minority concentrated areas, the poverty headcount ratio of rural households whose income is under the national income poverty line is 16.98%, which is slightly lower than the multidimensional poverty headcount ratio calculated with two dimensions considered. It demonstrates the differences between the income and multidimensional poverty in poverty identification. In other words, although increasing income is conducive to reducing multidimensional poverty, people may not be free of poverty after the income poverty eradication. However, from the perspective of multidimensional poverty, the poverty and deficiency problems that poverty-stricken population faces in popularization of Mandarin, medical care, electricity, water, communications, energy, roads, land, and topography mainly lie in insufficient public goods and services provided by the government and society. Therefore, these problems cannot be solved by solely increasing the income of poor peasant households. Working towards the goals of building a moderately prosperous society in all respects, the government should focus not only on reducing the income poverty for poor peasant households, but on eradicating multidimensional poverty and deficiency by providing more public goods and services in implementation of various anti-poverty strategies and policies.

Table 7.1 Dimensions, indicators, critical values and weights of multidimensional poverty measurement in ethnic minority concentrated areas

Dimension	Indicator and weight	Indicator description and value
Education (0.25)	Average schooling years of the laborer of the family (1/8)	If the average schooling of the laborer of the family workers (male: 16–60 years old; female: 16–55 years old) is less than 6 years, its value will be 1, otherwise it will be 0
	No "Basically Can't" for oral Mandarin skills or no "Basically Can't" for Chinese reading and writing skills (1/8)	If there is "Basically Can't" for the head of household's spoken Mandarin level or the literacy ability of Chinese, its value will be 1, otherwise it will be 0
Health (0.25)	Proportion of people without physical disabilities in the family (1/16)	If there is at least one disabled person in the family (and their normal work, study, and life are affected), its value will be 1, otherwise it will be 0
	Proportion of the family without labor whose normal work, school or life is affected by illness or injury for more than 30 days (1/16)	If there is at least one economically active people in the family whose normal work, school or life are affected by illness or injury for more than 30 days, its value will be 1, otherwise it will be 0
	Proportion of the family without economically active people who have "Common", "Relatively Serious" or "Very Serious" physical or psychological diseases in the past one month (1/16)	If there is at least one economically active people in the family who has "Common", "Relatively Serious" or "Very Serious" physical or psychological diseases, its value will be 1, otherwise it will be 0
	Proportion of the family without people who drink less than 4 times a week and smoke no more than 20 cigarettes per day (1/16)	If there is at least one person in the family who drinks alcohol more than 4 times a week, or smokes no less than 20 cigarettes a day, its value will be 1, otherwise it will be 0
Living standards (0.25)	Clean and convenient drinking water (1/28)	If the family's drinking water is from "River", "Lake and Pond", "Rainwater Cellar", "Other Sources", or "Outside the Courtyard" and the time walking to get water exceeds 15 min, its value will be 1, otherwise it will be 0
	Toilet (1/28)	If there is no toilet in the house, its value will be 1, otherwise it will be 0
	Use clean and convenient energy for cooking (1/28)	If the main energy used for cooking at home is "firewood", it's value will be 1, otherwise it will be 0
	Housing (1/28)	If the family has no house or the per capita housing area of the family is less than 9 square meters, its value will be 1, otherwise it will be 0

(continued)

Table 7.1 (continued)

Dimension	Indicator and weight	Indicator description and value
	No natural disasters happened to the village where the family lives (1/28)	If 2 or more natural disasters happened to the village from 2007 to 2011, its value will be 1, otherwise it will be 0
	Type of village where the family lives (1/28)	If the village is in mountainous area, its value will be 1, otherwise it will be 0
	Basic public services in the village where the family lives (1/28)	If there is no road, no electricity, no telephone, and no television channels in the village, its value will be 1, otherwise it will be 0
Assets (0.25)	Per capita productive fixed assets (1/12)	If the original value of the per capita productive fixed assets of the household is less than 808 yuan (20% of the average original value of the per capita productive fixed assets of the interviewed households), its value will be 1, otherwise it will be 0
	Durable consumer goods (1/12)	If there are no cars or tractors for the household, and at most two of the following household appliances like washing machines, refrigerators, water heaters, air conditioners, motorcycles, fixed telephones, mobile phones, color televisions, and home computers, its value will be 1, otherwise it will be 0
	Actual operating land area (1/12)	If the actual land area per capita of the household is less than 1 *mu* ($\approx$666.67m^2), its value will be 1, otherwise it will be 0

Note Values in parentheses indicate weight

Table 7.2 Results of multidimensional poverty estimation in ethnic minority areas

K (%)	Poverty headcount ratio (H, %)	Average deprivation share (A, %)	Multidimensional poverty index (M_0)
25.0	41.04	36.27	0.1489
37.5	15.78	45.44	0.0717
50.0	3.45	55.33	0.0191
62.5	0.21	68.39	0.0015

3.2 *MPI and Decomposition*

1. Measurement and decomposition based on regional grouping

Table 7.3 shows the decomposition result of the MPI based on provinces. It can be found that there are obvious differences in the multidimensional poverty of peasant households in different provinces. When investigating rural poverty in

Table 7.3 The MPI decomposed by province (k = 25%)

		MPI		MPI decomposition
		H (%)	M_0	M_0
Two provinces and one autonomous region in southwestern China	Hunan	73.03	0.1428	15.05
	Guangxi	70.25	0.1523	17.04
	Guizhou	73.52	0.1553	19.53
One province and three autonomous regions in northwestern China	Ningxia	49.46	0.0998	11.8
	Qinghai	73.22	0.1511	16.49
	Xinjiang	60.68	0.1013	12.47
	Inner Mongolia	50.11	0.0766	7.61

ethnic minority concentrated areas from any of the four dimensions, we can find that Guizhou contributed the most to multidimensional poverty, and the remaining provinces and autonomous regions in descending order of contribution are Guangxi, Qinghai, Hunan, Xinjiang, Ningxia and Inner Mongolia. In general, the multidimensional poverty situation in Guizhou, Guangxi, and Hunan in southwestern China is severer than that in Ningxia, Qinghai, Xinjiang, and Inner Mongolia in northwestern China. This is consistent with the trend of income poverty analysis. On the one hand, it shows that income poverty analysis and multidimensional poverty analysis have a certain degree of consistency in the identification of regional poverty; on the other hand, it also shows that income poverty and multidimensional poverty are related to regional factors. According to some related researches, southwestern China has many mountains where mostly are karst landforms, a very complex topographic structure, and dense population. With mountain agriculture as the main industry in the region, the rural poverty problem there is very serious.[23] This situation indicates that in terms of anti-poverty practices, the rural poverty reduction strategy and policy systems in these areas should not only generally and inclusively support economic development promotion, but also include things specially for mountainous areas and areas in harsh natural ecological environments, so as to alleviate poverty (both income poverty and multidimensional poverty) caused by regional factors.

2. Measurement and decomposition based on ethnic grouping

Tables 7.4 and 7.5 present the MPI and decomposition based on ethnic grouping. Obviously, there are evident differences in multidimensional poverty among peasant households of different ethnic groups. In general, the multidimensional poverty of ethnic minorities is severer than that of the Han, and contributes more than 70% of the total. The headcount ratio of it among rural residents of all ethnic groups in southwestern China is higher than that in the northwestern area; the ratios among the Han ethnic group and the ethnic minorities in Southwestern China are higher

[23] Liu Xiaomin, (2013), "A Comparative Study on the Poverty of Rural Residents from the Perspective of Ethnic Groups: Taking Guangxi, Guizhou, and Hunan as Examples", *Ethno-National Studies*, (4).

than those of the northwestern area. In this two regions, the ratios among ethnic minorities in the two provinces and one autonomous region in southwestern China and one province and three autonomous regions in northwestern China are higher than that of the Han.

In terms of the differences in multidimensional poverty of various ethnic groups, the main ethnic minorities, including the Zhuang, Miao, Dong, and Tujia ethnic groups in southwestern China suffer the severest multidimensional poverty while the main ethnic minorities in the northwestern area, such as the Sala and Uyghur ethnic groups face no better situation.

However, although the differences in multidimensional poverty and income are different in some ethnic minorities, they are basically similar in general. Moreover, resembling the income poverty, differences in multidimensional poverty and regions among ethnic minorities are to some extent connected.

3. Based on poverty dimensions

Table 7.6 shows the MPI and its decomposition in ethnic minority concentrated areas. The variables in each poverty dimension contribute distinctly to the multidimensional poverty. The schooling years, communication skills or literacy skills contribute the most. Other variables including village characteristics (topography), natural disasters, fixed assets, toilets, housing, cooking energy, and land also contribute significantly. Therefore, according to the decomposition of the poverty dimension, in the future rural poverty alleviation policies and projects, it shall increase education

Table 7.4 The MPI decomposed by Han and ethnic minorities (k = 25%).

	MPI		MPI decomposition
	H (%)	M_0	M_0
Ethnic minority areas	66.16	0.1456	100
Han ethnic group	55.33	0.099	29.49
Ethnic minorities	71.36	0.1503	70.5
Two provinces and one autonomous region in southwestern China	71.42	0.1532	51.63
Han ethnic group in southwestern China	66.46	0.1246	10.68
Ethnic minorities in southwestern China	74.07	0.1697	40.94
One province and three autonomous regions in northwestern China	61.6	0.1002	48.37
Han ethnic group in northwestern China	51.99	0.0798	18.81
Ethnic minorities in northwestern China	69.99	0.1466	29.56

Table 7.5 The MPI decomposed by ethnic groups (k = 25%)

	MPI		MPI decomposition
	H (%)	M_0	M_0
Total	66.16	0.1456	100
Han	55.33	0.099	29.49
Mongol	66.97	0.1012	2.5
Hui	66.67	0.1231	9.09
Tibetan	71.87	0.1287	4.69
Uyghur	73.5	0.1503	8.19
Miao	74.19	0.1496	16.34
Zhuang	74.33	0.1575	6.85
Dong	74.03	0.1543	8.91
Yao	70.81	0.1501	2.46
Tujia	73.84	0.1562	2.9
Kazak	70.01	0.1687	1.8
Sala	80	0.1721	1.94
Other ethnic groups	71.01	0.1507	4.82

investment in a targeted manner, especially enhance various training for economically active populations who have graduated from school to improve their communication and literacy abilities. For some mountainous areas with harsh living environments, it is necessary to intensify the implementation of ecological environmental protection projects and immigration relocation projects, improve both the supply of rural public goods and services and the ability of the poverty-stricken population to shake off poverty in ethnic minority concentrated areas.

4 Conclusion and Policy Recommendations

Based on the CHES2011 rural household statistics, in this paper, we measure the multidimensional poverty of rural households in ethnic minority concentrated areas of China by using the AF method, and obtain the following main findings and conclusions.

First, regional differences exist in multidimensional poverty. In general, the multidimensional poverty in Guizhou, Guangxi, and Hunan is severer than that in Ningxia, Qinghai, Xinjiang, and Inner Mongolia, which is consistent with the regional differences in income poverty.

Second, ethnic differences exist in multidimensional poverty. In general, the multidimensional poverty of ethnic minorities is severer than that of the Han, and contributes more than 70% of the total. The Zhuang, Miao, Dong, and Tujia ethnic

Table 7.6 MPI Decomposed by indicators (k = 25%)

		$H(\%)$	Decomposition of M_0
Education	Schooling years	64.33	28.99
	Communication skills and literacy	48.68	20.20
Health	Proportion of the people with disabilities	8.72	1.50
	Illness or injury	15.61	2.73
	Physical or mental difficulties	11.82	2.03
	Frequency of drinking and smoking per week	20.46	3.51
Living standards	Drinking water	5.34	0.52
	Toilet	51.32	5.04
	Cooking energy	49.21	4.89
	Housing	46.32	4.93
	Natural disasters	67.45	6.62
	Village characteristics	57.12	7.57
	Basic public services in the village	2.54	0.25
Assets	Per capita productive fixed assets	26.76	6.13
	Durable consumer goods	1.1	0.25
	Actual operating land area	21.32	4.88

groups, the main ethnic minorities in the southwest region, suffer the severest multidimensional poverty, while the main ethnic minorities in the northwest region, such as the Sala and Uyghur ethnic groups also face a serious situation. Although multidimensional poverty differences are different from income differences in some ethnic groups, they are basically at the same level in general. Moreover, similar to the income poverty, there is a certain degree of coupling between multidimensional poverty differences and regional differences among ethnic groups.

Third, the contributions of variables in each poverty dimension to multidimensional poverty are different to some extent. Among these variables including schooling years, communication skills, literacy, village characteristics (topography), natural disasters, fixed assets, toilets, housing, cooking energy, and land, the first three contribute the most. In other words, the most serious problems that poor peasant households face in ethnic minority concentrated areas lie in education, topography, natural disasters, fixed assets, and others.

Since the 18th CPC National Congress, the central government has gradually formulated a strategy of taking targeted measures for poverty alleviation and eradication and related theoretical systems. General Secretary Jinping Xi pointed out, "Targeted poverty alleviation is an important way to solve problems in poverty alleviation and development, such as unclear condition, blurry goals and poor results. In practice, we should carry out precise identification, targeted support, and dynamic management for poor villages and households, and help those in need and deliver genuine assistance."[24] Therefore, in view of the development status, multidimensional poverty characteristics and problems existing in anti-poverty in ethnic areas, we should adhere to the strategies of taking targeted measures for poverty alleviation and eradication in the future poverty alleviation work, and pay attention to the following aspects.

First, the implementation of the targeted poverty alleviation strategy requires a more comprehensive approach for accurate identification and targeting of the poor from a multidimensional perspective. Accurate identification is the basis and prerequisite for taking targeted measures for poverty alleviation and eradication. In the past, poverty measurement methods for identifying poor areas and poor people mainly started from the single dimension of farmer's income. However, it often failed to accurately identify poor individuals and their poverty characteristics, resulting in mismatch of the support for the people who should not be supported. At present, when implementing targeted poverty alleviation policies, governments at all levels have also begun to realize the problems and difficulties in the past poverty identification and targeting methods based only on income poverty standards, and have built multidimensional poverty standard systems including income. The most typical multidimensional poverty identification methods including the method Guizhou Province adopts, which involves four aspects including housing, food, labor force and education,[25] and the method Guangdong Province applies, which requires being clear about the family situation, listening to the suggestions of the masses, asking about the needs of the poor, and providing targeted support for those in need.[26] Obviously, a multidimensional poverty indicator system complying with the actual situation of each region needs to be established for rural poverty alleviation in ethnic minority concentrated areas in China, so that we can identify and target the poor more scientifically, and better implement the accurate identification of the poor really in need based on real data and corresponding facts.

Second, we should further increase support, accelerate the economic and social development, and alleviate multidimensional poverty in ethnic minority concentrated areas. The "13th Five-Year Plan" period is a critical period for China to achieve the goal of building a moderately prosperous society in all respects. To achieve this grand goal, the central government has issued a number of policies and measures to optimize the pattern of regional development and promote economic and social development in ethnic minority concentrated areas, such as formulating and implementing the "13th Five-Year Plan" for the large-scale development in the western region, supporting the development of ethnic minority concentrated areas, border areas, and poor areas,

---

[24] Liu Yongfu, (2014), Winning the tough battle for poverty alleviation to build a moderately prosperous society in all respect: Earnestly study and implement the guiding essence of Comrade Jinping Xi's important speeches on poverty alleviation and development, *People's Daily*.

[25] Meng Xingrong, (2015), Weining Autonomous County explores the approach from four respects involving house, food, labor force, and education to promote targeted poverty alleviation, *Bijie Daily*.

[26] Li Kun, (2015), On theoretical implications, practical experience and path optimization of targeted poverty alleviation based on the investigation and comparison of Guangdong Province and Enshi in Hubei Province, *Journal of Shanxi Agricultural University (Social Science Edition)*, (8).

and so forth. In other words, the "13th Five-Year Plan" provides great strategic opportunities for the economic and social development of these areas. Therefore, they must seize these opportunities to improve the production and living conditions here so as to improve the self-development ability of the poor and alleviate multidimensional poverty. We can improve the infrastructure here for the poor to gain access to road, electricity, telephone, television, and internet in rural areas, and improve the living environment of rural families by providing them with clean and convenient drinking water and energy resources. We also can strengthen the construction of medical and health services to reduce their risk of poverty due to illness, guide them to build sanitary toilets, and provide support for the rebuilding of dilapidated houses to the impoverished.

Third, for the problems poor peasant households in ethnic minority concentrated areas face in education, terrain, natural disasters, and fixed assets, in the future, we should increase the education-centered investment, promote the fairness of rural education, stop poverty from being passed on to the next generation, and increase various training for the economically active population who have left the school to improve their Mandarin proficiency. In this way, their employability and income-increasing ability will be strengthened. For some mountainous areas in harsh living environments, we should enhance the implementation of ecological environmental protection projects and relocation of residents to reduce the poverty risk brought by the environment and natural disasters to rural families. It is necessary for us to comprehensively accrue rural households' assets, further increase the subsidy standards for rural households to purchase agricultural machinery, and raise subsidies for household appliances and other durable consumer goods to the countryside. We also should do a good job in the transfer of surplus labor, and in the real urbanization of the relocated population from poor rural areas, especially the population migrating to urban areas, thus creating social conditions for the smooth circulation of rural land. It helps to reduce the abandonment but increase the land for farmers engaging in agriculture. In short, only by improving the supply of rural public goods and services, improving the competence of the poor and increasing their assets in ethnic minority concentrated areas, can the poor people's multidimensional poverty alleviation capabilities be improved.

Finally, a question worthy of further study is that, according to the goals of the current targeted poverty alleviation strategy, absolute poverty in rural China, including ethnic minority concentrated areas, will eventually be eliminated by 2020, but this may be mainly reflected in the initial stage of income poverty reduction. With the development of the whole society, after the absolute poverty is eliminated, the problem of relative poverty will become prominent, and it will be more manifested in other dimensions of poverty. In other words, poverty will continue to exist in other dimensions of multidimensional poverty, and will become the main factor hindering those who have shaken off income poverty from achieving balanced development in other areas. In fact, the multidimensional poverty research model developed in western developed countries aims to solve the problem of poverty caused by factors other than low-income (or the problem of social deprivation). It is impossible for

China to avoid such problems. Therefore, we need to continue to use multidimensional poverty research methods to study and monitor the relative poverty in agricultural and pastoral areas in ethnic minority concentrated areas, so as to shed light on new multidimensional targeted poverty alleviation in the future.

Chapter 8
Poverty and Its Causes in a Prototypical Pastoral Area: The Case of Zhiduo County in Yushu Tibetan Autonomous Prefecture, Qinghai Province

In this chapter, we discuss a field questionnaire conducted in the pastoral areas in Zhiduo County, Yushu Tibetan Autonomous Prefecture, Qinghai Province, to shed light on the work and life of local herders' households, including their income and expenditure, their participation in and comments on the project for the ecological conservation and improvement of Sanjiangyuan Nature Reserve, the implementation of the pasture contract responsibility system, the public services they received, their opinion of their own living and current policies for pastoral areas, and their actual needs. Through these empirical investigations and studies, we proceed to analyze the main economic, social and cultural causes of poverty in pastoral areas in Zhiduo County, so as to better understand why there is poverty and how it is influenced by different factors in those pastoral areas where ethnic minorities make up a majority of the population, thereby facilitating the poverty alleviation in these areas.

1 A Preliminary Analysis of Pastoral Household Poverty Data

Zhiduo County administers five townships and one town. In 2013–2014, I presided over a Chinese Academy of Social Sciences (CASS) national condition research project—a field survey designed to explore the situation of poverty and social security in this county, which is also a part of the Yangtze River source region. The research included a large number of individual interviews and a questionnaire survey of more than three hundred pastoral families. We introduced the scientific method of stratified sampling according to economic conditions (well-off, medium, and poor) of all the towns, townships and villages in Zhiduo County. Then we randomly sampled pastoral families from the households in the town/townships and administrative villages selected for the questionnaire. Considering that the pastoral areas in Zhiduo County are large but sparsely populated and herders there are all Tibetans,

X. Liu, *Complex Pictures of Poverty and Multiple Paths of Poverty Alleviation in Ethnic Areas of China*, https://doi.org/10.1007/978-981-97-4133-5_8

Table 8.1 Villages and households sampled in the Zhiduo County survey

Suojia township		Duocai township		Lixin township		Jiaji town	
Village name	No. of sampled households	Village name	No. of sampled households	Village name	No. of sampled households	Village name	No. of sampled households
Yaqu village	16	Lari village	35	Zhaxi village	8	Riqing village	4
Junqu village	12	Dasheng village	10	Yeqing village	18	Gaicha village	18
Dangqu village	4	Dangjiang village	3	Gangcha village	23	–	–
Relocated village	33	–	–	–	–	–	–

we entrusted Kegawa Animal Husbandry Cooperative to conduct the questionnaire survey. However, in the process of survey, investigators found that it was difficult to locate some of the sampled households as they had migrated to the town or moved to remoter summer pastures to graze their animals. Thus, the investigators had to adjust the interviewees, so the resulting sample was quite different from what we had randomly drawn in the first place. In addition, of the nearly three hundred questionnaires eventually collected, less than two hundred were valid, which shows the difficulty of conducting a household questionnaire survey in high-altitude cold pastoral areas.

In the end, a total of 194 questionnaires were found to be valid, and the sampled pastoral families, with 499 members, were from 13 villages of one town and three townships. In 2012, Zhiduo County had 8,763 households and a population of 36,751, making the sample size in this survey disproportionately small. Besides, as not all the pre-determined sampling principles were actually followed, the survey data finally obtained might not be fully representative in theory or methodology. Nevertheless, given the multi-level interviews with government officials at county and town/township levels, village heads, and ordinary households, we believe that the sample data are practically representative to some extent, especially as the one town and three townships selected can basically represent the overall situation in the county.[1] Accordingly, the analysis results allow us to build a framework for describing and explaining poverty among local herders, in a logical way that is consistent with the actual conditions in the county. Table 8.1 presents the villages from which the households are sampled.

[1] Among the "three townships" we selected, Duocai Township was purely pastoral with the most extensive impoverished areas in Zhiduo County; Suojia Township was an absolutely impoverished township far away from the towns; and Lixin Township was relatively well-off. Yeqing Village and Gangcha Village administered by Lixin Township, along with Gaicha Village in Jiaji Town, boasted the cordyceps militaris resources, and pastoral families there were thus relatively well-off. In summary, given their different economic conditions, the townships and villages we surveyed can basically represent the general situation of social and economic development in Zhiduo County.

1.1 Basic Information on the Households Interviewed in Zhiduo County

1. Household size and structure

A preliminary analysis of 194 households interviewed shows that the average family size is 3.64 (see Table 8.2). Among them, 187 households have an average of 2.25 members in the labor force; 120 households have an average of 1.75 children who are receiving school education; 28 households have an average of 1.39 elderly dependents.

Of the 194 sampled households, 96% are headed by men while 4% by women, showing that the household heads in Zhiduo County are predominantly male. These household heads have an average age of 42. They are generally poorly educated, with 76.8% of them being illiterate. In addition, the household heads who can only read account for 12.4%, those with primary education account for 6.2%, and those with junior high school education or above only account for 4.6%. They received significantly less education not only than the average rural residents nationwide, but also than residents in other agricultural and pastoral areas of Qinghai Province of the same year. The school-age members of these interviewed families are mostly attending school, because according to local government policies, failure to do so would make these families disqualified for government subsidies such as pasture rewards.

The majority of the household heads interviewed, that is, 96.9% of the total, are engaged in animal husbandry. In the other six household heads, two are self-employed, one is a teacher, one is a doctor, and two are engaged in other occupations. And 98.4% of the household heads work in their own villages, while only three persons are employed in other parts of Zhiduo County. We have conducted several field trips to the county, and our observations were consistent with the results of the questionnaire survey.

2. Main means of production for the households interviewed: contracted pastures

Pasture is what local herders rely on for productive activities. As early as 1984, Zhiduo County implemented a reform which contracted all pastures out to individual households. At that time, there were a total of 17,072 herders and 96,559,365.2 *mu* of pastures in Zhiduo County. The contracted pasture area per capita was about 5,656

Table 8.2 Basic information on households interviewed in Zhiduo County

	Mean	Minimum	Maximum	No. of sampled households
Family size	3.64	1	8	194
Workers	2.25	1	6	187
Students	1.75	1	4	120
Elderly dependents	1.39	1	2	28

Table 8.3 Units of pasture contracted to herders interviewed in Zhiduo County

	No. of households	Proportion (%)	Pasture area per household (*mu*)
No pasture	38	19.6	0
One unit	37	19.1	5,656
Two units	105	54.1	11,312
Three units	12	6.2	16,968
Four units	1	0.5	22,624
Five units	1	0.5	28,280
Total	194	100.0	1,651,552

mu. The contract system has since remained unchanged.[2] However, most herders did not know the exact area of pasture they had contracted. When asked about that in the interviews and questionnaire survey, they all said how big a plot was contracted to how many of them, as was recorded in the certificates for pasture use and ownership issued to them. Thus the per capita area in their certificates should still be 5,656 *mu*, the same as in 1984.

As the pasture and population size vary, so does the pasture area per capita in different townships and villages. However, due to the lack of relevant official statistics in Zhiduo County, we cannot track the changes in population and pasture size over the years. Therefore, here we would use the county average in 1984 as the per capita pasture size of each township and village today. For brevity, we refer to the pasture contracted by one person recorded in the certificates as one unit, that contracted by two as two units, and so on. The questionnaire survey shows, 38 of the 194 households interviewed have not contracted any pasture, and the rest have contracted a minimum of one unit and a maximum of five units (see Table 8.3). It should be noted that the number of pasture units contracted by a household is not necessarily equal to the family size.

The reason for such inconsistency between pasture units and family size is that since the 1984 reform, Zhiduo County has made no change to the size of the pasture a household contracted even if the family has more or fewer members. Thirty-eight households without contracted pastures are all migrants who moved from Suojia Township to the county seat because of the grazing ban on their originally contracted pastures.

3. Main source of livelihood for the households interviewed: raising livestock

In field surveys, we found that the number of households raising yak is the largest. For the households involved in the questionnaire survey, 77.8% raise yak and the largest raiser has 200 yaks; about 17% farm cows; and only a few raise sheep, but the size of their herd is relatively large. One pastoral family, for instance, has farmed 2,000 sheep (see Table 8.4). It should be noted, though the survey result shows only six

[2] Yushu Tibetan Autonomous Prefecture Local Chronicle Compilation Committee (2005). *Yushu Tibetan Autonomous Prefecture Chronicle*. Xi'an: Sanqin Publishing House.

sheep farmers, there are actually more of them. Some households entrusted others to raise sheep and some donated their sheep to monasteries. In most cases, monasteries would not take the sheep away, but keep them reared by the donors. Consequently, herders may have difficulty clearly describing the ownership of these animals. When interviewed, some herders would claim that they no longer had sheep while some would say that they still farmed sheep. A similar situation exists with regard to cattle raising. Interestingly enough, when raising cattle or sheep that had been donated to monasteries, the households could take possession of the by products, including milk, wool, calves, lambs, and so forth. As a result, it was difficult to ascertain the actual livestock headcount.

However, most school-age children, the main force for grazing sheep, were gathered in the county seat under the policy of universal nine-year compulsory education, so even fewer households went on raising sheep. Herders who used to breed horses for grazing use motorcycles now, which caused the number of horse-raising households to decrease considerably. Nonetheless, horse racing in pastoral areas gains increasing popularity in recent years, accompanied by the rising prize money. Therefore, this number has seen a growth as some herders begin to breed horses specifically for racing.

In a word, the economy of pastoral families in Zhiduo County is closely related to changes in external economic and social development. This phenomenon not only changes the way they live and work to some extent, but also influences the approaches selected and adjusted to eliminate poverty in impoverished pastoral areas.

4. Marketization of animal husbandry production for the households interviewed

Table 8.5 demonstrates the animal husbandry output of the households interviewed. We are interested in their annual output and allocation of the products for sale and for self-use. Further analysis of the data in Table 8.5 leads to two basic conclusions. First, the marketization degree varies across animals they breed, while in general, the total value of products for sale is often higher than that for self-use. To some extent, we can assume that as a whole, the production of pastoral areas in

Table 8.4 Livestock raised by households interviewed in Zhiduo County, 2012 Unit: Head

		Mean	Minimum	Maximum	No. of interviewed households
Raised livestock	Sheep	600	50	2,000	6
	Beef cattle	25.5	21	30	2
	Cow	72.7	1	400	29
	Horse	2	2	2	1
	Yak	40.6	8	200	133
Basic dams	Sheep	75	50	100	2
	Cow	9.8	2	35	39
	Yak	21.3	3	100	78
Improved livestock	Cow	1	10	10	10

Zhiduo County is initially market-oriented but still on its way toward further marketization as the average value of livestock products for self-use is only slightly lower in most cases. Second, there is a striking gap in terms of the total production among the sampled households. The maximum value of livestock products both for sale and self-use is several to several hundred times greater than the minimum one. Indeed, due to the incomplete information collected in the questionnaire survey, the result here only reflects a general trend rather than precise disparity among them.

1.2 Income and Living Expenditure of the Households Interviewed in Zhiduo County

1. Income inequality among the sampled households

All the valid samples have reported their income from animal husbandry (see Table 8.5), which was 7,420.36 yuan in 2012 according to a preliminary statistical analysis. However, 46 families, all the 32 interviewed in the relocated village of Suojia Township included, reported no income of this kind. Thus, the average value for the other 148 households was 9,726.69 yuan, with the lowest and highest being 1,000 yuan and 45,000 yuan respectively.

The high income shown in the survey can be explained in two aspects. For one thing, the market prices of yak and sheep grazed on pastures as well as livestock products (such as meat, milk, wool, hide, and so on) have been increasing in recent years. However, the high price of animal husbandry output of the interviewed households measured at the market price does not necessarily mean that they have a high income. In reality, a huge portion of their livestock products are for self-use in that their traditional production and lives are highly interconnected, and their food, for example, consists mainly of meat and dairy products from cattle and sheep they raise. If the value of livestock products for self-use measured at market price was deducted, their actual income would be much lower. This is especially the case for those raising fewer livestock. For another, the income from animal husbandry shown in Table 8.5 is only gross income, which shows the total price and value of livestock products when the costs of raising livestock are not subtracted. The vast majority of herders in pastoral areas of Zhiduo County who are engaged in pasture animal husbandry rely on nature to raise livestock. They rarely buy feed (except when facing extreme weather like snow disaster) or raise livestock in captivity. However, in addition to the manpower required for grazing livestock or processing products, they have to pay for the fuel (for grazing on motorcycles) and feed (during snow seasons). When these costs are deducted, their net income from animal husbandry is considerably lower than the gross income.

Most of the households interviewed also have income from cordyceps militaris, wages, government transfer (including various relief funds and subsidies), etc. The questionnaire survey shows 131 households had an average income of 30,843 yuan

Table 8.5 Animal husbandry output of the households interviewed in Zhiduo County, 2012: For Sale and for Self-use

			Mean	Minimum	Maximum	No. of sampled households
Sheep	For sale	Quantity (head)	8.2	4	10	10
		Average unit price (yuan/head)	1,210	1,200	1,300	10
		Total price (yuan)	9,890	4,800	12,000	10
	For self-use	Quantity (head)	20	–	–	1
		Value (yuan)	24,200	–	–	1
Cattle	For sale	Quantity (head)	4.77	1	30	35
		Average unit price (yuan/head)	4,181.18	2,500	5,000	34
		Total price (yuan)	17,066.47	4,000	45,000	34
	For self-use	Quantity (head)	2.37	1	5	19
		Value (yuan)	9,894.74	4,000	40,000	99
Meat products	For sale	Amount (*jin*)	168.4	1	280	5
		Average unit price (yuan/*jin*)	25	25	25	3
		Total price (yuan)	4,210	25	7,000	32
	For self-use	Amount (*jin*)	145	1	400	21
		Value (yuan)	3,636	25	10,000	95
Dairy products	For sale	Total price (yuan)	1,986.29	350	5,000	35
	For self-use	Value (yuan)	1,823.09	200	5,000	55
Wool and hides	For sale	Total price (yuan)	726	300	1,500	10
	For self-use	Value (yuan)	500	–	–	1

from cordyceps militaris in 2012, ranging from 1,000 to 10,000 yuan; 172 households reported other income, with an average of around 9,526 yuan; four had regular wages averaging 8,550 yuan; and two households received relief funds of 20,000 yuan and 4,000 yuan respectively. It is noteworthy that the "other income" they reported mainly came from the government transfer payments. Since 2012, Zhiduo County has put in place the national policy of rewards and subsidies for pasture ecological conservation, giving 3.5 yuan for each *mu* of pastures. The township governments distributed the rewards and subsidies allocated by the county government to each village according to their pasture areas. Then further distribution to households is carried out in a similar way. The more areas of pastures a pastoral household contracts, the more rewards and subsidies it can receive. We found that Junqu Village in Suojia Township received the highest rewards and subsidies of 4,100 yuan per capita, and thus a family of five here could get over 20,000 yuan in 2012; Zhijia Village of Zhahe Township received the lowest amount, with 1,450 yuan per capita.

With regard to the income composition, the households interviewed face a lack of diversity in the source of income, which mainly includes pastoral livestock production and cordyceps militaris. Industries are hardly seen here and the commerce is limited and mostly run by outsiders due to the small population here. Local herders lack both the technical skills and the capital to start or participate in non-agricultural business.

The income gaps in this county are also striking. A few families reported no income in 2012, while the highest family income that year was 110 thousand yuan, with an average of 38,600 yuan. The highest per capita income reported was 39,500 yuan and the average was 10,974.6 yuan, 3,058 yuan higher than the national per capita net income of rural residents (7,916.6 yuan) in the same year. However, as mentioned above, the income shown in our questionnaire survey is not the net income as it includes costs. Compared with the per capita net income of rural residents in Qinghai Province in 2012, which was 5,364.4 yuan, that of the households interviewed in Zhiduo County was still at a relatively high level among farmers and herders in the whole province.

There remains income inequality among the interviewed households. In respect of the gap of their gross income, a preliminarily statistical analysis shows that the Gini coefficient was 0.3738, the income distribution inequality index[3] was 2.27, the Theil index GE (0) and GE (1) were 0.2801 and 0.2278 respectively, and the Atkinson index was 0.24429. There are several factors contributing to such inequality, and the most important one is the difference in resource endowments of different townships or villages. The top 10 households in family income are from Yeqing Village and Gangcha Village in Lixin Township and Gaicha Village in Jiaji Town, all of which are main cordyceps militaris-producing areas in Zhiduo County. Herders who collect cordyceps militaris every year include both villagers in these areas and those

[3] The income distribution inequality index, also known as the Oshima index, is the ratio of the income proportion of the top 20% of the population to that of the bottom 20% of the population. The index reflects the unequal distribution of income in a society to some extent. Its lowest value is one (1), and a higher value indicates a greater gap between the rich and the poor as well as more striking income inequality.

of other villages in the county. According to local practice, to dig for cordyceps militaris, villagers from other areas should pay a certain amount of turf fees to the herders contracting the pastures. The amount varies according to the diggers' relation with administrative villages which cordyceps militaris producing areas belong to. Diggers from other villages in the same township, other townships in the same county, other counties in the same prefecture, other prefectures in the same province, and other provinces pay an escalating turf fee in sequence. However, local governments would take various measures to restrict outsiders (including those from other counties, prefectures and provinces) from digging for cordyceps militaris. In any case, herders from these producing areas can not only dig for cordyceps militaris conveniently, but collect hefty turf fees from diggers of other villages. Moreover, we found in interviews that with the continuously increasing market price of cordyceps militaris in recent years, some herders from the above villages started cordyceps militaris or hide business, and some even acted as loan sharks. Naturally, their income rose accordingly. In addition, such government subsidies as the pasture ecological rewards and subsidies are calculated based on the area of pastures herders contracted, which, as mentioned above, varies greatly among households (see Table 8.3). Accordingly, a huge gap appears in the amount of rewards and subsidies they received. The pastures were equally distributed in the 1984 reform without adjustment for more than 30 years. However, the family size of pastoral households has undergone considerable changes in the same period. Though this policy has stabilized the pasture contracting, it makes a great "contribution" to income inequality among herders.

2. Production and living expenditure of the households interviewed

Overall, the households interviewed have low production expenditure. The questionnaire survey presents only two households with expenditure on pasture rental, one thousand yuan and 1,800 yuan respectively. Eight families reported production expenditure on other items with a minimum of two hundred yuan, a maximum of 1,800 yuan, and an average of 813 yuan. In reality, however, other households may have productive expenditure as well. For example, many herders need to pay for fuels as they usually ride motorcycles to graze their livestock; they pay for fodder when it snows in winter, and the fees, depending on the number of livestock they keep and the snow, can amount to several thousand yuan in a normal year; and they pay turf fees to dig for cordyceps militaris. They did not report above-mentioned expenditures not because they have no such expenditure. It is more than likely that they are not deemed productive.

The overall living expenditure of the households interviewed is still relatively low (see Table 8.6). In 2012, the average value of 190 families interviewed was 10,345.3 yuan and the average household had 3.64 members, according to the data in Table 8.2. Thus, the per capita living expenditure in Zhiduo County was only 2,842.1 yuan in 2012 while that of rural households nationwide was 5,908 yuan, 2.08 times higher. Nonetheless, it should be noted that their actual living expenditure could be higher than the reported amount. Many of them might not count in the value of home-grown livestock products (including meat, dairy and hide products) they consumed at market prices, which was found considerable in our field observations and interviews.

Table 8.6 Living expenditure and consumption structure of households interviewed in Zhiduo County

Items	Expenditure per household (yuan)	Percentage(%)
Food	4,271.6	41.3
Clothing	1,349.0	13.0
Education	284.5	2.8
Health care	1,668.2	16.1
Gifting	153.7	1.5
Transport	671.2	6.5
Communications	497.5	4.8
Water and electricity	157.6	1.5
Recreation and culture	11.3	0.1
Others	1,280.9	12.4
Total	10,345.3	100.0

The consumption structure in Table 8.6 reveals an overall moderately prosperous life of the households interviewed, with an Engel's coefficient of 41.3%. In general, families with an Engel's coefficient ranging from 40 to 50% are deemed well-off.[4] However, the actual figure would be higher because of a wide disparity in living standards and the fact that many of them, as stated, might not report the value of their home-grown livestock products they consumed at market prices. If we calculated the Engel's coefficient of each household before working out the average value, the figure would be 48%.

On the whole, the consumption pattern of the households interviewed was still subsistence-oriented. Expenditure on development-oriented items such as education, transport, communications, recreation and culture accounted for only a small portion in their overall living expenditure. In addition, their expenditure on health care was mainly for medical treatment rather than for health improving.

Similarly, there is a significant gap in living expenditure between a maximum of 87,000 yuan and a minimum of 1,000 yuan in 2012. Of the 190 households, 162 had no education expenditure, 111 had no transport expenditure, 57 had no expenditure on communications, and only two had expenditure on recreation and culture. The maximum value in each item is hundreds of times greater than the minimum. In terms of the Engel's coefficient, we find that the figure of 28.4% of the 190 households is 60% and higher (see Table 8.7), and they are deemed poor from the perspective of consumption. As a result, households under the poverty line or barely meeting daily needs (27.4%) altogether accounted for as high as 55.8% of all households interviewed. Meanwhile, we notice 31.1% of affluent families, which shows the pronounced inequality in living expenditure among herders in Zhiduo County.

[4] Li, P. L., & Zhang, Y. (2003). Stratification of Consumption by Class and Strata. Chinese Sociology, Chinese Academy of Social Sciences. http://www.sociology.cass.cn/shxs/xpxz/t20030916_1044.htm.

Table 8.7 Engel's coefficient in 2012 of households interviewed in Zhiduo County

Engel's coefficient	No. households	Percentage (%)	Living standard
29% and lower	34	17.9	Wealthy
30–39%	25	13.2	Relatively affluent
40–49%	25	13.2	Moderately well-off
50–59%	52	27.4	Barely meeting daily needs
60% and higher	54	28.4	Poor
Total	190	100.0	-

1.3 Assets and Liabilities of the Households Interviewed in Zhiduo County

Production and income of the households interviewed are significantly influenced by family assets that mainly include sheds, pens, silage, and productive vehicles and machinery the herders built or purchased. A total of 148 households in our questionnaire survey provided information on fixed productive assets and their estimated value. By our calculation, each household had such assets of 39,800 yuan on average. However, there exists a considerable gap in this aspect. Some households reported no fixed productive assets while some estimated theirs at over a hundred thousand yuan to hundreds of thousands of yuan. There is no doubt that households with fixed productive assets of high value are affluent.

Indebtedness is uncommon in Zhiduo County with only 20 households reporting liabilities of about 15,350 yuan on average and of a maximum of 60,000 yuan. The primary reason for indebtedness was illness as seven families borrowed for medical treatment. Then four families borrowed for improving production conditions. These liabilities mainly arose from private lending with exorbitant interest rates in many cases. For instance, of the fifteen households who provided information on the source, six households borrowed from relatives or friends and nine from usurers or unqualified credit institutions (also usurers in nature). Since some herders could not pay back the usurious loan or even its interests, their cattle and sheep would be taken away by usurers at a price greatly lower than the market price. As a result, some of them were forced into poverty and could not pull themselves out in a short period of time. In interviews, the households generally reported the difficulty in getting loans from banks or rural credit cooperatives. They could only borrow from usurers in most cases once they needed money urgently for medical treatment of family members or for tuition fees.

2 Analysis of Poverty and Its Causes in the Pastoral Areas of Zhiduo County

In reality, poverty is pretty common among households in pastoral areas of Zhiduo County. Statistics of local Office of Poverty Alleviation and Development show that of the county's population of less than 30,000, a total of 13,000 people were living under the poverty line in 2012, who fell into poverty for various reasons. To better understand the main reasons, we have conducted several field surveys in recent years, and collected a lot of documents and first-hand data through symposiums and interviews with relevant departments of the governments of Yushu Tibetan Autonomous Prefecture and Zhiduo County, heads of Duocai Township government, and many households. With comprehensive and in-depth analyses, we come to the conclusion that poverty in pastoral areas of Zhiduo County results from multiple factors including the county's natural conditions, economic and social development, historical and cultural characteristics, and many other practical issues. In this section, we attempt to systematically explore the poverty here and main reasons behind it from these perspectives.

2.1 Special Geographical and Ecological Conditions

Zhiduo County is located in the hinterland of Qinghai-Tibet Plateau, with towering terrain and an average altitude of above 4,500 m. Lying in the largest eco-regulation region and China's biggest high-frigid species property repository, the county plays an important role in ecology. However, it is also one of the regions with the worst conditions for animal husbandry because of its extremely fragile ecological environment and harsh natural conditions. The average annual temperature here is below minus three degrees centigrade with the cold season lasting eight months. Such harsh weather conditions lead to a lack of diversity in animal husbandry production. Besides, the county is trapped in a pronounced imbalance between pastures and livestock when the livestock-carrying capacity of pastures is declining due to climate- or human-induced degradation, desertification, alkalization, soil erosion and infestation of rodents and insects. As ecological conditions keep deteriorating, local herders suffer more in their production and lives, and the poverty headcount ratio increases correspondingly. In a word, the fragile ecological environment is a basic characteristic of the pastoral areas in Zhiduo County, which is neither conducive to human habitation nor to the development of animal husbandry production on which the poor rely to meet their basic needs. This harsh environment is a root cause of herders' poverty and vulnerability, making them easy to relapse into poverty.[5]

---

[5] Su, H. H., & Du, Q. H. (2008). *Research on Anti-poverty Strategies in China's Tibetan Ethnic Areas.* Lanzhou: Gansu Ethnic Publishing House.

2.2 Natural Disasters

Zhiduo County is frequently hit by such natural disasters as snow disaster, wind disaster, drought and frost which cause considerable losses. According to officials at local Office of Poverty Alleviation and Development, natural disasters, mainly snow disasters that bring the most serious impact, are so frequently seen that the law of "a big disaster once every ten years, a medium one every five years, a small one every three years, and disasters definitely seen every year" has formed. In a big disaster, herders would suffer losses almost equivalent to their livestock income of several years or even a dozen years. For instance, the 2008 snowstorm lasting more than one month with thick snow cumulatively led to direct economic losses of 3.4 million yuan. All the five townships and one town in Zhiduo County with a population of 25,524 were affected and more than seventeen thousand heads of livestock died. As a result, the poverty-returning rate that year reached 12% with 928 people from 265 households relapsing into poverty.[6]

2.3 Diseases

For many herders in Zhiduo County, unforeseen diseases are also a reason behind their impoverishment. Our field survey comes to a similar conclusion. Although it may be the case for all rural areas nationwide, the impact of diseases is particularly noticeable for herders here. A report from local Office of Poverty Alleviation and Development shows the county is known as a "forbidden zone for life" since the high altitude and low oxygen content in air (half the level in low-altitude regions) make an extremely harsh living environment. Its pastoral areas are confronted with high incidence of endemic diseases including tuberculosis, hepatic hydatid cyst, arthritis, compensatory ventricular hypertrophy and other circulatory and respiratory diseases. With high mortality from diseases and high incidence rate of infectious diseases that keep rising year by year, the herders' average life expectancy is only about 55.8 years.[7] Besides, considering the poor medical conditions and limited income, herders would rather wait out minor diseases and endure serious ones than go to hospital for treatment unless they can no longer bear.

Diseases become a crucial factor in herders' poverty because they, especially serious ones, will bring about interlocking impacts to herders who fall ill, especially those whose families are financially vulnerable. Diseases add to the burden of medical expenses on agricultural or pastoral families, so when they cannot afford the daunting medical expenses of serious illnesses, they have to cut other living expenses. They may naturally first reduce expenses of food and beverages, which

---

[6] Office of Poverty Alleviation and Development of Zhiduo County. (2011). Plan on Poverty Alleviation and Development of Zhiduo County During the 12th Five-Year Plan Period.

[7] Office of Poverty Alleviation and Development of Zhiduo County. (2012). *Research Report on Poverty Alleviation in Zhiduo County (Internal Report).*

increases the future risk of diseases for nutritional deficiencies will undermine their health. The second countermeasure may be to force their children out of school for the purpose of reducing educational expenditures and letting the children take care of the sick and livestock. However, reducing the investment in human capital like children's education will inevitably weaken the family potential and ability to cope with the risk of poverty. The herders would also sell livestock or fixed productive assets, which of course undercuts their productive conditions and thus affects their per capita income. Other households, in desperation, may resort to usury to tide over the difficulty temporarily. It undoubtedly is another heavy burden for pastoral households that are already impoverished.

2.4 Lack of Human Capital

Zhiduo County is underdeveloped both economically and socially, which greatly limits the self-improvement of its people. The labor force here is generally of low quality, with a lack of knowledge and awareness necessary for developing modern agriculture or other industries. Statistics show that in pastoral areas,90% of the workforce has received no more than primary school education. Therefore, these areas are confronted with several problems including low skills and low education level of the labor force, low conversion rate of scientific and technological achievements in the animal husbandry development, and the lack of personnel with know-how, scientific knowledge or managerial skills.[8] As mentioned above, the household heads interviewed were mainly in their middle age and mostly illiterate or semi-literate. They engaged only in livestock production, and barely worked outside the village. Meanwhile, we also found in our field survey that many eco-migrants and migrants from pastoral areas to the town were often impoverished though at their working age. Suffering from a lack of human capital, they were unable to get employed due to low employability.

2.5 Inadequate Education-Caused Poverty Under New Circumstances

Inadequate education-caused poverty was a new phenomenon in rural China in the 1990s. To solve this problem, the government implemented a policy of exempting primary and secondary students under the nine-year compulsory education in rural areas of ethnic minority concentrated areas in western China from paying tuition and miscellaneous fees, and provided them with free nutritious lunches and certain living allowances. Students in boarding schools were also exempt from paying boarding

[8] Zheng, H. F. (2012). Analysis of Non-Economic Factors Constraining Economic Development of Zhiduo County (Internal Report).

fees and living expenses. In theory, these measures should have greatly relieved the financial burden of the families with primary and secondary school students in these areas.

However, China adjusted the distribution of rural primary and secondary schools since 2001, and implemented the "combination of schools"[9] nationwide. Zhiduo County also concentrated its students to schools at the county seat or townships. Generally, students at township schools were picked up by their parents every day given the short distance between school and home while those from pastoral areas to farther schools at the county seat had to board. Though relevant policies had exempted these students from paying boarding fees and living expenses, most of their parents had to stay with them for various reasons. Therefore, herders would move to the county seat by participating in the "eco-migration" project, or move there voluntarily after selling their livestock.

There was no secondary industry in Zhiduo County, and the underdeveloped commerce was almost managed by outsiders. As a result, herders moving to the county seat, though still in the prime of their lives, could hardly find jobs. With only income from government transfer and cordyceps militaris dug in June every year, they had to bear much higher living expenses than when they had been in pastoral areas. Some of them thus began to fall into poverty.[10]We called this phenomenon as "inadequate education-caused poverty under new circumstances". In field surveys, we found that the vast majority of herders who had moved to the county seat with their children were living in or on the edge of poverty, except those from the cordyceps militaris producing areas.

2.6 *Shortage of Public Goods and Services*

At high altitudes, pastoral areas in this county are large but sparsely populated due to inconvenient transport. Living dispersedly, many of the herders here are far away

---

[9] "Combination of schools" is an "educational reform" in the end of 1990s. It was officially started in 2001 to rearrange the distribution of rural primary and secondary schools nationwide. Specifically, it is to dismantle a large number of such schools, and concentrate students in schools at the county seat or townships. From 1997 to 2010, 371,470 primary schools were dismantled nationwide, in which 302,099 were in rural areas, accounting for 81.3% of the total.

[10] Of course, the main impact of "combination of schools" was positive. For one thing, this reform was undoubtedly conducive to the improvement of education in pastoral areas in Zhiduo County and obvious reduction in student dropout rates here (since students didn't have to leave school to graze animals anymore). For another, it "accidentally" facilitated the relocation of residents and urbanization in Zhiduo County. Previously, herders in pastoral areas were unwilling to participate in the relocation project. After this educational reform, those whose children studied in the county seat had to make a move, and a few of them who had not yet got houses from the "Nomad Settlement Project" decided to build houses at the county seat. Nevertheless, the "poverty under new circumstances" caused by increasing living cost and reduced source of income still deserves special attention. Some people call it the "cost of reform", indicating that one generation pays the price to harness the reform for the sake of future generations. Hope such price is not perpetual misery.

from public service institutions, facing a serious shortage of such public goods and services as road, water, electricity, radio, television and communications. This is also a main reason behind the poverty of some herders. Moreover, inadequate infrastructure and public services make them greatly isolated from the external market economy and difficult to participate fully in economic exchanges to develop their family economy, which further "solidifies" their poverty. Then they fall into long-term impoverishment.

Our survey shows that many public infrastructures are not sufficiently accessible to herders in pastoral areas. Specifically, according to answers of 107 households to the question about the distance between their homes and the nearest road, the average distance was 11.25 km and the longest was as large as over 60 km; among 190 households, homes of 125 families were not electrified, accounting for 65.8%, and 110 families had no phone. Nevertheless, mobile phones were increasingly popular with herders, which could make up for the low usage rate of wire telephone in a way. Obviously, there was a really low penetration of public infrastructures and services in pastoral areas of the county in 2013. In recent years, when China makes unremitting efforts to eradicate poverty, Zhiduo County has promoted the construction of public infrastructures, which definitely improves the situation.

It is important to note that serious shortage of public services featuring backward financial industry and seriously insufficient credit services will, to a large extent, hinder the herders' capability to develop production and cope with risks. In Zhiduo County, some herders get stuck in poverty mainly because they cannot receive formal and standard credit services when facing key risks.

3 Achievements of Poverty Alleviation and Development in Zhiduo County

Zhiduo County has made good progress on poverty alleviation and development. Statistics show that since the 12th Five-Year Plan period, this county has witnessed a dramatic reduction in poverty-stricken population in rural areas. In 2008, by the poverty standard, there were 11,101 poor people from 2,649 households, accounting for 50.3% of the county's total population. By 2012, based on the poverty standard in 2010, the number had been reduced to 8,817 and 32.6% respectively, the poverty headcount ratio showing a decrease of 17.7% meanwhile.[11] It is noteworthy that the poverty standard in 2010 is much higher than that in 2008. In another words, if measured by the standard in 2010, the poverty headcount ratio in 2008 would be much higher than 50.3%.

[11] Calculated based on the data from *Yushu Statistical Yearbook: 2008 (compiled in 2009)* and *Yushu Statistical Yearbook: 2012 (compiled in 2013)* by Statistics Bureau of Yushu Tibetan Autonomous Prefecture.

3.1 Poverty Alleviation and Development Projects in Zhiduo County

The county has launched a series of important projects to promote poverty alleviation and development. Since the 11th Five-Year Plan period, it has rolled out the projects of whole-village pushing forward, relocation of rural poor for poverty alleviation, workforce training and employment transfer, ecological improvement, and development of industries with local advantages. In general, these projects have certainly made some achievements as most of them are designed and implemented in line with the reasons behind poverty in Zhiduo County. Below is a brief review of these projects and a preliminary assessment of their effectiveness in poverty reduction.

1. "Whole-village pushing forward"

Before the 11th Five-Year Plan period, almost all villages in pastoral areas of Zhiduo County were stuck with backward infrastructure and social undertakings, which is one of the key factors in herders' difficulty of getting rid of poverty. In a bid to improve the infrastructure of poor villages,[12] strengthen the self-development ability of poor herders, and lift them out of poverty, the county had rolled out the "whole-village pushing forward" project in 20 impoverished villages from five townships and one town since 2005. On the premise of environmental protection and ecological restoration, it invested a total of 12.47 million yuan in 18 villages in 2005–2009, and supported 7,448 poor herders from 2,178 households. It purchased 300 cows, 40 small four-wheelers and 3,450 solar power heaters for domestic use, constructed 254 km of simple gravel road, trained 2,500 people for this project, and built 17 storefronts run by poor villages (mainly for collecting rent). In 2010, the project was also completed in another two poor villages. By implementing the "whole-village pushing forward" project, Zhiduo County accelerated the infrastructure construction and enhanced the support for production in poor villages, effectively promoting the development in such areas and increasing the income of the poverty-stricken population.

During the 12th Five-Year Plan period, the county listed five villages which were poorer and harder to support among the said 18 villages as the "follow-up" objects to continue the "whole-village pushing forward" project and consolidate achievements they had made during the 11th Five-Year Plan period. The five villages are Yaqu Village and Junqu Village from Suojia Township, Zhisai Village and Kouqian Village from Zhahe Township and Lari Village from Duocai Township, with a population of 3,584 from 1,047 households. In addition, Zhiduo County, after the careful

[12] Poor villages refer to administrative villages with large poor population that cannot meet daily needs or barely meet daily needs but face unstable life. Such villages pose great difficulties and heavy tasks to poverty alleviation and development. They are defined based on the per capita annual net income of no more than 1,500 yuan in 2009, with reference to the number of sheep per capita, infrastructure including water, electricity and road, and the development degree of education, science and technology, culture, health and other social undertakings. Moreover, poor villages must be administrative villages rather than natural villages, as determined by the civil affairs department. (Poverty Alleviation and Development Bureau of Zhiduo County: *Poverty Alleviation and Development Plan During the 12th Five-Year Plan Period in Zhiduo County*).

selection by herder committees of the five villages and township (town) governments administering them, appointed the Office of Poverty Alleviation and Development to carry out field investigation. Based on the previous experience in project implementation and opinions from the industry sectors, the county adjusted the project contents and determined two follow-up projects with a gross investment of about 19,167,500 yuan, namely, construction of fine breed production base and labor skills training. The former focused on construction of the breeding base and forage grass base, and purchase of livestock, and the latter involved training of skilled manpower in feeding, forage grass planting and epidemic prevention. It was estimated that the follow-up projects will lift 3,584 people from 1,047 households out of poverty. When we investigated in Zhiduo County in 2013, initial success had been achieved, while the final effect should be evaluated in the future. In the light of the plan for the "whole-village pushing forward" project during the 11th Five-Year Plan period, all poverty alleviation and development projects involving capital input and tangible construction could be completed on schedule.

2. "Relocation of the rural poor"

Indeed, "relocation of the rural poor" is actually an "eco-migration" project. As mentioned above, most of the poor people in Zhiduo County live in "inhospitable areas" at an altitude of 4,100–4,400 m, facing harsh natural environment, fragile ecological environment, poor infrastructure and a severe shortage of roads and electricity. Besides, pasture degradation, serious desertification, and declined livestock bearing rate restricted the development of animal husbandry in pastoral areas. Under such external conditions, it is scarcely possible for the herders to increase their income and improve their production and living standards through traditional animal husbandry. Moreover, the frequent occurrence of natural disasters and endemic diseases make them vulnerable to long-term and overall poverty, so it is difficult for them to get rid of poverty in their living places. To help them reduce poverty, and protect and restore the pasture ecosystem, the county learnt from its experience of the "relocation of the rural poor" project during the 11th Five-Year Plan period, and formulated the *Relocation Plan of Zhiduo County for Poverty Alleviation and Development During the 12th Five-Year Plan Period*, which has been implemented since 2011.

The project during the 12th Five-Year Plan period involved 5,164 people from 1,064 poor households in 20 herder committees under five townships and one town who still lived at an altitude of 4,100–4,400 m with harsh living conditions. In a span of five years, the project has been rolled out by these herder committees by stages and in groups. When we investigated in Zhiduo County in 2013, the 2011–2012 implementation plan had been basically completed, and the 2013 plan was under way.

Actually, target herders in the project during the 12th Five-Year Plan period were not all relocated. There were two options for them: migration to the seat of the township government or resettlement in their hometowns. Finally, a total of 368 households chose the former relocation mode and 696 households chose the latter who were mainly in Suojia, Zhahe, Duocai and Zhiqu townships. All the households involved in Lixin Township and Jiaji Town were relocated to the seat of the township government. The government provided housing for all relocated herders, built necessary facilitiesof water, electricity, roads and sanitation, and tried to build follow-up industries for them. We had inspected some of the completed settlements and found that the construction projects had actually been implemented. Despite low quality, these construction projects still significantly improved the production and living of relocated households.

3. "Workforce training and employment transfer"

In poverty alleviation and development, Zhiduo County has been paying attention to the workforce training and employment transfer. This project includes the following three items. The first is skills training for the households of 20 herder committees under five townships and one town which engage in animal husbandry. The second is training in practical skills mainly about home appliance maintenance, machine maintenance, automobile driving, folk handicraft, etc. With an investment of 34.25 million yuan, such training had been carried out many times during the 11th Five-Year Plan period, and the county planned to train one thousand practical technicians during the 12th Five-year Plan period, which can support 3,425 poor people. The third is the training in professional knowledge of poverty alleviation for all county and township officials concerned, which was implemented during the 12th Five-Year Plan period. It was planned to train 40 officials every year, and the training shall be completed in five years.

4. "Ecological improvement"

Since 2003, Zhiduo County had implemented a number of ecological improvement projects including restoring grazing land to pasture, integrated black soil land management, pest and rodent control, closing hillsides to cultivate grass (forest), eco-migration and so on. During the 12th Five-Year Plan period, local government planned to invest 20,042,400 yuan to continuously protect the grassland eco-environment, covering 20 herder committees under five townships and one town. This project focuses on integrated black soil land management, pest and rodent control and closing hillsides to cultivate grass (forest), going along with the integrated management project of Sanjiangyuan ecological environment. By then, 30,994 people from 7,158 households will benefit from it. In other words, the implementation of the ecological improvement project is to benefit the whole county.

5. "Development of industries with local advantages"

Since the 11th Five-Year Plan period, in the process of poverty alleviation and development, Zhiduo County had explored and promoted the development of industries with local advantages. In particular, it implemented the project from eight aspects during the 12th Five-Year Plan period.

First, construct a fine breed production base which mainly focuses on the cultivation and breeding of high-quality hybrid yaks and Tibetan sheep, in a bid to solve the problem of strain degradation caused by inbreeding of livestock in the whole county. The project adopted a mode of intensive cultivation combined with family cultivation. In total, the county planned to invest 19,167,500 yuan to establish nine breeding bases and purchase 4,575 hybrid yaks and 8,320 quality Tibetan sheep. Taking sale of hybrid male animals and high-quality livestock products as the main profit model, the county aimed to drive its industrialization of animal husbandry and support 3,584 herders from 1,047 poor households. In 2013, the base was basically constructed and put into operation.

Second, construct a production base of Chinese and Tibetan medicinal materials. On the basis of integrated black soil land management, Zhiduo County planned to invest 1.5 million yuan to help each household cultivate 30 *mu* (2,250 *mu* in total) of Tibetan medicinal materials including common turnip, rhubarb, costusroot and Tibetan capillaris, which supported 255 people from 75 poor households. By our investigation in 2013, the base had been partially built and was being improved.

Third, construct an artificial grass base by focusing on the intensive and integrated planting of herbage storing for winter. With a planned investment of 2.7 million yuan, the county constructed a planting base covering 7,150 *mu* to support 10,978 poor people from 3,169 households. The construction began in 2011 and had been partially completed by 2013.

Fourth, conduct the breed improvement project. Zhiduo County planned to invest 54 million yuan, organize 120 thousand *mu* of pasture, establish three livestock fattening bases, and purchase twelve thousand livestock and six hundred tons of granular feed. The livestock was cultivated and fattened in a semi-enclosed mode and sold in due time. Once implementation, this project could support 1,321 people from 4,391 poor households. The county has started the project in 2012 and rolled out it smoothly.

Fifth, construct a byproducts processing base. Giving full play to the geographical advantage of Tongka Village in Zhiqu Township, the county planned to invest 2,430 thousand yuan to establish a yak milk base with five hundred cows and eight thousand *mu* of pasture. The base, which can support 1,455 poor people from 441 households, mainly produces fresh milk and dairy products. Its construction began in 2011 and is progressing smoothly.

Sixth, develop handicraft industries with ethnic features, including Mani stone carving and processing of ethnic clothing and ornaments. It was planned to invest 1,210 thousand yuan in the project of Mani stone carving for building three processing sites of scriptures in stone carving, each equipped with processing workshops of two hundred square meters and a set of ancillary facilities and devices. The project supporting 3,779 people from 1,041 poor households was started from 2012 and basically completed in 2013. In addition, Zhiduo County planned to invest 1,536 thousand yuan in the processing project of ethnic clothing and ornaments, in which two corresponding workshops were built, each covering an area of 500 square meters with a set of equipment and facilities. At the same time, shops with an area of eighty square meters to sell the ethnic clothing and ornaments were built. This project, started in 2011 and nearly completed in the next year, supported 274 people from 80 poor households who had relocated to the county seat.

Seventh, develop characteristic plateau tourism involving four sub-projects started in 2011 and basically completed by 2013. The first one is Qidukou scenic spot in

Masai Village of Zhahe Township covering an area of 2,500 square meters. With an investment of 1,760 thousand yuan, the project entailed the construction of a relic and Tibetan style park at Qidukou, an important pass along the Tea-horse Ancient Road. The second sub-project is the construction of Gongsa Temple, a national AA level tourist attraction built in Nieqia Village of Duocai Township with the highest indoor Buddha statue in the world. Zhiduo County planned to invest 1,360 thousand yuan into the project to build selling points for souvenirs and handiwork with ethnic features as well as ancillary tourist facilities, together with a tourist accommodation and dining venue in the county seat, which covers a total area of 800 square meters. The third project is about the construction of tourist areas along the Yangtze River in the Gangcha Village and Yeqin Village of Lixin Township. With a planned investment of 5,120 thousand yuan, the project took the development of comprehensive tourism along the Yangtze River as the mainstay, and aimed to build 29 km of gravel road and 20 signs for publicity and to construct tourism infrastructures based on folk customs. It was anticipated that there would be accompanying development of local catering and service industries. The last one is the Kangyur stone carving scenic spot in Zhijia Village of Zhiqu Township, which has been listed as a key cultural relic protection unit by the related department. The county planned to invest 16,140 thousand yuan to build roads of 47 km from the scenic spot to the seat of the township government, where a site covering an area of 500 square meters for catering and accommodation and supporting facilities would be constructed.

3.2 *Achievements of Poverty Alleviation and Development in Zhiduo County*

In general, the aforementioned projects had considerably boosted the poverty alleviation in Zhiduo County. Through the implementation of the 11th Five-Year Plan, in particular, remarkable results had been made here, which are mainly shown in the following five aspects.

1. The number of poor people had been reduced year after year. At the beginning of the 11th Five-Year Plan period, there were 17,420 herders and 4,926 poor households in Zhiduo County. Through the efforts for five years, the numbers dropped to 11,715 and 3,425 respectively by the end of 2009, with reduction rates of 30.5% and 32%. When poverty alleviation standards were improved in 2012, there were still 8,817 people and 3,115 households living in poverty. The proportion of poor people in this county was further reduced.
2. The income of poor people increased rapidly through continuously diversified channels. During the 11th Five-Year Plan period, Zhiduo County accelerated the construction of infrastructures, and developed and expanded productive projects. By the end of 2009, the per capita income of poor herders was 1,796.65 yuan, an increase of 817.65 yuan or 83.52% over the 979 yuan in 2003. The channels for increasing the poor's income also expanded from the animal husbandry only to

the combination of the animal husbandry, collecting industry and other industries. It is noteworthy that China launched a subsidy and incentive mechanism in 2011, aiming to protect the eco-environment, change production modes of the animal husbandry, increase the income of herders, and take the grassland ecological protection and animal husbandry development onto a sound track. Since the year 2012, each herder in Zhiduo County had received about 2,800 yuan under this mechanism, and their per capita income had risen rapidly, reaching 4,012.83 yuan in 2013.

3. Infrastructures in poor villages had been improved significantly. At the beginning of the 11th Five-Year Plan period, 14 herder committees in Zhiduo County had no access to traffic routes and 20 had no access to electricity. Thenceforth, the county had built78 kilometers of simple roads, and purchased 3,450 sets of solar power panels for domestic use. By the end of 2009, the number of poor herder committees having no access to traffic routes dropped to four, and to zero by 2013, with a majority of them having electricity.
4. The social undertakings were developed. With arduous work in poverty alleviation and development during the 11th Five-Year Plan period, Zhiduo County had witnessed all-round progress in all social undertakings. In 2009, the enrollment rate of school-age children in poor villages here reached 98.5%, and the literacy rate among young and middle-aged people continued to rise; medical facilities had been further improved, and the shortage of medical services and medicines had been significantly relieved; most of the poor villages with electricity were able to purchase radio and television; people's cultural life had been improved, and their mental outlook had changed a lot.
5. The social security system in the pastoral areas had been established and improved year by year. Zhiduo County made nearly all herders covered by the new rural cooperative medical system, which effectively alleviated the dilemma of "poverty caused by illness" they faced. It is particularly worth noting that many poor households, such as those who enjoy the "five guarantees" (for food, clothing, medical care, housing and funeral expenses) and the minimum living guarantee, had received particular support from the above medical system and medical assistance system. They could be reimbursed for their medical cost entirely by the insurance of this medical system and the civil administration department of the county. In 2013, to make the said poor herders all able to afford the medical treatment, local administration office for new rural cooperative medical system created a "two reimbursements and one remission" system after careful investigation, which conformed to the actual conditions of this county. In this system, the poor are allowed to seek medical care in designated hospitals and enjoy entirely free medical care. Moreover, remarkable performance had been made in the new rural pension insurance scheme launched in 2010, where all people above the age of 60 were covered for free. The aged under this scheme could get pensions every month which rose from55 yuan in 2010 to 85 yuan in 2013. Owing to the governments' vigorous promotion in the three years, 13,000 herders participated in the pension insurance scheme in 2012 with a participation rate of 92%, increasing from 4,992 in 2010.

The "five guarantees" policy in the pastoral areas of Zhiduo County had been implemented thoroughly. In 2012, it supported 555 people, including 121 in a centralized way and 434 in a decentralized way. According to Qinghai's standards for supporting the poor in the "five guarantees" policy, people who were supported in a centralized way shall receive 80% of the herders' per capita net income of the previous year, and the decentralized support shall be about seventy70% (about two thousand yuan). All these standards were basically met in this county.

Since 2007, Zhiduo County had fully rolled out the rural subsistence allowance system, kept improving it based on the actual situation, and supported it by adopting measures in terms of medical treatment, education, housing and heating. As China kept raising the rural subsistence allowance standard, the number of poor people assisted by this system also increased year by year. In 2007 when the standard was an annual income of no more than 720 yuan, there were 4,300 people enjoying the subsistence allowance, while in 2011 when the standard was raised to no more than 1,320 yuan, the corresponding number was 5,251. In 2013, the county changed this standard again, rising to 1,800 yuan. To support the subsistence allowance system, it also took many measures. For example, poor people covered by the system were exempted from the premiums for the new rural medical and pension insurance schemes, which were covered by the transfer payment of the civil administration department; people included in the system were deemed key subjects of medical assistance, whose reimbursement ratio under the new rural medical scheme was 10% to15% higher than that of ordinary herders.

4 Problems and Difficulties in Poverty Alleviation and Development in Zhiduo County and Suggestions

Since 1950, central and local governments had made great efforts to advance economic and social development of Zhiduo County, and people's living standard had been improved gradually. Since 1986, in particular, with the unified deployment of Yushu Tibetan Autonomous Prefecture and Qinghai Province, the county had implemented large-scale poverty alleviation and development in an organized way according to relevant policies issued by the central government and the province, and had made some but not so satisfactory achievements. There are mainly six reasons behind this result.

First, the harsh environment and frequent natural disasters make the living environment of herders here so vulnerable, so it is difficult to consolidate the achievements made in poverty alleviation and development.

Second, it is the low quality of labor force in the county. Poor herders felt diffident in self-development even if they participated in several simple workforce training and employment transfer projects.

Third, the construction of facilities lags behind the needs of economic and social development due to the weak foundation and insufficient investment. The low-grade infrastructures of transportation, electricity, communications and water conservancy are few and small,, with obsolete, aging and backward functions and at a low degree of modernization, integration and systematization; they perform poorly in resisting major disasters and supporting economic development.

Fourth, there is insufficient funding for poverty alleviation and development, which makes the government unable to deal with important problems in industries and improve infrastructures. In recent years, the ever-growing price of living materials, coupled with long transportation distance as poor people live scattered in remote area, cause the cost of poverty alleviation and development to rise sharply, while the capital invested in this task is deemed insufficient. In result, the efficiency is low for the poor herders to get rid of poverty.

Fifth, the government attached importance to implementing poverty alleviation and development projects, but ignored the subsequent supporting measures. For example, the relocation project mainly focuses on the choice of relocation site, the construction of houses and the publicity and mobilization work, but the follow-up industrial development, urban adaptation and other needs of relocated herders have not been reasonably considered, which leads to many problems now.

Sixth, the unbalanced regional development affects poverty alleviation and development. In villages and towns near the county seat with remarkable achievements, infrastructures of water, electricity, road, education and health developed more quickly than those of villages and towns far away from the county seat, such as Suojia Township and Zhahe Township. They are in remote areas with problems like harsh environment, backward infrastructures, and low-skilled herders who find it difficult to get out of poverty. These places have made small achievements in poverty alleviation and development, but they are exactly the poorest areas in Zhiduo County where poverty alleviation and development is most needed.

Therefore, to tackle the problems in the previous work of poverty alleviation and development, we believe that Zhiduo County should pay attention to the following points.

First, industrial development should be combined with environmental protection. It is no doubt that many industrial development projects in poverty alleviation and development can improve the income by creating jobs for poor herders. However, only by improving the ecological environment of pastoral areas can we improve the production and living environment of herders, thus raising their income and realizing stable poverty alleviation.

Second, poverty alleviation and development should be combined with disaster prevention and mitigation. Due to the family production mode of animal husbandry, herders in Zhiduo County are susceptible to natural disasters occurring frequently, which constitute the main cause of their poverty. In poverty alleviation and development, we should strength the cooperative production and management and enhance the infrastructure construction for the animal husbandry to reduce the impact of natural disasters.

Third, poverty alleviation and development should be combined with the construction and improvement of the social security system, which has been widely recognized by academic circles at home and abroad. The pastoral areas of Zhiduo County are on the whole poor, and the poor people are mostly from ethnic minority groups and are fragile. The long-time poor people account for the majority while those in temporary poverty make up a high proportion. Therefore, further strengthening the social security is an important way to eliminate poverty.

Fourth, in the new era, the direction of poverty alleviation in Zhiduo County should be changed from mere economic development to overall economic and social progress. In poor alpine pastoral areas where science, education, culture and health undertakings lag behind, the low-income group whose cultural, productive and life concepts cannot adapt to the new trend of social and economic development has weak production and operation capacity. Thus, to coordinate poverty alleviation, we need to abandon such unary economic indicators as the monetary income of a household and the per capita monetary income of an administrative village to measure the advance of poor households and poor villages. Instead, when we endeavor to help poor households increase their income and raise the level of poor villages' economic development, we should vigorously develop science, education, culture and health, integrate poverty alleviation projects and make economic, social and cultural development more balanced. The overall social progress in poverty alleviation and development should also be reflected between different townships and villages. In another word, we should balance the investment in villages and towns near the county seat and those far away from the county seat, eliminating the unbalance of this kind within the county. In general, the overall social planning in poverty alleviation and development should be conducive to strengthening the endogenous development capacity of the poor people and poor villages, to the benefit of these villages for long-term development and of such people in improving the self-development ability.

Chapter 9
Poverty Alleviation and Development in Farming-Pastoral Regions: A Case Study of Wuqia County, Xinjiang Uighur Autonomous Region

Wuqia is a farming-pastoral county where animal husbandry outweighs farming. In 2013, there were 2,392 hectares of cropland and 1,463 hectares of pastureland in county. However, the output of agriculture was not on a par with that of animal husbandry due to the poor cropland. In the yearly total output of agriculture and animal husbandry, the output of agriculture, forestry and animal husbandry accounts for 26.97%, 1.89%, and 63.97%, respectively. Wuqia is faced with a relatively severe problem of poverty and is one of the poorest counties in the contiguous areas with particular difficulties in the three prefectures of southern Xinjiang.[1] This chapter mainly analyzes the characteristics and influence factors of the poverty in the agricultural and pastoral areas of Wuqia in the new era and explore the basic path to accelerating poverty alleviation in the areas.

[1] IT refers to Hotan Prefecture, Kashgar Prefecture and Kizilsu Kirghiz Autonomous Prefecture at the southwestern edge of the Taklimakan Desert, which are known collectively as the Three Prefectures in Southern Xinjiang. It is a region where rural poor people of ethnic minority groups live in concentrated communities, and the number of poor people in the region accounts for 80% of the poor people in Xinjiang (*Poverty, Poverty Alleviation and Development in Xinjiang*, compiled by the research group of the Policy Research Office of the CPC Xinjiang Uygur Autonomous Region Committee, Xinjiang People's Publishing House, 2010, p.109). The three prefectures have been designated by the State Council as a contiguous area with particular difficulties. Wuqia is under the jurisdiction of Kizilsu Kirghiz Autonomous Prefecture (hereinafter referred to as Kizilsu).

X. Liu, *Complex Pictures of Poverty and Multiple Paths of Poverty Alleviation in Ethnic Areas of China*, https://doi.org/10.1007/978-981-97-4133-5_9

1 Current Situation and Characteristics of Agricultural and Pastoral Areas in Wuqia

1.1 Overview

Wuqia is located in the west of the Tarim Basin, the east of the Pamirs, and the junction between Tianshan Mountains and Kunlun Mountains. It has a mountain climate, with an annual average temperature of 6.5°C. Wuqia has 2,146 million cubic meters of water resources, and its annual per capital water availability is 49,633 cubic meters, at the level of the warning line of the world's annual per capital water availability. Due to the lack of heat resources, only cold-resistant crops can grow here. As the westernmost county of China, Wuqia borders Kyrgyzstan in the west and in the north, with a 485 km-long borderline. It has two state-level Class-I open ports, namely Torugart and Irkeshtam, which link China and the Central Asia and the Western Asia and serve as bridgeheads for opening-up.

Wuqia covers an area of 22,000 square kilometers, of which the area of mountains, Gobi deserts and wastelands accounts for 99.8%. It has 2,392 hectares of farmland, and its per capita arable land is 0.04 hectares, which is one sixth of per capita arable land of Xinjiang. It has 1,463 hectares of pastureland, but the natural pastures are sparsely vegetated and most of them are desertificated and severely degraded due to overgrazing.[2]

In 2013, Wuqia had a population of 59,948, 32,389 of whom were engaged in agriculture and animal husbandry, accounting for 54.03% of the total population. The population of ethnic minorities accounted for 88.13% of the total population of the county. As the main ethnic group of Wuqia, Kirghiz accounts for 70.93% of the total population of the county.[3]

Wuqia is rich in mineral resources, but has little arable land. Wuqia has an extremely fragile ecological environment since it is frequently hit by ecological disasters such as earthquake, hail, drought, and flood, which restrict its industrial development. Before 2000, the economic and social development of the county was relatively slow.

In the twenty-first century, Wuqia embarked on a fast lane of economic growth, and particularly its industrial economy grew continuously and rapidly. Between 2000 and 2013, its GDP increased from 111 million yuan to 1,565 million yuan, with an average annual growth of 16.73% (calculated at comparable prices), 6.4% points higher than the average growth rate of Xinjiang in the same period, and nearly 7.1% points higher than the average growth rate of China in the same period.[4] However,

---

[2] *Manual for Leading Officials of Wuqia* (2014), compiled by Wuqia Bureau of Statistics.

[3] Ditto.

[4] The 1999-2012 data of China and Xinjiang are from the "NSDP" of China's official website of the National Bureau of Statistics, the 2013 data are from *China Statistical Abstract: 2014*; the data of Kizilsu before 2013 are from *Kizilsu Statistical Yearbook: 2013* compiled by Kizilsu Bureau of Statistics; and the 2013 data are from the *Analytical Report on the Economic Development of*

Wuqia's economic development started from a low starting point, its GDP ranking 48th amongst the 68 counties (autonomous counties) in Xinjiang in 2013.[5]

Compared with the level and growth rate of income of residents in Xinjiang and other places of China, that of farmers and herders in Wuqia is relatively low. Between 2000 and 2013, the per capita net income of farmers and herders of Wuqia increased from 1,115 yuan to 4,356 yuan, with an annual average nominal growth rate of 11.05%. In the same period, the annual average increase of per capita annual net income of farming and herding families in Xinjiang was 12.28%, and the annual average increase of per capita net income of China's rural families was 11.14%, which were slightly higher than the annual average increase of per capita annual net income of farmers and herders in Wuqia. In 2000, the per capita net income of farming and herding families in Wuqia accounted for merely 68.91% of that of rural families in Xinjiang; in 2013, the percentage declined to 59.7% with fluctuations.[6]

Correspondingly, compared with Xinjiang and other places of China, the agricultural and pastoral areas in Wuqia face more severe poverty problems. In 2013, there were nine townships, two towns, eight neighborhood committees, and 34 villages; all of the nine townships were key poor townships designated by Xinjiang, and 25 villages were state-designated key poor villages. There were 17,971 poor people in 4,577 families, with a poverty headcount ratio of 55.48%, 46.98% points higher than the average poverty headcount ratio of rural areas of China in the year, and 29.88% points higher than that of the eight provinces and autonomous regions where people of ethnic minorities live in concentrated communities.[7]

To sum up, Wuqia is a sparsely populated county with abundant resources and a poverty-stricken border county with a strategic location. Since the beginning of the twenty-first century, Wuqia has seen sustained and rapid economic development,

---

Kizilsu authored by Xu Xianyi (the official website of the People's Government of Kizilsu, http://www.xjkz.gov.cn/ccd67880-2c3f-4dcd-b619-3034977217a4_1.html); the data of Wuqia are from the *Social and Economic Statistics of Wuqia (1954-2004)* compiled by the General Office of the People's Government of Wuqia and the Development, Planning and Statistical Commission of Wuqia County and the *Manual for Leading Officials of Wuqia* (2007-2014). The calculations here are made on the basis of relevant data.

[5] Xinjiang Statistical Yearbook (2014) compiled by Xinjiang Bureau of Statistics, China Statistics Press, 2014; the *Social and Economic Statistics of Wuqia (1954-2004)* compiled by the General Office of the People's Government of Wuqia and the Development, Planning and Statistical Commission of Wuqia County and the *Manual for Leading Officials of Wuqia* (2007-2014). The calculations here are made on the basis of relevant data.

[6] The official website of the National Bureau of Statistics "NSDP"; Xinjiang Statistical Yearbook (2014) compiled by Xinjiang Bureau of Statistics, China Statistics Press, 2014; the *Social and Economic Statistics of Wuqia (1954-2004)* compiled by the General Office of the People's Government of Wuqia and the Development, Planning and Statistical Commission of Wuqia County and the *Manual for Leading Officials of Wuqia* (2007-2014). The calculations here are made on the basis of relevant data.

[7] The calculations are made on the basis of relevant data in the *Manual for Leading Officials of Wuqia (2014)* and the *Poverty of Rural Ethnic Minority Concentrated Areas in China in 2013* complied by the Department of Economic Development under the National Ethnic Affairs Commission of the People's Republic of China, http://www.seac.gov.cn/art/2014/4/21/art_151_203095.html.

steady improvement of its people's living standards, and reduced poverty. Comparatively speaking, Wuqia ranks 48th in economic development amongst the 68 counties (autonomous counties) in Xinjiang and is one of the poorest counties of China.

1.2 The Current Situation and Characteristics of Agricultural and Pastoral Areas in Wuqia

Next, we will make a quantitative analysis of the sample survey data of Wuqia in *The Comprehensive Survey on the Economic and Social Development in China's Ethnic Minority Areas in the Early Period of the 21st Century*, make a survey by using the documents and materials of in-depth interview with farming households obtained by the research group of "A Survey of the Economic and Social Development of Wuqia, Kizilsu Kirghiz Autonomous Prefecture, Xinjiang" in Wuqia in July and August 2014, and make a comprehensive study on the current situation and characteristics of the rural areas of the county.

The research group took samples of 392 households at eight villages (neighborhood committees) of Wuqia Town and Heiziwei Township. The questionnaire involved the economic and social characteristics, conditions of employment, income and consumption of the respondents, as well as their understanding and assessment of local resources and environments, ecological protection, public services and government administration, providing important empirical data for us to understand and analyze the poverty and characteristics of the county.

To sum up, Wuqia is a sparsely populated county with abundant resources and a poverty-stricken border county with a strategic location. On the basis of such unique conditions of the county, our field survey indicates that poverty of the agricultural and pastoral areas of Wuqia has multiple characteristics.

1 Overall and persistent poverty

Overall poverty

On the one hand, more than half of the population in the agricultural and pastoral areas of Wuqia lived in poverty. In 2013, the poverty headcount ratio of the agricultural and pastoral areas stood at 55.48%, far higher than that of China's rural areas (see Fig. 9.1); on the other hand, the poverty in Wuqia was widespread; amongst the 34 administrative villages of the county, 25 were poor villages designated by the autonomous region, accounting for 73.5% or nearly 3/4 of the administrative villages were poor villages designated by the autonomous region. In addition, a considerable proportion of farmers and herders in other administrative villages than the designated poor villages were also impoverished.

Persistent poverty

According to statistics, the poverty headcount ratio of agricultural and pastoral areas in Wuqia was 59.18% in 2004 and dropped to 55.48% in 2013. This shows that the poverty in agricultural and pastoral areas of Wuqia has become a chronic and

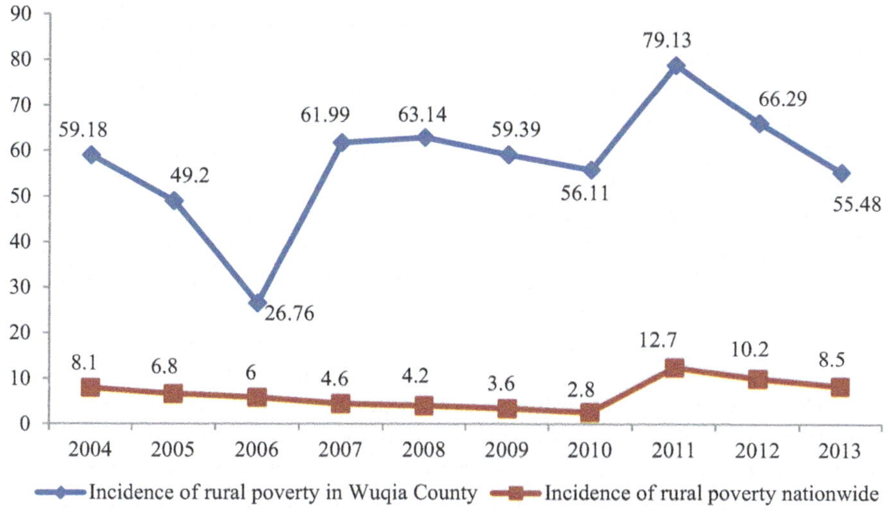

Fig. 9.1 Comparison between the poverty headcount ratio of the agricultural and pastoral areas of Wuqia with that of rural areas of China (%). *Data source* The data of Wuqia are based on the *Manual for Leading Officials of Wuqia* (2005–2014) compiled by Wuqia Bureau of Statistics; the 2004–2008 national data are calculated on the basis of relevant data in the *Poverty Monitoring Report of Rural China·2011* compiled by the Department of Household Survey of the National Bureau of Statistics of China, China Statistics Press (2012), and the 2009–2013 data are from the *Poverty of Rural Areas in Ethnic Minority Areas in China in 2013* complied by the Department of Economic Development of the National Ethnic Affairs Commission of the People's Republic of China (http://www.seac.gov.cn/art/2014/4/21/art_151_203095.html).

persistent problem. It should be noted that, as Fig. 9.1 shows, the poverty headcount ratio was extremely high in 2011 since the state raised the rural poverty line in the year, making some of those who were not originally poor people fall under the poverty line (targets of the poverty alleviation program).

The overall and persistent poverty in agricultural and pastoral areas of Wuqia is caused by many reasons, among which the harsh and fragile natural and ecological environment is the main reason. Located at the southwestern edge of the Taklimakan Desert, Wuqia has a harsh natural and ecological environment. It is one of the four major ecologically-fragile regions in China and one of the worst living areas in the world.[8] This is the basic condition of Wuqia and the main reason for overall and persistent poverty of the county. First, Wuqia has complicated geological structure and intensive neotectonic movements as well as frequent and intensive earthquakes due to active fault movements. According to the statistics of Kizilsu Earthquake Administration, 89 earthquakes with a magnitude above 4.7 occurred in Wuqia and its nearby areas between 1903 and 2012, causing geological disasters such as house

[8] Research group of the Policy Research Office of Xinjiang Uygur Autonomous Region CPC Committee, *Poverty and Poverty Alleviation and Development in Xinjiang,* Xinjiang People's Publishing House, 2010, p.103.

collapse, ground fracturing, ground collapse, landslide, mudslide, and ground depression, etc. According to incomplete statistics, by the end of 2012, 49 geological disasters had occurred in the county, resulting in a death toll of 3, a direct economic loss of over 12 million yuan and a population of 1,350 under threat.[9] Therefore, once geological disasters occur, the affected farmers and herders are very likely to fall into poverty. Second, 97.6% of the land areas of Wuqia are mountains. Except for Wuqia Town, the county seat, which is mostly located on a plain, most of the towns and townships are located in ecologically-fragile mountain areas with cold, complicated and changeable climate, frequently hit by natural disasters such as earthquake, hail, strong wind, frost, floating dust, storm, and drought. Third, due to the special ecological, natural and geological environments, local residents in the agricultural and pastoral areas have to engage in the traditional animal husbandry. Compared with farming, traditional animal husbandry relies more on natural and ecological environments, which in turn make animal husbandry a fragile industry, and farmers and herders live at the mercy of the elements and are incapable of resisting natural disasters. Therefore, it can be said that the fragile ecological environment is the main reason for the overall and persistent poverty in agricultural and pastoral areas of Wuqia.

2. Uneven distribution of poverty among different ethnic groups and regions

The poverty of the agricultural and pastoral areas of Wuqia is relatively concentrated in ethnic minority concentrated areas and shows certain ethnic features. The Kirghiz lives in Wuqia for generations and is the main ethnic group of the county. According to statistics, in 2013, Wuqia had a total population of 59,948, including 42,520 Kirghiz residents who account for 70.93% of the total population of the county. At some towns and townships of Wuqia, nearly all residents are Kirghiz people. For example, at the Urukchati Township, the population of Kirghiz accounts for 99.95% of the total population of the township. Therefore, it is understandable that there are quite a few poor Kirghiz people in Wuqia.

Since we have not found data on ethnic distribution of poor people in the agricultural and pastoral areas of Wuqia in official statistics, we will make a brief analysis by using the above sample survey data (see Table 9.1). The analytical data in Table 9.1 are related to farming and pastoral households rather than individual farmers and herders. Therefore, the analytical result partially reflects the fact, though it is different from the analyses based on individuals. As seen from Table 9.1, the proportion of poor rural households of the Han ethnicity is significantly lower than that of poor families in the total population; in Uyghur, the proportion of poor families is significantly higher than that of poor families in the total population; in Kirghiz, the proportion of poor families is only 1.89% points higher than that of poor families in the total. As seen from the ethnic distribution of poor families in the respondent farming and herding families, except for the Han ethnicity, the proportions of both Uyghur and Kirghiz respondent farming and herding families to the total farming and herding

[9] The People's Government of Wuqia: *Geological Disasters Prevention and Control Plan for Wuqia* (2013-2020), April 2013.

families are lower than the proportions of respondent poor farming and herding families to the total respondent poor families. The above results indicate that, poverty of the agricultural and pastoral areas of Wuqia is mostly concentrated in ethnic minority farming and herding families. Comparatively speaking, such ethnic differences are not particularly obvious.

Meanwhile, the poverty distribution in agricultural and pastoral areas of Wuqia differs from region to region. First of all, the field survey results indicate that, the poverty headcount ratios of farming and herding families in different townships and towns of Wuqia are different. Second, the poverty headcount ratios vary greatly even between different administrative villages in the same township (town). Take the Heiziwei Township as an example. As seen from data in Table 9.2, its six administrative villages can be divided into three types by poverty headcount ratio. Specifically, the Ayibrack Village is of a type, which has the highest poverty headcount ratio (60.4% in 2013) and a low speed of poverty reduction (the poverty headcount ratio declined by merely 4.4% points in three years). The Yekterak Village and the Yekterak Village are of the same type and their poverty headcount ratios are basically the same (more than 20% points lower than that of the Ayibrack Village, and 10–15% points higher than that of the other three villages); the poverty alleviation of both the villages advanced at a fast speed, and their poverty headcount ratios declined by about 20% points in three years. The other three villages are of a third type; their poverty headcount ratios were significantly lower than that of the villages of the first and second types; the speed of their poverty alleviation varied, and the poverty headcount ratios of the three villages dropped by 15.3% points, 11.5% points and 5.3% points in three years, respectively.

3. Wuqia has a large poor population and its poverty alleviation effect fluctuates

Table 9.1 Poverty distribution in a single ethnic group/in different ethnic groups in agricultural and pastoral areas of Wuqia Unit: household, %

	Distribution of respondent farming and herding families in different ethnic groups		Distribution of respondent poor farming and herding families in different ethnic groups		Proportion of poor families in the total population of a single ethnic group
	Number of respondent households	Proportion	Number of poor families	Proportion	
The Hans	30	17.65	8	12.12	26.67
Uyghur	27	15.88	12	18.18	44.44
Kirghiz	113	66.47	46	69.70	40.71
Total	170	100.00	66	100	38.82

Data source The survey data of Wuqia from The Comprehensive Survey on the Economic and Social Development in China's Ethnic Minority Areas in the Early Period of the 21st Century. Any use of the survey data hereinafter will not be indicated.

Table 9.2 Comparisons of the poverty headcount ratios among administrative villages of Heiziwei Township of Wuqia Unit: %

	2010	2011	2012	2013
Ayibrack village	64.8	62.5	61.5	60.4
Yekterak village	57.6	53.7	46.4	39.9
Kangxiwan village	58.8	52.5	46.8	39.8
Kulazek village	44.4	39.6	32.1	29.1
Jianger village	40.1	35.8	33.7	28.6
Kanjiugan village	29.7	27.7	26.5	24.4

Data source Statistical tables of the Ethnic and Religious Commission of Heiziwei Township, Wuqia (restricted document).

Due to historical reasons and natural and environmental restrictions, Wuqia has a weak economic base and is faced with severe poverty problems. In 1986, it was designated by the State Council and Xinjiang Uygur Autonomous Region as a key poor county. According to records of *Wuqia County Annals*, at the end of 1990, measured by the poverty line of per capita income of 250 yuan of the year,[10] the county had 238 poor households, with a poor population of 1,310, accounting for 5.48% of local agricultural population of the year. In 1994, the government of Wuqia formulated the *Plan of Wuqia on Alleviating Poverty of 80 Million People in Seven Years* and made great achievements in poverty alleviation and development. According to Wuqia County Annals, between 1994 and 2000, a total of 6,128 persons of 1,380 households were lifted out of poverty (see Table 9.3). However, there was a serious problem of relapse into poverty in Wuqia due to illness and disaster, as the poverty line increased year after year, particularly since the adoption of the national poverty line in 2007, the size of poor population of the county significantly increased, and the poor population and the poverty headcount ratio fluctuated (see Fig. 9.1). In 2013, all the nine townships of Wuqia were key poor townships, and 25 villages were key poor villages, with a poor population of 17,971 from 4,577 poor families, and the poverty headcount ratio was 55.48%. Clearly poverty continues to afflict many Wuqia residents.

As seen from Fig. 9.1, the changes of the poor population and the poverty headcount ratio of Wuqia between 2004 and 2013 can be analyzed in three phases. Specifically, the first phase is 2004–2006, during which the poor population and the poverty headcount ratio of the county declined year by year, and the difference between the poverty headcount ratio of the county and that of China narrowed year by year, indicating that Wuqia had achieved remarkable effects in poverty alleviation during the phase. The second phase is 2007–2010, during which the poor population and the poverty headcount ratio of Wuqia increased sharply in 2006, and then narrowed down with fluctuations. It shows that Wuqia has become poorer compared with the other places of China. The third phase is 2011–2013. In 2011, since the state-designated

[10] In 1990, the government of Wuqia set its rural poverty line at 250 yuan, lower than China's absolute poverty line (300 yuan) of the year.

Table 9.3 The trend of poverty alleviation in Wuqia between 1990 and 2010 Unit: household, person

Year	Number of households	Population	Year	Number of households	Population	Year	Number of households	Population
1990	71	296	1997	116	487	2004	1222	5329
1991	137	934	1998	109	518	2005	260	1012
1992	159	810	1999	262	1359	2006	271	1211
1993	85	365	2000	312	1310	2007	90	405
1994	125	525	2001	526	2209	2008	115	535
1995	186	781	2002	382	1604	2009	150	675
1996	270	1150	2003	1000	2048	2010	168	725

Data source Wuqia County Gazatteer Compilation Committee: *Wuqia County Gazatteer* (1990–2010), final draft.

rural poverty line was significantly increased to 2,300 yuan (at the constant price in 2010), the poor population significantly increased to 25,650 and then decreased year after year. Correspondingly, its poverty headcount ratio reached 79.13% in 2011, and then declined year after year, and the gap between the poverty headcount ratio of the county and that of other places of China narrowed down year by year. It shows that in this phase Wuqia had made remarkable results in poverty alleviation and consolidated its achievements to some extents. In a word, due to the fragile ecological environment and animal husbandry in agricultural and pastoral areas, farmers and herders were severely influenced by natural disasters and fluctuations of the farming/livestock product market. In a bumper year or a year when farming/livestock products enjoy a stable price, the poverty of farmers and herders will be alleviated to a great extent, and the poverty headcount ratio will drop. If natural disasters occur or farm/pasture product prices decline, more farmers and herders will return to poverty due to natural disasters or income reduction as a result of market fluctuations, the poor population will increase, and the poverty will intensify. Therefore, the poverty of agricultural and pastoral areas in Wuqia is characterized with fluctuations.

4. Insufficient infrastructures and public services in the agricultural and pastoral areas of Wuqia

In the agricultural and pastoral areas of Wuqia, there is a severe lack of infrastructures and public services and the working and living conditions of farmers and herders are poor, affecting the development of agriculture and animal husbandry. According to the results of our field survey in Wuqia, the water conservancy and transport infrastructures in the agricultural and pastoral areas are still poor and there is a lack of controlling water conservancy projects. Three townships and 10 villages have no access to electricity, 20 herders's settlements have no access to the telephone network, 25,400 farmers and herders have no access to safe water, one township and 15 villages have no access to asphalt road, and in particular five villages of them suffer from poor road conditions throughout the year. Some poor residents find it difficult to have access to medical services and education, and their social security level is low.[11]

5. Poor farming and herding families are large and have a larger dependency ratio

As our questionnaire surveys indicate, in 2013, the average respondent farming and herding family in Wuqia had 4.22 members, and the average rural household in China had 2.98 members,[12] the former being 1.42 times the latter; the total dependency ratio of respondent farming and herding families of Wuqia was 68.75%, and the average total dependency ratio of rural families of China was 35.3%,[13] the former being 1.95 times the latter. It shows that, compared with China's rural households, the farming and herding families of Wuqia have a bigger family size and heavier labor burden.

The survey data also show that, compared with non-poor families in agricultural and pastoral areas of Wuqia, poor families have larger population size and heavier labor burden. Specifically, in 2013, the average respondent poor family had 5.39 members while that of other respondent families was 3.5, the former being 1.54 times the latter. In the same year, the average dependent ratio of the respondent poor families was 88.54% while that of other families was 47.57%, the former being 1.86 times the latter. In a word, the farming and herding families of Wuqia have significant features of large size and heavy burden.

6. Insufficient economic development resources in agricultural and pastoral areas

Economic development resources are an important basis for regional development and poverty reduction. The agricultural and pastoral areas of Wuqia had limited economic development resources. On the one hand, mountain, Gobi deserts, and wastelands account for 99.8% of its total area (22,000 km). On the other hand, among the utilizable lands, there are nearly 1,072,000 hectares of desertificated pasture and less than 2,010 hectares of arable land. Therefore, the agricultural and pastoral areas have insufficient natural resources. The scarce arable land and grassland affect the development of agriculture and animal husbandry of the county, and the income level of farmers and herders who rely mainly on agriculture and animal husbandry is relatively low.

[11] Wuqia Office for Poverty Alleviation and Development: The Implementation Plan on Regional Development and Poverty Alleviation in Wuqia, Kizilsu Kirghiz Autonomous Prefecture, Xinjiang Uygur Autonomous Region (2011-2015), April 2013.

[12] National Bureau of Statistics: China Statistical Yearbook (2014), China Statistics Press, 2014, Table 2.9.

[13] Ditto, Table 2.4.

2 Effects and Problems of Poverty Alleviation and Development in Wuqia

Wuqia, which was designated as a key poor county by the state and Xinjiang in 1986. Since the adoption of the policy on large-scale poverty alleviation and development, it has adhered to the major principles of development-oriented poverty reduction, focused on lifting local residents out of poverty, implemented a raft of projects of poverty alleviation and development, and achieved certain effects in poverty alleviation.

2.1 Poverty Alleviation and Development of Wuqia

Since the start of the 11th Five-year Plan period, Wuqia, in accordance with the "one body with two wings" poverty alleviation and development strategy formulated by the State Council Leading Group Office of Poverty Alleviation and Development and the way of thinking about "one aim and three priorities", has made poor villages its main battlefields against poverty and poor families its main targets, focused on overall village-based poverty elimination, poverty elimination through industrial development and poor labor training, improved the comprehensive quality of the poor population, and enhanced their self-development capacity so as to ultimately realize the common ideal of assisting poor villagers in meeting their basic needs, getting rid of poverty and becoming rich over time. By following such principles and visions, the government of Wuqia has implemented a series of projects for poverty alleviation.

1. Overall village-based poverty elimination

First, invest more funds in overall village-based poverty elimination so as to accelerate the process of poverty elimination. For example, in 2009, Xinjiang allocated a total of6.4 million yuan to Wuqia for poverty alleviation, of which 4.9 million yuan went for overall village-based poverty elimination, accounting for 77% of the total. Besides, an additional fund of about 70 million yuan was used for poor villages through providing employment as a form of relief, vitalizing border areas and enriching local people, and supporting the housing project for earthquake relief. By the end of 2009, the overall village-based poverty elimination project had been basically completed and passed the acceptance check, which improved the infrastructures of relevant poor villages and the living and working conditions of poor rural families.[14]

Second, between 2011 and 2015, Xinjiang designated 25 villages of Wuqia (15 border villages and 10 mountain villages) to carry out the "overall village-based poverty elimination" project. In 2013, it allocated a special poverty alleviation fund

[14] Wuqia Office for Poverty Alleviation and Development: *2009 Work Summary of and 2010 Work Plan on Poverty Alleviation and Development in Wuqia*, December 6, 2009, for internal circulation only.

amounting to 28.58 million yuan to carry out 35 "overall village-based poverty elimination" projects, solving the problems hindering infrastructure construction and industrial development of poor villages. In line with the acceptance standard set by Xinjiang for overall village-based poverty elimination, 944 houses and 1,130 covered pens for livestock were built, and the construction of supporting infrastructures of water supply, electric power supply and roads was accelerated in three border villages and 10 mountain villages.[15]

2. Poverty elimination through industrial development

Since the adoption of the "11th Five-year Plan" on poverty alleviation, the government of Wuqia has based itself on its realities, made in-depth investigations and studies, relied on the vast wastelands and Gobi deserts, worked hard to advance facility agriculture, characteristic fruit industry and breeding industry, carried out the project of poverty elimination through industrial development, and promoted structural readjustment.

(1) Facility agriculture. In order to assist farmers and herders and particularly poor farmers and herders in changing their lifestyles and working practices, overcoming the practical difficulties caused by insufficient natural resources and harsh climate, and shaking off poverty and becoming prosperous through settlement, the CPC Wuqia Committee and Wuqia government, by relying on the vast Gobi deserts and the soil-less cultivation technique, made the development of facility agriculture an important task for increasing the income of farmers and lifting them out of poverty. With the aims of building 1,000–3,000 greenhouses during the 11th "Five-Year Plan" period, building 8,000–10,000 fresh vegetable greenhouses during the 12th "Five-Year Plan" period, building 15,000 greenhouses in 2020 and making every farming and herding family have a greenhouse on average, Wuqia made investments in building 1,000 vegetable, melon and fruit greenhouses (for the first phase) in Heiziwei and Maykak by using the soil-less cultivation technique. By 2011, a total of 511 greenhouses had been built. Specifically, the number of newly-built greenhouses in Maykak, the towns and townships and neighboring areas of Wuqia were 214, 46 and 307, respectively, cultivating solanaceous fruits, melons, leaf vegetables, tubers, dwarfed fruit trees, and beans, etc. Meanwhile, businessmen from Dalian were brought in to grow edible mushrooms in greenhouses and businessmen from Shandong were brought in to grow flowers. The melons, fruits and vegetables produced here were sold to Kashgar, two ports as well as factories, mines and enterprises of the county. In 2011, a total of 350 tons of vegetables from facility agriculture were sold, with a sales revenue of 700,000 yuan; 15 tons of fresh mushrooms were grown, with a sales revenue of 210,000 yuan, one ton of dried mushrooms were produced, with a sales revenue of 400,000 yuan. According to statistics,

[15] Wuqia Office for Poverty Alleviation and Development (Immigration Administration): *2013 Work Summary of and 2014 Work Plan on Poverty Alleviation and Development in Wuqia*, September 30, 2013, for internal circulation only.

the gross sales revenue of facility agriculture of the whole county was 1.31 million yuan, with a profit of 700,000 yuan.

(2) Characteristic fruit industry. Due to its special climate, Wuqia focuses on the late-maturing fruit industry and strives for a balance between economic benefits and ecological benefits. In 2009, it planted 2,345 hectares of fruit trees, including economic forests (1,541 hectares) and ecological forests (804 hectares), growing over 1.7 million fruit trees such as peaches, desert dates, large-fruit sea buckthom, walnuts, red dates, wild apricots, cherry apples, and dark plums, etc. At present, the survival rate of seedlings is 85%. The area of water-saving and sprinkling irrigation has increased from 134 hectares in 2008 to 837.5 hectares (specifically, 301.5 hectares at Ake, 402 hectares at Kangxiwan, and 134 hectares at Heishuihe).

(3) Characteristic breeding industry. Since the adoption of the "11th Five-year Plan" on poverty alleviation, the government of Wuqia has accelerated the development of greenhouse crop farming and breeding in Gobi deserts, and has given priority to characteristic breeding industries for increasing the income of farmers and herders and lifting them out of poverty. Meanwhile, it gives priority to geographical advantages, strives for reasonable industrial distribution, regulates the construction of incubation and nursing bases, strengthens management by using science and technology, and forms a coordinated industrial development model of "incubation → nursing → raising → processing → selling" and the pattern of "enterprise participation, small group cooperation, and tens of thousands of families engaging in fowl farming". In order to protect and restore the grassland ecosystem, Wuqia divides itself into 10 characteristic breeding areas, four fattening and stock breeding areas and four breeding centers, builds two fowl hatching and breeding bases (each is capable of supplying 400,000 fowls a year) and two animal husbandry technology demonstration parks, established two or three breeding and fattening sales associations for each township, and applied for registration of the trademarks of Simuhana series for livestock and fowl farming. In 2010, 500,000 fowls were raised, four breeding centers and 20 cooperatives were established, and 1,500 households began to engage in breeding by taking advantage of the operation of the meat processing factory. As a result, the number of fowls raised by each farming and herding household exceeded 50. In 2011, 250,000 special fowls were raised in the county; as each special fowl generated a net profit of 5–20 yuan on average, the total revenue reached 3,000,000 yuan, and the per capita income of farmers and herders stood at 300 yuan.[16]

---

[16] Wuqia Office for Poverty Alleviation and Development: *2009 Work Summary of and 2010 Work Plan on Poverty Alleviation and Development in Wuqia*, December 6, 2009, for internal circulation only; Wuqia Office for Poverty Alleviation and Development: *2011 Work Summary of and 2012 Work Plan on Poverty Alleviation and Development in Wuqia*, October 13, 2011, for internal circulation only; *General Office of the Leading Group for Poverty Alleviation and Development in Wuqia*: *The Plan on Overall Village-based Poverty Elimination in Wuqia of Xinjiang Uygur Autonomous Region (2011-2015)*, March 2011.

3. Labor training

Wuqia took targeted measures to carry out skills training and cultural training, in order to help poor laborers meet the needs for industrial development and increasing their adaptability to nonfarm work. In addition, it focuses on training for leaders of Party organizations and governments and Party members of poor villages, aiming to prepare them for leadership roles in which they can help local residents overcome poverty and achieve prosperity.

(1) Skills training for industrialization. The training involves knowledge about pasture utilization and protection, animal epidemic prevention and control, techniques for fattening cattle and sheep, fruit tree grafting, pest control, and greenhouse soilless culture technique. In 2009, Wuqia trained 250 persons for animal epidemic prevention and control, pasture utilization and protection, and fattening of cattle and sheep. In 2010, it carried out three practical agricultural technology training sessions for 600 farmers and herders, and one practical animal husbandry technology training for 50 epidemic prevention and control personnel. In 2013, it carried out 12 training sessions for poverty alleviation (including three technical training sessions for standard management and cultivation of fruit trees and three technical training sessions for chicken breeding), covering 725 poor farmers and herders.

(2) Labor transfer training. In order to assist poor herders in changing their lifestyle and mindset, increase their quality and diversity their sources of income, the Wuqia CPC Committee and Wuqia County fully mobilized various training resources and strengthened vocational training. In 2009, it held 41 training workshops for over 6,000 farmers and herders, involving various skills such as electric welding, cooking, and farm machinery operation. A total of 9,587 rural surplus laborers were transferred to urban areas as migrant workers, generating a total revenue of 32.84 million yuan, and a per capita income of 3,425 yuan for transferred laborers, and a per capita income of 959 yuan for farmers and herders. In 2012, Xinjiang allocated 480,000 yuan to carry out five poverty alleviation training projects in Wuqia, and held 13 poverty alleviation training workshops for 2,090 local poor farmers and herders, involving border patrolling, auto repair, knowledge about Chinese and English languages, and construction skills, etc., promoting the development of labor services in the county. In 2012, 10,618 laborers were transferred to work outside as migrant workers, generating a total income of 70,866,800 yuan and a per capita income of 6,673 yuan. In 2013, on the basis of the labor demands of those provinces and municipalities aiding Xinjiang and local enterprises, the government of Wuqia carried out over 40 practical technical training sessions for 13,303 training farmers and herders, involving knowledge about border patrolling, auto repair, knowledge about Chinese and English languages, and construction skills, and more than 3,000 farmers and herders obtained the "Qualification Certificate for Technicians". In 2013, Wuqia allocated 480,000 yuan to carry out special training projects for poverty alleviation, trained 725 poor farmers and herders in 12

poverty alleviation training sessions, and transferred about 10,400 laborers to work outside as migrant workers, generating an income of100 million yuan.[17]

(3) Training projects for poverty alleviation officials at poor villages. It is training for officials who are in charge of poverty alleviation in poor villages in Wuqia. For example, in the winter slack season of 2009, Wuqia carried out the "Winter of Science and Technology" training and the training on labor transfer for officials at all levels, poor farmers and herders and agricultural technicians in key poor townships and key poor villages who are engaged in poverty alleviation and development.

4. "Mutual-aid fund" project and interest-free loan project for poor villages

Lack of capital is one of the factors for poverty of farmers and herders. In order to support poor farmers and herders to develop production and enhance their self-development capacity, Wuqia launched a pilot "mutual-aid fund" project at poor villages in 2011. In the year, three villages were designated by the government of Xinjiang as pilot poor "mutual-aid fund" villages and were granted 150,000 yuan each as the initial fund. By the end of October 2011, three cooperatives had been registered, three mutual-aid groups had been established, 150 farming households including 128 poor households had joined the cooperatives, mutual-aid funds worth a total of 300,000 yuan had been granted, the number of person-times of borrowing had reached 130, and the average occupancy expense of borrowing had reached 6‰.[18]

In 2013, when implementing the "mutual-aid fund" project at poor villages, Wuqia granted poor households with interest-free loans. By the end of 2013, it had granted 108 farming families with a interest-free loan of 946,000 yuan and a fiscal allowance of 52,500 yuan via rural credit cooperatives.[19]

5. Poverty alleviation through pairing assistance

The poverty alleviation through pairing assistance in Wuqia is conducted at three levels: pairing assistance of other provinces and municipalities for Wuqia, pairing assistance of organizations directly under the central government of Wuqia, and pairing assistance for Kizilsu, pairing assistance of departments directly under the government of Kizilsu Prefecture and departments directly under the government of Wuqia County.

---

[17] Wuqia Office for Poverty Alleviation and Development: *2009 Work Summary of and 2010 Work Plan on Poverty Alleviation and Development in Wuqia*, December 6, 2009, for internal circulation only; Wuqia Office for Poverty Alleviation and Development: *2012 Work Summary of and 2014 Work Plan on Poverty Alleviation and Development in Wuqia*, December 20, 2012, for internal circulation only; Wuqia Office for Poverty Alleviation and Development (Immigration Administration): *2013 Work Summary of and 2014 Work Plan on Poverty Alleviation and Development in Wuqia*, September 30, 2013, for internal circulation only.

[18] Wuqia Office for Poverty Alleviation and Development: *2011 Work Summary of and 2012 Work Plan on Poverty Alleviation and Development in Wuqia*, October 13, 2011, for internal circulation only.

[19] Wuqia Office for Poverty Alleviation and Development (Immigration Administration): *2013 Work Summary of and 2014 Work Plan on Poverty Alleviation and Development in Wuqia*, September 30, 2013, for internal circulation only.

(1) Pairing assistance of other provinces and municipalities and organizations directly under the central government

According to the guiding principle of the CPC Central Committee (1996) No.7 document and the instructions of the Organization Department of the CPC Central Committee, the Ministry of Personnel and the People's Government of Xinjiang Uygur Autonomous Region, Jiangxi Province is in charge of pairing assistance for Kizilsu, mainly in the form of talent assistance. From July 1997 to July 2005, Jiangxi Province dispatched a total of 18 managerial staff members and technicians to assist Wuqia for four consecutive times, donated one Isuzu pickup truck and one Jiangling minivan, and a fund of 1.2 million yuan, and trained over 50 officials for the county.[20]

In accordance with the requirements of General Office of the CPC Central Committee (2005) No.15 document, since 2005, Liaoning Province has been in charge of pairing assistance for Kizilsu and, Dalian, a city in Liaoning Province, has been in charge of pairing assistance for Wuqia. From July 2005 to July 2009, Dalian assigned 26 officials and professionals in two batches to work in Wuqia, donated funds and materials amounting to 60.85 million yuan, trained 124 officials and completed 21 projects in aid of the county.[21]

In 2010, the CPC Central Committee and the State Council convened a work conference on aid to Xinjiang. According to the instructions of the central government, the new round of pairing assistance for Xinjiang aims to support the coordinated and all-round development of Xinjiang in the aspects of economy, officials, talents, education and technology. It gives attaches greater importance to key points, and has a greater coverage and a more profound impact. According to the instructions, Changzhou city of Jiangsu Province and China Huadian Corporation were tasked to support Wuqia. The efforts for poverty alleviation through pairing assistance for Wuqia have been significantly increased. In 2011, 2012 and 2013, Changhzhou city of Jiangsu Province and China Huadian Corporation allocated 92.64 million yuan, 58.72 million yuan and 61.82 million yuan respectively to support the county.[22]

(2) Poverty alleviation through pairing assistance from Xinjiang

In 1990, the People's Government of Kizilsu decided to carry out the pairing assistance program of the Construction Department and the Coal Industry Department of Xinjiang in Wuqia, starting the pairing poverty alleviation of Xinjiang

---

[20] Wuqia County Gazatteer Compilation Committee: *Wuqia County Gazatteer* (1990-2010), final draft.

[21] Wuqia County Gazatteer Compilation Committee: *Wuqia County Gazatteer* (1990-2010), final draft..

[22] Wuqia Office for Poverty Alleviation and Development: *2011 Work Summary of and 2012 Work Plan on Poverty Alleviation and Development in Wuqia*, October 13, 2011, for internal circulation only; Wuqia Office for Poverty Alleviation and Development: *2012 Work Summary of and 2014 Work Plan on Poverty Alleviation and Development in Wuqia*, December 20, 2012, for internal circulation only; Wuqia Office for Poverty Alleviation and Development (Immigration Administration): *2013 Work Summary of and 2014 Work Plan on Poverty Alleviation and Development in Wuqia*, September 30, 2013, for internal circulation only; Wuqia County Gazatteer Compilation Committee: *Wuqia County Gazatteer* (1990-2010), final draft.

in Wuqia. Besides, the following government departments and enterprises have supported poverty alleviation of the county through pairing assistance: Xinjiang Coal Industry Department, Xinjiang Earthquake Administration, Xinjiang Labor Employment and Insurance Management Bureau, Xinjiang Tianshan Building Materials Co., Ltd., Xinjiang High-grade Highways Administration, China Development Bank Xinjiang Branch, CNPC Transportation Company Xinjiang Branch, Urumqi Customs, Xinjiang Labor and Social Insurance Administration and Tianshan Wool Fabric (Group) Co., Ltd.

According to the overall requirements, specific pairing assistance programs are directly carried out by supporting units at designated villages and key poor families are provided with living costs. Between 2002 and 2004, Xinjiang High-grade Highways Administration offered assistance to the Bostanterak Township through pairing programs. During the period, it invested more than 400,000 yuan to assist Wuqia in bringing in good varieties, making great efforts for breed improvements, and enhancing the market competitiveness of their animal products. Besides, it provided jobs for 605 surplus rural laborers from the county in 2003 and 2004. Between 1996 and 2010, the support units of Xinjiang donated 3,600,400 yuan as well as coal, rice, flour and computers valued at 510,000 yuan. Between 2011 and 2013, the support units of Xinjiang continued to donate materials to Wuqia, with a total value of 2.04 million yuan.[23]

(3) Poverty alleviation program of Kizilsu and Wuqia through pairing assistance

Since 1994, departments directly under the government of Kizilsu have begun to assist poor families in Wuqia through pairing programs, together with over 20 units including Kizilsu Armed Police Border Detachment, Kizilsu Military Sub-command, the General Office of the Standing Committee of the People's Congress of Kizilsu, and the People's Court of Kizilsu. The departments directly under Kizilsu Autonomous Prefecture are mainly in charge of pairing assistance at the township level. Between 1994 and 2010, the above units donated funds and materials worth 1,434,100 yuan to the country.[24]

The departments directly under the government of Wuqia assign personnel to stay with farmers and herders so as to gain an understanding of their living and working conditions and solve their difficulties. Since 2007, the departments directly under the government of Wuqia have implemented the "1221" working mechanism for poverty alleviation through pairing assistance, that is, officials are assigned with tasks of

---

[23] Wuqia County Gazatteer Compilation Committee: Wuqia County Gazatteer (1990-2010), final draft; Wuqia Office for Poverty Alleviation and Development: *2011 Work Summary of and 2012 Work Plan on Poverty Alleviation and Development in Wuqia*, October 13, 2011, for internal circulation only; Wuqia Office for Poverty Alleviation and Development: *2012 Work Summary of and 2014 Work Plan on Poverty Alleviation and Development in Wuqia*, December 20, 2012, for internal circulation only; Wuqia Office for Poverty Alleviation and Development (Immigration Administration): *2013 Work Summary of and 2014 Work Plan on Poverty Alleviation and Development in Wuqia*, September 30, 2013, for internal circulation only.

[24] Wuqia County Gazatteer Compilation Committee: *Wuqia County Gazatteer* (1990-2010), final draft.

poverty alleviation of certain townships, villages and households. Specifically, the principal leader of the county takes charge of poverty alleviation of a village, two county-level officials take charge of that of a township, two departments directly under the county government take charge of that of a village, and one government official supports a poor family and takes charge of ten families of farmers and herders. It archives poor families of the county for each household and each village and the supporting units purchase daily necessities such as rice, edible vegetable oil and clothes every year for poor families, so as to solve their difficulties in life. Between 1994 and 2010, the donations of the whole county amounted to 8,034,700 yuan.[25]

After 2011, the departments directly under the government of Kizilsu Autonomous Prefecture and the departments directly under the government of Wuqia County continued to take actions for poverty alleviation through pairing assistance. In 2011, the departments directly under the government of Kizilsu Autonomous Prefecture and the departments directly under the government of Wuqia County donated funds and materials amounting to 100,000 yuan to their points of contact. In 2012, 25 support units of Kizilsu established assistance relationships with 25 key villages of Wuqia, 108 departments directly under the county government assisted 34 administrative villages in nine townships, 22 county-level leaders contacted with 11 townships (towns), and members of the standing committee of CPC Wuqia Committee served concurrently as honorary secretaries of eight communities so that poor farmers and herders were all covered by pairing assistance. In the year, the supporting units of Kizilsu Autonomous Prefecture and Wuqia County made donations with a total value of 1.21 million to their points of contact. In 2013, the supporting units of Kizilsu and the departments directly under the government of Wuqia county offered funds of 226,100 yuan and 753,500 yuan for poverty alleviation, respectively.

2.2 *Main Effects and Problems of Poverty Alleviation and Development in Wuqia*

1. Main effects of poverty alleviation and development in Wuqia

(1) Remarkable progress has been made in infrastructure construction and the economic and social development conditions have been improved over time. In the process of poverty alleviation and development, Wuqia has built a large number of major infrastructures of water conservancy, transport, electric power, urban construction, trading of farm/pasture products, fodder base, and land reclamation, etc., improving the basic conditions of economic and social development, promoting economic and social development and driving income growth of poor farmers and herders. Since the 11th Five-year Plan period, Wuqia

[25] Wuqia County Gazatteer Compilation Committee: *Wuqia County Gazatteer* (1990-2010), final draft.

built a water reservoir, reinforced a water reservoir, built a water-saving irrigation system with an area of 2,010 hectares, seepage-proofing trenches (68 km) and farm trenches (111.9 km), reclaimed lands with an area of five square kilometers, and ensured safe water supply for 21,000 rural residents. It has built a total of 1,911 greenhouses in Gobi deserts and1,526 planting vegetable greenhouses, and completed the construction of the three major vegetable production bases, namely Maykak, the suburban agricultural science and technology demonstration park, and the Gobi desert industrial park. It laid emphasis on technology introduction, built a smart seedling greenhouse covering an area of 4,200 square meters, and established a logistics distribution center for highland organic green vegetables. Wuqia upgraded its rural roads and transport network over time, made all its administrative villages have access to highroad, and completed the construction of the Wuqia section of the G3013 highway. So far, the total mileage of highways in the county has reached 1,716.29 km, the county-township-village power grid transformation project has been basically completed, and 1,715 houses have been built for poverty alleviation.[26]

(2) Wuqia accelerates the development of its social programs and keeps improving its people's livelihood. Thanks to years of efforts for poverty alleviation and development, the development of social programs in agricultural and pastoral areas of Wuqia has accelerated and the level of service and security has been increased. Rapid progress has been made in the development of education, and the two basic education projects have been completed. By 2013, the ratio of children enrolled in preschool had reached 93.2%, the ratio of compulsory education had reached 100%, the primary school enrolment rate had reached 100%, and the junior high school enrolment rate had reached 94%. The cultural programs have also developed. It has built the Kirghiz Cultural Industrial Park, township (town) and village cultural plazas, cultural stations (rooms) and reading rooms. The radio and television network covers all natural villages that have access to electricity. The basic public health service has been carried out in an all-round way, the health awareness and the level of healthcare have been markedly enhanced, and the inoculation rates of all vaccines have exceeded 95%. The rural areas have been fully covered by the social security network, the participation rate of the new-type rural pension insurance has reached 100% and that of the new-type rural cooperative medical care system has reached 99.2%, and insurance services have been provided to all those who are covered by the minimum living allowance system.

(3) Progress has been made in structural adjustments in agriculture. The project of poverty elimination through industrial development has accelerated the structural adjustment in agriculture of Wuqia. As a result, the scale of featured advantageous industries increased over time, not only strongly supporting the supply of main agricultural products of Wuqia, but also opening up a path for poor

[26] The General Office of the Leading Group of Wuqia for Poverty Alleviation and Development: *Plan of Xinjiang Uygur Autonomous Region on Overall Poverty Alleviation and Development of Poor Villages in Wuqia* (2011-2015), March 2011.

farmers and herders to get rid of poverty and become rich. Specifically, Wuqia boasts "Gobi desert industries" characterized with facility agriculture, modern animal husbandry, characteristic fruit industry and Gobi desert fodder industry. First, in recent years, Wuqia has built a science a technology demonstration park for facility agriculture and about 2,000 greenhouses, putting an end to history of full reliance on buying vegetables from other localities and pushing for a fundamental transformation in the way of production of farmers and herders. Second, characteristic fruit industries have been further developed. In 2013, Wuqia experimentally planted fruits and vegetables including red grape and nectarine in Gobi desert greenhouses and promoted its practices, used high-efficient water-saving drip irrigation technologies to plant 400,000 fruit trees (335 hectares) and 1.31 million ecological trees (covering 683 hectares) in Kangsu, Akko, and Wuheshalu, and experimentally planted 200,000 big-fruit sea buckthorn (12 hectares) in Maykak. Third, remarkable development has been achieved in modern animal husbandry. In 2013, 16 breeding and fattening units were built, eight cooperatives were established, 130,000 domestic animals were improved, 190,000 cattle and sheep were fattened, 1,987 Dolang sheep were raised, and a mutton sheep breeding base was established, integrating "breeding sheep and mutton sheep, and demonstration and promotion". Meanwhile, it adopted the "base + company + cooperative + farmer" model to energetically develop the characteristic breeding industry, built seven bases for keeping special fowl, and raised over 800,000 special fowls throughout the year.

(4) The income increase of farmers and herders accelerates and the channels for income increase diversify over time. In recent years, Wuqia has carried out various key projects in the process of poverty alleviation and development, including overall village-based poverty elimination, poverty elimination through industrial development, labor training, infrastructure construction, and pairing assistance, etc., promoting its economic and social development, creating conditions for increasing the income of farmers and herders of Wuqia and widening their income channels, and benefiting poor farmers and herders. According to the statistics of the Office of Poverty Alleviation of Wuqia, in 2013, the per capita net income of farmers and herders of Wuqia reached 4,356 yuan, up 32% over the previous year. Specifically, the income from the modern agriculture and forestry increased by 98 yuan, that from modern animal husbandry increased by 290 yuan, that from the secondary and tertiary industries in rural areas increased by 65 yuan, and that from transfer of labor increased by 603 yuan.[27]

(5) The basic needs of local residents have been further met and the poverty has been notably alleviated. According to the poverty line of the year, between 2008 and 2010, the poor population of Wuqia dropped from 19,773 to 18,001, and the poverty headcount ratio declined from 63.14% to 56.11%. In 2011, as

[27] Wuqia Office for Poverty Alleviation and Development (Immigration Administration): *2013 Work Summary of and 2014 Work Plan on Poverty Alleviation and Development in Wuqia*, September 30, 2013, for internal circulation only.

China significantly raised its line of poverty alleviation, the poor population of Wuqia increased significantly. However, as greater efforts were made to alleviate poverty, between 2011 and 2013, the poor population declined from 25,650 to 17,971, and the poverty headcount ratio dropped from 79.13% to 55.48%. Clearly, poverty in Wuqia has been significantly alleviated.

2. Problems of and difficulties in poverty alleviation and development in Wuqia

Since 1986, Wuqia has carried out large-scale poverty alleviation and development in an organized and planned way, and made certain achievements. However, it still has problems and difficulties in poverty alleviation and development. By 2013, in the rural areas of the county there had been 4,577 poor families with a population of 17,971 and a poverty headcount ratio of 55.48%, which was 46.98% points higher than the average poverty headcount ratio of the rural areas of China. Although the income of rural poor farmers and herders increases year by year, it still lags far behind the per capita net income of rural families of other places in Xinjiang and China. The gap widened between 2000 and 2010 (see Fig. 9.2) on the whole and began to narrow in 2011. In 2013, the per capita net income of farming and herding families in Wuqia accounted for 59.7% of that of rural families in Xinjiang, 20% points higher than 39.8% in 2010, but was not on a par with that in 2000. The same trends holds for the gap between Wuqia and the national average for rural areas. The situation is not conducive to reducing poverty in Wuqia.

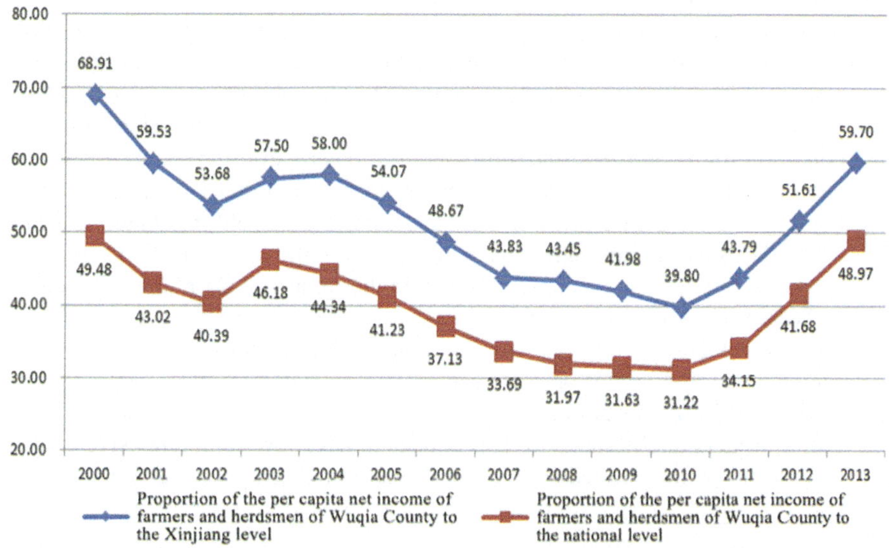

Fig. 9.2 Comparisons between the per capita net incomes of farmers and herders of Wuqia and Xinjiang, and China. *Source* Relevant data in the *Manual for Leading Officials of Wuqia* compiled by Wuqia Bureau of Statistics (2005–2014) and the official website of the National Bureau of Statistics of China.

According to our analytical results, the main problems and difficulties that Wuqia faces in poverty alleviation are mainly reflected in the following aspects.

(1) Wuqia is located in cold highland areas with a poor natural environment and frequent natural disasters, so the poor farmers and herders live in a fragile environment and find it difficult to get rid of poverty. In fact, most agricultural and pastoral areas of the county suffer from inadequate transportation and poor natural environment. Particularly, 15 border key poor villages and 10 key poor mountain villages are far from towns, with a fragile ecological environment, infertile land and meadow, and poor infrastructures. It is very hard to change the situation in the short run and to carry out poverty alleviation and development in such areas.
(2) Led by the government, poverty alleviation and development are inadequately taken part in by poor farmers and herders. As seen from poverty alleviation and development practices of Wuqia in previous years, the governments at all levels basically lift poor families from poverty by purely relying on government inputs rather than guiding them to get rid of poverty by means of government inputs. It is characterized with more "giving" policies on poverty reduction and less guiding measures for poverty alleviation, more short-term measures for poverty alleviation and less long-term measures for poverty alleviation. Such policies tend not to mobilize poor farmers and herders to take initiatives to get rid of poverty; instead, they tend to encourage to some extent the "reliance mentality" of some poor farmers and herders.
(3) Although Wuqia has intensified its efforts for poverty alleviation and development, the fund it has invested in poverty alleviation and development is insufficient. On the one hand, since the funding for poverty alleviation is limited, only a few poverty alleviation funds are invested in infrastructure construction and public welfare. Basically, only a few simple devices are added in line with local conditions of the villages, and infrastructure construction and social welfare are still less developed.[28] On the other hand, 15 key poor border villages and 10 key poor mountain villages are basically scattered in cold highland pasturing areas. The cost for infrastructure construction and maintenance such as road works and wiring in such areas is much higher than that for plains. Therefore, in Wuqia, the cost for poverty alleviation is relatively higher and the current poverty reduction funds are still insufficient. Due to shortage of funds, some fundamental and urgent projects cannot be completed in due course, directly affecting the effectiveness of poverty alleviation.[29]
(4) Some farmers and herders are less-educated, have low comprehensive quality and are not willing to leave their native places to seek personal development.

[28] Wuqia Office for Poverty Alleviation and Development: Plan for Overall Village-based Poverty Alleviation and Development of the Yimyk Village of Bostanterak Township (2011—2015), March 2011.

[29] Wuqia Office for Poverty Alleviation and Development: *2009 Work Summary of and 2010 Work Plan on Poverty Alleviation and Development in Wuqia*, December 6, 2009, for internal circulation only.

In recent years, although some young adults have worked in other places than their hometown, some farmers and herders adhere to the traditional ideas of production and living and lead a herding life, so it is difficult for them to get rid of poverty. As seen from the results of the field survey we have conducted in Urukchati Township, some herders move to pastures in summer and stay at the settlements in other seasons. For many years, they have led a traditional herding life in mountain areas and their income is low.

(5) Low quality of labor transfer training. On the one hand, there is a shortage of labor transfer trainers; on the other hand, labor transfer training is not targeted and is disconnected with the market. The main problem is that labor training is generally ordinary skills training and there are few training sessions meeting the current needs of enterprises. Therefore, among those working outside as migrant workers, there is a surplus of unskilled workers and general workers and a shortage of skilled technicians and managers. Of course, it is related to the language barrier and low education level of farmers and herders.

3 Policy Suggestions for Poverty Alleviation and Development of Wuqia

For the problems related to poverty alleviation and development of Wuqia, we believe that we should pay attention to the following points for poverty alleviation and development of Wuqia in the future.

First, for poverty alleviation and development in the future, we should give top priority to improving ecological environment and strengthening infrastructure construction. No doubt, some industrial development projects related to poverty alleviation are important for creating more jobs for poor farmers and herders and increasing their income. However, only by improving the ecological environment and infrastructures of poor areas, can we improve the work and living environments of poor farmers and herders, increase their income and lift them out of poverty. In addition, the frequent natural disasters are the main reason for the fragility of the poor population in Wuqia. Therefore, on the one hand, Wuqia should do a thorough job in conducting the "four 10,000 herders" project,[30] support 10,000 herders to engage in the traditional animal husbandry, and guide other farmers and herders to resettle and engage in other industries in towns. We should try everything possible to ensure ecological immigration. On the other hand, as a single farmer or herdsman is weak and tends to be affected by natural disasters, we should guide those farmers

[30] Since the new round of poverty alleviation and development work has been launched, Wuqia has carried out the"four-10,000 herders" project in line with their local conditions, namely, 10,000 herders engage in the traditional industry at border areas, 10,000 herders quit the traditional industry and engage in the labor economy, 10,000 herders settle down in cities and engage in the secondary and the tertiary industries, and the settlement of 10,000 old herders and students as well as industrial development. Liu Wei: *The Happiness of Herdsmen in the Border Areas: Wuqia Energetically Implements the 'Four-10,000 Herdsmen' Project to Accelerate Poverty Alleviation*, Kizilsu Daily (Chinese), January 9, 2015, Edition 4.

and herders from agricultural and pastoral areas to join in specialized cooperatives to enhance their abilities against natural disasters and minimize the impacts of natural disasters.

Second, in the process of poverty alleviation and development, we should expand the scope of poverty alleviation so as to cover more households and people. China's poverty alleviation policy has exerted a much greater effect as it has shifted its focus from poor counties to poor villages. In fact, even overall village-based poverty elimination projects focusing on poor villages do not give priority to those poor residents who are in most need of assistance and do not benefit much poor families, so it is necessary to further narrow the scope of targets of poverty alleviation and carry out relevant projects for poor families and poor residents.

Third, in the process of poverty alleviation and development, we should adopt a differentiated approach, and give specific guidance and support. For example, when carrying out the "four 10,000 herders" project, for the 10,000 border herders, we should provide them with adequate public services and industrial support by means of the poverty alleviation program for border key poor villages, and make social security and particularly subsistence allowance in agricultural and pastoral areas tilting toward them. They not only support the development of the traditional animal husbandry, but also take the heavy responsibility of safeguarding the homeland in the bad natural environment. For poor young residents, we should make great efforts to conduct training for those who work outside as migrant workers, guide those who are young, educated and skilled to transfer to the county seat or the areas beyond the county seat to engage in the "Gobi desert industry" featuring facility agriculture, modern animal husbandry, characteristic fruit industry and Gobi desert fodder industry as well as the secondary and the tertiary industries, help aged herders and school-age children settle in the county seat, and provide them with convenience in terms of pension insurance and school attendance, thereby making all poor residents take part in and benefit from the power alleviation projects and achieving the goal of lifting poor residents out of poverty.

Fourth, as China's national financial strength keeps increasing and the local economy grows rapidly, we should continue to invest more funds for poverty alleviation, and track and support relevant projects. Moreover, in the process of implementation of poverty alleviation and development projects, we should provide project locations with comprehensive support, guide project locations to establish cooperatives and bring in leading enterprises, ensure successful implementation of poverty alleviation projects and try to increase the effect of such projects.

Fifth, we should further develop the human capital of the poor regions. In June 2014, the central government decided that the students in the three southern prefectures of Xinjiang can gain free access to education in senior high schools, namely, 12-year free compulsory education. The move is of great significance to economic development and social stability of southern Xinjiang. On the basis of ensuring implementation of the 12-year compulsory education, we should improve the compulsory education, accelerate the development of vocational technical schools including vocational high schools, and ensure that students of vocational high schools are entitled to free education that is same as regular high school education, so as to enhance the occupational skills and labor market competitiveness of young laborers. In addition, in order to further increase the income of poor farmers and herders and help more of them work outside as migrant workers, we should intensify our efforts to implement the labor transfer training project, increase the efficiency, and make them receive targeted skills training before entering the labor market. For those farmers and herders living in border areas, we should offer more training related to advanced animal husbandry technologies in terms of livestock species, disease prevention and pandemic control.

Sixth, in the process of poverty alleviation and development, we should strengthen the social security system. The agricultural and pastoral areas of Wuqia are poor on the whole, and the poverty is persistent and exists mostly among ethnic minorities. For this, we need to further strengthen and improve the social security system and make it an important measure. First of all, for those poor farmers and herders who are lacking in ability to work, are advanced in age and poor in health, we must support them by means of social assistance, so as to ensure that all poor residents benefit from such poverty alleviation measures. Second, the agricultural and pastoral areas of Wuqia suffer from high incidence of endemic diseases and chronic diseases. As for poverty alleviation in Wuqia, efforts should be intensified for the building of the system of cooperative medical care in agricultural and pastoral areas and the level of medical insurance shall be increased, so as to help poor farmers and herders afford medical services and try to reduce the phenomena of "poverty due to illness". Third, the frequent occurrence and insufficient disaster relief are also a key reason for the persistent poverty of the agricultural and pastoral areas of Wuqia. Therefore, social assistance including emergency management and disaster relief shall be strengthened.

Chapter 10
The Model of Targeted Poverty Alleviation for Ethnic Autonomous Areas in Eastern China: A Case Study of Jingning She Autonomous County

1 Introduction

"We must ensure that by the year of 2020 all rural poor residents will have been lifted out of poverty. It is the most arduous task for completing the building of a moderately prosperous society in all respects". Since the 18th National Congress of the CPC, the central government has incorporated the poverty alleviation and development work into the Four-Pronged Comprehensive Strategy, made it key work for achieving the first Centenary Goal and given higher priority to it. Thanks to the innovations in poverty alleviation and development, a sound theoretical system of the targeted poverty alleviation strategy has gradually taken shape. General Secretary Jinping Xi has pointed out that "targeted poverty alleviation is an important approach to solving such problems as unclear population size, inaccurate target and poor effect in the work of poverty alleviation and development."[1] At such a critical time for completing the building of a moderately prosperous society in all respects, targeted poverty alleviation is a new policy for efficiently allocating poverty alleviation resources and achieving the poverty alleviation goals.

The strategic thinking of targeted poverty alleviation is an innovation by the CPC on China's existing thoughts on poverty reduction. Since the start of the 1980s, after several rounds of rural poverty alleviation and development, the number of people living in poverty in rural China has decreased sharply, and the poverty of the remaining poor people has been effectively mitigated. Nevertheless, as of the end of 2015, according to the current rural poverty line of China, there was still a poor population of 55.75 million in the rural areas of China.[2] Currently, China still has to face some problems and challenges in its anti-poverty efforts. First, in

[1] Liu Yongfu: Winning the Battle against Poverty and Completing the Building of a Moderately Prosperous Society in All Respects: Earnestly Studying and Implementing the Guiding Principles from Jinping Xi's Speeches on Poverty Alleviation and Development, People's Daily, April 9, 2014.

[2] National Ethnic Affairs Commission of the People's Republic of China: *Rural Poverty of Areas with Concentration of Ethnic Minorities in 2015*, the official website of the National Ethnic Affairs

X. Liu, *Complex Pictures of Poverty and Multiple Paths of Poverty Alleviation in Ethnic Areas of China*, https://doi.org/10.1007/978-981-97-4133-5_10

the process of the sustained and rapid growth of the national economy, the equality between different regions, urban and rural areas, and social strata of China remains relatively high and has a nonnegligible adverse impact on China's anti-poverty efforts in rural areas. According to statistics, the ratio between per capita disposable personal income of Chinese urban households and rural households was 2.73: 1 in 2015, a marked decline compared with the ratio of 3.33: 1 in 2008, but still remained high compared with that of many countries in the world. Second, previously, there were some serious problems of deviation in identifying poor people and areas in poverty alleviation for China's rural areas,[3] and some poverty alleviation funds and resources were not used to meet the needs of poverty-stricken areas and people.[4] Third, the poverty alleviation efforts of China's rural areas have been plagued by an overall difficult situation: the total poverty alleviation resources increase continuously and steadily, but it is hard to truly achieve the goal of transformation from "externally-driven" poverty alleviation to "internally-driven" poverty alleviation.[5] It is precisely because of such practical problems as "unclear population size, inaccurate target and poor effect" of poverty alleviation and development, the fundamental way of China's efforts for poverty alleviation and development is to carry out poverty alleviation work in a more targeted way and implement the strategies of targeted poverty alleviation and elimination.

Studies show that, to solve such problems as low efficiency of poverty alleviation and insufficient funding channels in China's current poverty alleviation and development due to the deviation in identifying poor people and areas and the high investment leakage rate, we must increase policy elasticity and differentiation.[6] Therefore, it is imperative to adapt to the new situation of poverty alleviation and make innovations in the poverty alleviation mechanism. At present, a widely-recognized measure is to introduce the market mechanism into the traditional organizational model which relies purely on government efforts for poverty alleviation, channel market awareness and market-based operating mode into poverty alleviation and elimination, connect relatively closed poverty-stricken areas with the external markets, and use the market mechanism to enhance the capability of people living in poverty to adapt to market and economic changes, so as to increase the internal impetus and self-development capacity of poverty-stricken areas, foster a mechanism of internal growth, avoid

Commission of the People's Republic of China, April 11, 2016, http://www.seac.gov.cn/art/2016/4/11/art_31_251389.html, last access: March 9, 2017.

[3] YE Chusheng, Zou Xin: Performance Assessment and Mechanism Design of Targeted Poverty Alleviation, Journal of Huazhong Agricultural University (Social Sciences Edition), Issue 1, 2012.

[4] Xu Yuanyuan: *A Study on Targeted Poverty Alleviation in Rural Areas of China*, a doctoral dissertation from Sun Yat-Sen University, 2006.

[5] Fang Jing: The "Involution" Predicament of China's Rural Poverty Alleviation and its Solutions, Social Construction, Issue 2, 2014.

[6] Zhang Xinwei: Low Efficiency of Poverty Alleviation Policy and Thinking on Market-based Anti-Poverty, Chinese Rural Economy, Issue 2, 1999; Kuang Yuanpei: A Summary of Researches on China's Innovations in Poverty Alleviation Policy and Mechanism, Issues in Agricultural Economy, Issue 8, 2005; Guo Jingguang: The Fragility and Trends of China's Poor Population, Statistical Research, Issue 9, 2011.

falling back to poverty and ensure that poor people are lifted out of poverty.[7] Moreover, increasing the level of rural households' engagement in the market is a must-have condition for reducing the probability of falling into poverty.[8] It can be said that the key to powering the rural economic development is to imbue people living in poverty with thinking of market-oriented economy and ensure that they play a leading role in poverty reduction and elimination.[9]

As China's only She autonomous county, Jingning County, is a key underdeveloped county and a major battlefield for poverty alleviation and development due to its poor natural endowments, bad natural conditions and underdeveloped economy and society. Since the 18th National Congress of the CPC, the government of Jingning has given top priority to "eliminating households with per capita annual income of 4,600 yuan and below"[10] and made it the most important program for improving its people's wellbeing, improved weak links in poor rural areas, targeted people living in poverty, fully implemented the targeted poverty alleviation and elimination strategy in consideration of different reasons for poverty and development conditions, made innovations in poverty alleviation model, explored and practiced and made remarkable results in poverty alleviation in the aspects of policy, industry, relocation, finance, education, and social security. As a result, it has taken the lead in many aspects of poverty alleviation in areas where ethnic minorities concentrate. Through innovation and practices in poverty alleviation model, the government of Jingning helped and guided poor rural households to enhance their awareness of market-based economy, increased their abilities of self-development and engagement in market competition, and preliminarily established a long-term mechanism for ensuring income growth of poor rural households. The extensive study on and summary of the model and practices of targeted poverty alleviation and elimination in Jingning set an example for other poor areas where ethnic minorities and poor counties in innovating the poverty alleviation mechanism and improving the efficiency of poverty alleviation, and hold great theoretical and practical significance.

[7] Lu Xiaohua: Anti-Poverty and Market Introduction, China's Underdeveloped Regions, Issue 5, 1997; Xu Yuebin, Liu Fengqin, Zhang Xiulan: A Reflection on the Anti-poverty Policy on China's Rural Areas – A Shift from Social Assistance to Social Protection, Social Sciences in China, Issue 3, 2007; Xu Zhiming: Low Efficiency in Poverty Alleviation Investment and Establishment of the Market-based Anti-Poverty Mechanism, Rural Economy, Issue 9, 2008; Tan Xuewen, Li Chenggui: A Review on the Economic Fragility of Poverty and Poverty Reduction Strategy, China Rural Survey, Issue 5, 2010; Zhang Tongchao, Yan Tingwu, He Ke, Zhang Junbiao: A Study on Rural Households' Multi-dimensional Poverty Based on Market Participation: Taking Contiguous Areas of Extreme Poverty as an Example, Journal of Zhongnan University of Economics and Law, Issue 3, 2016.

[8] Zhang Yuan, Wan Guanghua, Liu Xiuyan, Xu Qing: Market Participation and Poverty of Rural Areas: A Perspective of Micro-analysis, The Journal of World Economy, Issue 9, 2009.

[9] Yu Mingjiang: The Establishment of the Anti-Poverty Mechanism in China's Rural Areas: A Study from the Perspective of 'Government - Market' Double Orientation, Journal of Anhui Agricultural University (Social Sciences Edition), Issue 5, 2010.

[10] The 4,600 yuan (price of 2010) is the designated standard for rural poverty alleviation in Zhejiang Province.

2 Characteristics of Rural Poverty in Jingning She Autonomous County

Located in the mountainous area and old revolutionary base area on the border between Fujian and Zhejiang, Jingning She Autonomous County is the only ethnic minority autonomous county in eastern China and the only She autonomous county in China. Under the jurisdiction of Lishui city, Jingning is relatively underdeveloped and geographically remote, more than 259 km from Hangzhou, the provincial capital of Zhejiang, and over 170 km from Wenzhou. Covering an area of 1,950 square kilometers, it is mountainous, rich in water resources but scarce in arable land. In 1986, Jingning was designated as one of the first 301 poor counties to which priority was given, and was the poorest of the six poor counties in Zhejiang. Since the implementation the "Seven-Year Priority Poverty Alleviation Program", poverty has been eliminated in Jingning. However, compared with other regions in Zhejiang, Jingning, due to its underdeveloped economy and society and relatively serious poverty problems, was still listed as one of the 26 underdeveloped counties of Zhejiang in 2005. In 2011, Jingning was listed as one of the six key underdeveloped counties of Zhejiang due to its poor economic performance and arduous tasks of ecological protection as well as the hard lives of its people, and was given priority by the provincial government of Zhejiang. It would be fair to say that Jingning has been a frontier in Zhejiang for poverty alleviation and development.

As one of the most developed provinces in eastern China, Zhejiang takes the lead in the fight against poverty in China. In 1997, Zhejiang became the first province in China to eliminate poverty in poverty-stricken counties where the residents lived below the state-designated poverty line. As of 2015, Zhejiang had been ranking among the top three in China for 31 years in terms of the income of rural residents, and its index of moderate prosperity in all respects had exceeded 95%, eliminating absolute poverty (where the annual per capita household income is below the state-designated poverty line) and becoming China's first province winning the war against poverty. In other words, since 1997, the poverty of underdeveloped counties of Zhejiang Province has certain differences from that of poverty-stricken areas in central and western China. In 2011, the provincial government of Zhejiang set its standard for rural poverty alleviation (4,600 yuan in constant price in 2010), which was in line with its economic and social development and twice the national standard for poverty alleviation (2,300 yuan in constant price in 2010). Obviously, Jingning has different poverty characteristics due to its unique conditions.

First, the poverty in rural areas of Jingning is mainly the so-called "transformed poverty"[11] and "relative poverty". It is not "absolute poverty", but "relative poverty"

[11] Before the reform and opening-up, most poor rural areas in China were in a state of absolute poverty due to natural, geographic, historical and institutional constraints. After the start of reform and opening-up, some regions underwent rapid industrialization and urbanization while some other regions with relatively bad natural conditions were slow in industrialization and urbanization and became impoverished. So it can said that the poverty is "transformed poverty" caused by slow economic transformation (industrialization and urbanization). Zhao Qiangshe: *A Probe into the*

caused by insufficient development ability. In other words, the anti-poverty efforts of Jingning have shifted from focusing on meeting people's basic needs to increasing development ability and narrowing the gap in development, and such aspects as ensuring equal access to basic public services, enhancement of the self-development ability of poor people, and solving prominent problems hindering development are given higher priority to. It may be the reason why the poor rural households (population) in Jingning are called "low-income rural households (population)". Based on the research purpose of this chapter, we use "new-type poverty" to denote the so-called "transformed poverty" or "relative poverty", and use "rural households in new-type poverty/population" to denote "low-income rural households/population" mentioned by all governments at all levels of Zhejiang Province. In addition, when managing low-income farmers dynamically, the government of Jingning not only considers their income factors, but also considers such factors as health, housing, assets, and disaster, etc.[12] That is, in accordance with the requirements on dynamic management of poverty-stricken families, the poverty of rural areas mentioned by the government of Jingning has turned from single-dimensional poverty (low-income) to multi-dimensional poverty.

Second, there are many "new-type poor households" in rural areas in Jingning. In accordance with the new standards for poverty alleviation in rural areas developed by Zhejiang Province in 2011, the specific standard for poverty alleviation in rural areas of Jingning was per capita net income of 5,500 yuan for rural households in 2013, based on which it is estimated that there are 47,740 people living in new-type poverty in rural areas of Jingning, with a poverty headcount ratio of 33.6%.

Third, the distribution of people in new-type poverty in rural areas of Jingning shows a tendency of "being concentrated in certain places that are scattered in the 21 towns and townships (subdistricts) across the county", mainly in the eight underdeveloped towns such as Shawan Town, Yingchuan Town, Hongxing Sub-district, Dongkeng Town, Hexi Sub-district, Bohai Town, Jiulong Township and Dadi Township in mountainous areas, where there are 26,264 poor residents in 8,952 households, accounting for 54.7% and 55% of rural households in new-type poverty and people in new-type poverty of the county, respectively.

Fourth, there are some differences in the distribution of the population in new-type poverty in rural areas of Jingning. The natural and geographical conditions of most ethnic minority concentrated villages tend to be inhospitable, the working and living conditions of ethnic minorities are relatively poor, and their incomes are relatively low. Therefore, ethnic minority concentrated villages and ethnic minorities in the county have prominent problems manifesting new-type poverty. According to statistics, Jingning currently has 254 administrative villages, including 148 key villages of poverty alleviation, accounting for 58.3% of all the administrative villages.

Evolution of Poverty Alleviation Model and Countermeasures for Poverty Alleviation in the New Era, West Journal, Issue 2, 2013.

[12] NoTice of the General Office of the People's Government of Jingning She Autonomous County on Dynamically Managing Former Low-income Rural Households with an Annual Income of 4,600 yuan and Below, Jingzhengbanfamingdian [2016], No.31.

Amongst all the administrative villages, there are 46 ethnic minority concentrated villages, 35 of which are key poverty alleviation villages, accounting for 76.1% of all the ethnic minority concentrated villages, 17.8% points higher than the proportion of key poverty alleviation villages among all administrative villages. According to statistics about the standards for poverty alleviation in rural areas in Zhejiang in 2013, there were 47,740 residents living in new-type poverty in Jingning, accounting for 27.5% of all the registered population of the county, 6,237 new-type poor ethnic minority residents, accounting for 31.7% of all the registered ethnic minority population of the county, with a poverty headcount ratio 4.2% points higher than that of the total registered population of the county.[13]

Fifth, the poor rural residents of Jingning live mainly in rural areas facing bad natural and ecological environments and sluggish economic development. Domestic and overseas research results show that geographical conditions and economic circumstances are key factors to social and economic development. Poverty often goes hand in hand with fragile ecological environment.[14] There are 148 key poverty alleviation villages in Jingning, including 65 villages in old revolutionary base areas and 35 ethnic minority concentrated villages. Most of these key poverty alleviation villages are scattered in mountains and reservoir areas, which are geographically remote, have poor traffic and environmental conditions, and low capability against natural disasters. There are 31,632 persons (including 4,958 persons in 2,690 households entitled to subsistence allowances, and 224 childless and infirm rural residents who are entitled to five forms of support (food, clothing, medical care, housing, and burial expenses) from 10,562 poor rural households in 148 key poverty alleviation villages, accounting for 79.5% and 66.3% of the total poor rural households in the county, respectively.[15] Jingning is mountainous and has little arable land, and its mountainous areas with a slope of less than 25 degrees only account for 8.28% of

[13] The registered population mentioned here is derived from the *2013 Statistical Yearbook of Jingning She Autonomous County* compiled by the Bureau of Statistics of Jingning County, and the number of people living in poverty is derived from the *Summary of 2013 Poverty Alleviation Work and the Way of Thinking about 2014 Poverty Alleviation Work of Jingning She Autonomous County* compiled by the Office of Jingning She Autonomous County for Poverty Alleviation. It should be noted that, as mentioned above, the headcount ratio of new-type poverty in rural areas of Jingning County is 33.6%, which is calculated on the basis of the registered rural population and its statistical caliber is different from that used here. We can find the total registered rural population of ethnic minorities in the statistics of Jingning, therefore, the headcount ratio of relevant new-type poor populations is calculated on the basis of the total registered population. Considering that the urbanization rate of Jingning has reached 48.9%, the actual headcount ratio of registered new-type rural poor residents in Jingning (including that of the registered new-type rural poor ethnic minority residents in Jingning) is undoubtedly underestimated, but the data roughly reflect the headcount ratio of new-type poverty of different ethnic groups in rural areas of the county.

[14] David W. Pearce, Jeremy J. Warford: World without End, China Environmental Science Press, 1996; Wei Xiaowen, Zhu Xinlin: A Study on Combating Poverty of Farmers and Herdsmen in Xizang from the Perspective of Environmental Resources, Journal of Technical Economics and Management, Issue 2, 2012.

[15] The Agricultural Office of Jingning She Autonomous County (Office of Poverty Alleviation): *A Survey Report on Key Poverty Alleviation Villages of Jingning She Autonomous County* (Internal Report), August 8, 2013.

the total area of the county. As many as 25,000 farmers live in remote mountains, and it is the main reason why there are lots of poor people in rural areas in Jingning.

Sixth, Jingning's rural poor villages and poor people have insufficient human capital. The labor forces of key poverty alleviation villages have relatively low comprehensive quality such that lots of poor rural families fall into the vicious cycle of "poverty—low education level—lack of knowledge and skills—poor entrepreneurial ability—poverty". Most people in new-type poor rural families have not received good education, and those people who are illiterate, semi-illiterate and those who have only received primary school education account for 57.02% of all the new-type residents living in poverty. Most of them lacking in knowledge and skills to respond to market demands, therefore they earn little money and only do some dangerous physical work even if they work in cities, incapable of saving money or giving financial support to their family members. Most people stay at mountainous areas and do simple agricultural work.[16]

Seventh, Jingning's new-type poor rural residents mainly engage in traditional agricultural work and their income sources are few. The economy of key poverty alleviation villages is basically small-scale peasant economy, and most new-type poor rural families engage in traditional agricultural work. However, due to the unfavorable geographical environment and the failure of the ideological concepts of such rural families in keeping up with the social development process, they mainly engage in small-scale planting, and their agricultural products are mainly used to meet the living needs of their family members, and the commodity rate is relatively low. All of these are important factors behind backward economic development, single income structure of rural households in new-type poverty and low income level of key poverty alleviation villages.[17]

3 The Model of Targeted Poverty Alleviation in Jingning County

Poverty alleviation model is a generic term of methods and mechanisms aiming at poverty reduction and lifting poor rural areas and people out of poverty.[18] The targeted poverty alleviation model of Jingning covers a series of practical "anti-poverty" activities that are based on the actual situation of Jingning and new features of new-type poverty in rural areas and are in line with the goals and tasks of targeted poverty alleviation of the county.

To sum up, the establishment of a poverty alleviation model first of all requires five important supporting points, namely "government guidance, social participation, self-reliance, poverty alleviation through development, and overall development".

[16] Ditto.

[17] Ditto.

[18] Zhao Qiangshe: A Probe into the Evolution of Poverty Alleviation Model and Countermeasures for Poverty Alleviation in the New Era, West Journal, Issue 2, 2013.

The five supporting points are five poverty alleviation mechanisms that connect with and support each other. Especially, to successfully push forward the work related to poverty alleviation as a whole and achieve long-term effects in areas with extensive and concentrated poverty, it is essential to establish the five mechanisms in an integrated way and create a complete practical logic for poverty alleviation. At the present stage, the establishment of the five supporting points or a poverty alleviation mechanism is nothing new. However, in many places, the five supporting points can neither be truly established, nor make organic connections, norform an overall and sustainable poverty alleviation strategy and action system, nor create a strong synergy. On the contrary, in most cases only one or two supporting points work; particularly, "government guidance" is likely the poverty alleviation mechanism that can be most easily implemented while other supporting points or mechanisms are very likely to be forcibly established to coordinate with the process of "government guidance". It is neither active nor sustainable; stakeholders of such mechanisms consider relevant actions as "tasks" (and even "political tasks"), but tend not to believe that it will generate benefits to complete such tasks. Therefore, it is very difficult to form an internal driving force. These problems, in the process of poverty alleviation of Jingning, have been solved in varying degrees. Second, in the process of overall establishment of the five supporting points or mechanisms, all actors have relatively advanced ideas. For example, from the dimension of "government guidance", the government of Jingning County, either by accident or on purpose, makes such thinking run through many of its practices; it takes poverty alleviation and development not only as a solution for new-type poverty in rural areas of the county, but also an approach to and opportunity for promoting economic and social development of the county. It alleviates poverty not for the sake of poverty alleviation, but for the purpose of the overall economic and social development of the county, thereby making poverty alleviation and development in rural areas an integral part of the economic and social development of the county. In result, the work of poverty alleviation will be easier to be promoted and its effect will be better. Third, the formation and operation of the poverty alleviation model of the county has its unique local advantages. Specifically, Jingning is under the jurisdiction of Zhejiang Province, which enjoys a relatively high level of economic development, and the rapid economic development of the neighboring areas facilitates the development of Jingning. It also means that, compared with other poverty-stricken ethnic minority concentrated areas, Jingning is much nearer to the outside market. As long as Jingning takes the initiative to integrate itself into the developed market economic system in its surrounding areas, it can obtain more spaces and opportunities for market development and promote its economic and social development. Meanwhile, as long as it takes various effective measures for poverty alleviation, creates more opportunities for residents living in poor rural areas and assists them in developing self-development ability, it can bring people living in poverty more effectively into market-based development, truly achieve development through self-reliance, and get rid of poverty. Of course, the distance to the market system may not be a decisive factor, and the key is to introduce market-based ideas in the overall poverty alleviation mechanism, involving grasping the real needs of the market and the capabilities and conditions of poor local residents, and taking the initiative to connect the people living in poverty with the market needs by training and educating those people in light of market needs. Jingning has rich experience in rural poverty alleviation and establishment of development model.

The above characteristics of the poverty alleviation and development model are fully reflected in the specific practices of poverty alleviation and development of the county in nearly all forms. Next, we will explore the specific contents and practice logics of poverty alleviation and development model the rural areas in Jingning.

3.1 Policy-Based Poverty Alleviation

For many poor counties, key resources and opportunities for policy-based poverty alleviation are provided by the central, provincial and city-level governments. It is the case for Jingning. The central government, Zhejiang Province and Lishui City have provided Jingning with great support such as transfer payment, special support fund as well as preferential fiscal and tax policies, which mean resources and opportunities. Nevertheless, what is more critical is how poor counties effectively use their own resources and favorable conditions and incorporate the resources and opportunities offered by the government at a higher level into their development system and action structure, so as to bring out the best in each other. In other words, Jingning increases the effect of policies of the government at a higher level by improving the driving force and action structure of development, and uses the policy support from higher-level governments to improve its driving force and action structure of development, and stimulates its potential. The government of Jingning County has made effective attempts in poverty alleviation and development practices in rural areas.

A key point of the practices of Jingning is to make full use of its status as an ethnic minority county and make the general support policies of the central government and the provincial government of Zhejiang on Jingning into special support policies. Since its establishment, the county has been benefiting from the policies of CPC Zhejiang Provincial Committee and Zhejiang Provincial Government. In 2008, CPC Zhejiang Provincial Committee and Zhejiang Provincial Government issued the *Guidelines on Supporting the Accelerated Development of Jingning She Autonomous County* (Zhewei 2008, No.53). In 2012, the CPC Zhejiang Provincial Committee and Zhejiang Provincial Government issued the *Guidelines on Further Supporting the Accelerated Development of Jingning She Autonomous County* (Zhewei 2012, No.115), giving two rounds of special support to the county for a 10-year period. Meanwhile, Jingning was listed as one of the six key underdeveloped counties of Zhejiang Province in 2011, was included in the special support programs of Zhejiang Province for 2011–2013 and 2014–2016 (granted with 200 million yuan per year), and was included by CPC Zhejiang Provincial Committee and Zhejiang Provincial Government in the program of key mountainous counties of Zhejiang Province in 2014 (granted with 10 million yuan per year for industrial support). In addition, the CPC Lishui Municipal Committee and Lishui Municipal Government have allocated a land covering an area of four square kilometers in Lishui to Jingning to establish the Lijing Ethnic Minority Industrial Park for the purpose of industrial development. The park has been approved by China's National Ethnic Affairs Commission as an experimental site for offsite poverty alleviation and development. According to incomplete statistics, Jingning has obtained support funds amounting to more than 8 billion yuan from the higher-level governments since 2008.[19]

The above major policies have laid a foundation for the overall economic and social development of Jingning and stimulated it to get out of the difficulties through development and build a moderately prosperous society in all respects. More importantly, the use of such special support funds is integrated closely with economic and social development, and poverty alleviation and development of the county; it plays a role in promoting economic and social development of the county and supporting the development of new-type residents living in poverty in rural areas, and lays a solid foundation for the county to achieve the goal of eliminating low-income rural households with an annual per-capita income of less than 4,600 yuan by 2015. Specifically, the policy-based poverty alleviation system of Jingning County plays an effective role in laying a foundation for overall poverty alleviation and development in rural areas.

3.2 Non-governmental Poverty Alleviation

The non-governmental poverty alleviation of Jingning was also impressive. The most important part of non-governmental poverty alleviation is "paired assistance" where the developed areas of Zhejiang Province as well as provincial (Zhejiang), city (Lishui) and county (Jingning County) government organs and public institutions paired with key poverty alleviation villages and poverty-stricken families of Jingning to provide the latter with assistance. The paired assistance is given by provincial (Zhejiang), city (Lishui) and county (Jingning County) government organs and public institutions to poor villages and rural families of the county by various means such as financial support, intellectual support, economic cooperation, and talent training.

1. Provincial and city-level paired assistance. Jingning carries out provincial, city-level and county-level coordinated policy on paired assistance, and actively advances the paired assistance on both sides to maximize the effects of assistance by establishing the mechanism of "three-tier guidance and assistance". In accordance with the *Notice of the General Office of the CPC Zhejiang Provincial Committee and the General Office of the People's Government of Zhejiang Province on a New-Round of Poverty Alleviation and Paired Assistance* (Zheweibanfa (2014), No.8). The members of the new-round provincial assistance program include Zhejiang Development and Reform Commission,

[19] Lan Lingli, Deputy Secretary of the CPC Jingning She Autonomous County Committee, Head of the Government of Jingning She Autonomous County: *The Report Materials for the Special Research Meeting of the National People's Congress*, on the afternoon of June 3, 2016.

Zhejiang Finance Department, Zhejiang Radio and TV Group, the First Hospital of Zhejiang Province, and Yinzhou District (10 towns and townships). The above units pair with 65 key poverty alleviation villages of Jingning County. Leaders of Lishui government as well as 17 units including city-level departments (General Office of the CPC Lishui Committee, CPC Lishui Discipline Inspection Commission, Lishui Department of Water Resources, and Lishui Department of Construction) paired with 28 key poverty alleviation villages of Jingning County.

2. Implementation of county-level paired assistance. In order to further improve the system of paired assistance, the CPC Jingning County Committee and Jingning County Government issued documents related to paired assistance to make greater efforts for assistance to key poverty alleviation villages in addition to provincial and city paired assistance. Currently, "paired assistance" has covered all poor villages.
3. Jingning motivates all sectors of society to extensively take part in poverty alleviation in the county. In our opinion, it is actually the real "non-governmental poverty alleviation" or public participation of poverty alleviation" where the key actors of poverty alleviation are nongovernmental organizations or individuals rather than governmental organs and departments. Poverty alleviation resources do not come from government finance but from individuals, non-public enterprises and nongovernmental organizations. Poverty alleviation actions are not taken by the government but are taken voluntarily by social actors. In this regard, Jingning has made initial success though it is still in the process of development. For example, Jingning, by using the mechanism of "mountain-sea coordination", keeps strengthening contact and cooperation with developed counties in the principle of "joint development, joint administration and sharing", innovates the way of non-governmental poverty alleviation, carries out the projects of "Enterprise-Agriculture Cooperation" and "Returning of Jingning Businessmen", mobilizes and contacts with more non-governmental organizations including industrial and commercial enterprises, public organizations and charitable organizations, and encourages them to participate in poverty alleviation and development in various forms. In 2016, Zhejiang Overseas Chinese Chamber of Commerce carried out assistance activities in Jingning. It assisted 10 rural schools in improving students' living and working conditions and facilities, assisting 100 poor families in getting rid of poverty by means of industrial assistance, employment assistance and award granting to students from families in difficulties, and creating non-agricultural employment opportunities for 1,000 rural laborers. In this way, Zhejiang Overseas Chinese Chamber of Commerce has gained good social reputation and realized its value of serving the hometown.

3.3 Industrial Development

Poverty alleviation through industrial development is an important part of the special poverty alleviation work of Jingning and a main approach to increasing the self-development ability of people living in poverty and lifting them out of poverty. In recent years, considering that the residents living in new-type poverty living in rural areas of Jingning mainly engage in traditional agricultural activities and have a single income structure, Jingning vigorously boosts the endeavor of shifting from the traditional planting and breeding industry to the modern rural industrial system in which the primary, secondary and tertiary industries are attached equal importance, so as to achieve good results in leading poor villages and households out of poverty.

First, Jingning focuses on poor villages, makes full use of its resource advantages, supports the development of business operations with distinctive local features, gives high priority to supporting leading industrial projects such as moso bamboo, tea, Chinese torreya, mountain vegetables, edible mushrooms, Chinese herbal medicines, and cultivation that have a certain foundation and bright development prospects, and leads poor households to get rid of poverty. In 2013, it made an investment of 72.44 million yuan for the development of poor rural households, growing featured crops (23,500 mu), aquatic products (1,300 mu) and edible mushrooms (450,000 bags), and raising livestock (8,400) and fowl (61,900). Specifically, many products are in high demand, boosting the earnings of rural households in new-type poverty targeted by these projects.

Second, Jingning ensures the development of businesses such as specialty farmer cooperatives, family farms, and large planting and breeding families, etc., and sets a good example. Between 2013 and 2015, the county invested 6.911 million yuan from the provincial fund for development of low-income rural households in supporting 245 specialized agricultural cooperatives, 41 large breeding families, and 6,576 farmer households, including 3,184 low-income rural households.

Third, Jingning develops secondary and tertiary industries such as materials for processing and rural tourism. With an excellent ecological environment, the county, by using its superior resources, vigorously develops rural tourism including peasant families hosting urbanite guests in their farm guesthouses,, plans to achieve the goal of "making lucid waters and lush mountains invaluable assets" in due course and lift disadvantaged groups out of poverty by tourism. Considering that a large number of young people work in cities as migrant workers and leave behind women, Jingning actively develops processing industry with supplied materials. As of 2015, there has been 155 brokers and 14,500 laborers in 20 villages engaging in the industry, and they have earned a total of 91.37 million yuan from the processing industry.

3.4 Poverty Alleviation Through Labor Force Training

Training the labor force in poverty is an important part of and measure for government-led development-oriented poverty alleviation. Based on the problem of insufficient human capital of poor rural villages and people in new-type poverty, Jingning has carried out various labor force training projects in a targeted manner. Specifically, the most important training projects are listed below.

First, quality training of rural labor force. The Office of Poverty Alleviation (Agriculture Office) of Jingning County, guided by the goal of increasing the competence and employment and business startup skills of farmers including disadvantaged groups, carries out skills training for rural laborers through multiple channels, at multiple levels and in various forms. Between 2013 and 2015, a total of 18,294 persons were trained, including 3,680 rural practical talents, non-agricultural employment opportunities were created for 3,336 persons, and 11,278 persons received general training. The trainings have significantly increased the specialized agricultural skills and employment skills of rural laborers, opened new channels for business startup and employment of farmers including the people in new-type poverty, and created a number of models who have got rid of poverty, achieved prosperity and started up businesses.

Second, setup of county-level bases for practical training of farmers. To further implement the projects for enhancing the competence of farmers including the people in new-type poverty, vigorously promote the development of rural new-type labor force living in poverty, and enhance relevant labor force training projects in a more targeted and effective way, the following eight practical training bases for farmers have been established in Jingning: Zhejiang Qier Tea Co., Ltd. (tea practical training base), Chinese Torreya Practical Training Base at Jinqiu Village, Chengzhao Township, Zhejiang Chunyi Bamboo Development Co., Ltd. (moso bamboo practical training base), mountain vegetables practical training base at Chalin Village, Daji Township, Daziran Foods Co., Ltd. (edible mushrooms practical training base), Shanshan Shopping Mall (e-business practical training base), Nongjiale practical training base at Gendixian Village of Dongkeng Town, and Jingning County Center for Processing with Supplied Materials.

Third, brand building for farmer training. Jingning boasts distinctive training brands including "She Xiang Tea Master" and "She Xiang Maternity Matron". The "She Xiang Maternity Matron" training project is particularly successful. In 2013, "Ruihe Training", an organization engaging mainly in maternity matron training, began to operate in Jingning, but it was in a difficult situation and even could not enter the rural market. The Poverty Alleviation Office of Jingning, to meet the needs of poverty alleviation and development, assisted the employees of "Ruihe Training" in entering the market of Jingning. Since the introduction of the two-child policy in China, the demands for maternity matrons in some cities, particularly the first-tier cities, were steadily on the rise. Maternity matrons have a bright future and are in short supply. Currently, the "She Xiang Maternity Matron" training platform has more than 2,000 primary nursery teachers, whose monthly salaries are between 6,000 yuan and 26,000 yuan.[20] Usually, a maternity matron can earn at least 40,000 yuan. Moreover, different from that of ordinary rural migrant workers in cities, the board and lodging of maternity matrons are provided by their employers. Beyond doubt, the families of the 2,000 "She Xiang maternity matrons" can be lift out of poverty, and the maternity matrons will enjoy greater space for development as the market demands increase.

3.5 Relocation

Relocation refers to relocating local residents who live in inhospitable areas lacking in water and land resources such as mountainous areas and areas susceptible to geological disasters to areas rich in water and land resources in a planned, step-by-step and phased way. As a way of poverty alleviation, relocation can substantially improve the living and working conditions of poor rural households.

In Jingning, some rural residents live in areas with poor natural and ecological environment and scare regional advantages, and relocating them from such inhospitable areas is an important solution to assisting them in getting out of poverty. Between 2013 and 2015, the Poverty Alleviation Office of Zhejiang Province provided Jingning with 45.72 million yuan for relocation, and 3,802 persons were relocated. Specifically, 2,629 persons were relocated from mountainous areas, 1,173 persons were relocated from areas with geological disasters, 3,536 persons were resettled in a centralized way and 266 persons were resettled in a decentralized way. The relocation promoted a new type of urbanization of mountainous areas and advanced the building of the brand "Jingning, a famous county of She ethnic minority group in China".

3.6 Education

To eradicate poverty, one the most important things is to stop poverty from being passed on to the next generation. Education plays a key role in stopping poverty from being passed on to the next generation. The government of Jingning County works actively to explore education-based poverty alleviation and takes measures in light of the actual situation of the county.

First, based on the new-round (2014–2016) special support policies, the government of Jingning County implemented two special programs to support the board and lodging of students from rural families and those students who can't afford education expenses. It assists over 1,000 students from rural families each year and ensures that

[20] Mao Huaqing: *The Speech Delivered at the Forum of "Targeted Poverty Alleviation in Rural Areas"*, The Second Forum on the Development of China's She Ethnic Minority Group in Jingning County, November 27, 2016.

they will not drop out due to financial difficulties. The government has established a fund for assisting poor rural households (low-income rural households) in education, so as to fully improve the schooling conditions of children of rural households in poverty, and encourage them to study hard.

Second, since 2015, the government of Jingning County has implemented the *Notice on Assisting Members of Low-Income Rural Households in Receiving Vocational Education* (ZHEFUPINBAN 〔2015〕, No.40) issued by the Poverty Alleviation Office of Zhejiang Province, the Department of Education of Zhejiang Province, and Zhejiang Provincial Department of Human Resources and Social Security, further guided and supported members of low-income rural households (namely rural households in new-type poverty) to receive vocational education, and intensified education-based poverty alleviation. For "low-income rural households with an annual per-capita income of less than 4,600 yuan" (including households entitled to subsistence allowance) and their children receiving secondary and higher vocational education (including substituted post exercitation), the government gives each student a one-off subsidy of 3,000 yuan.

Third, it is a fact that ethnic minority concentrated areas are poorer than the areas populated by the Hans. To enhance the level of ethnic minority education, Jingning adopts special policies on supporting ethnic minority education. First, a system is adopted for providing ethnic minority students with free basic education (15-year education from kindergarten to senior high school). Second, each ethnic minority student of junior and senior high schools in Jingning is given a living subsidy of not less than 500 yuan, and each primary school student is given 300 yuan each school year. Third, each rural poor ethnic minority student, who rents a house in the county and studies at a school that has no boarding conditions and is beyond the urban bus service scope, is given a rental subsidy of 1,500 yuan each school year. In addition, the "fund for helping and giving awards to ethnic minority students in poverty" aims to subsidize poor ethnic minority students and give awards to ethnic minority students who have been admitted to a university. An ethnic minority student who has been admitted into a key university (covered by 985 and 211 programs) will be given an award of 30,000 yuan, an ethnic minority student admitted into an ordinary university will be given an award of 5,000 yuan, and an ethnic minority student admitted into a technical college will be given an award of 2,000 yuan. In a word, through education-based poverty alleviation, the learning environment of students from poor families or low-income families has been improved, their rights to learn are safeguarded, the phenomena of "poor education-caused poverty" and "poverty-caused dropout" have been basically eliminated, and equal and fair access to education is better ensured.

3.7 Poverty Alleviation Through Financial Means

Poverty alleviation through financial means is the most distinctive measure amongst the poverty alleviation practices in Jingning. In recent years, the government of Jingning County, has taken the opportunity of setting up poverty alleviation pilot reform areas in Lishui, actively made innovations in the poverty alleviation mechanism based on financial means, strived to meet the loan needs of poor rural households, solved the problems of backward production conditions and poor self-development abilities of some rural households, and kept increasing the vitality of their new businesses to help increase the farmers' income.

First, Jingning initiates the "Zhengyinbao" poverty alleviation mechanism based on financial means for poor groups, namely the new-type petty-loan mechanism consisting of government interest-free loan, bank loan, and insurance. In 2011, the *Guideline for the Development of Poverty Alleviation Loan Program for Low-income Rural Households* was developed and released; in November 2016, Jingning, by means of the special support fund and the new-type petty-loan mechanism for poverty alleviation, granted the 8,083 households of the county with an interest-free loan of 390 million yuan, of which 28.7 million yuan was granted to rural households in new-type poverty. A total of 16,057 "Harvest Love Cards" were granted, of which 4,501 cards were granted to rural households in new-type poverty.[21] Quite a few rural households tend to raise funds by themselves for business startup after obtaining the loans. In general, Jingning comes out first in China in terms of interest subsidies, scale of loan, and implementation effects. It is of significance in the four aspects below. First, it has solved the difficulties of poverty-stricken families and marginal poor households in obtaining funding support. Previously, poverty-stricken families and marginal poor households had insufficient savings and lost many development opportunities. By means of the "ZHENGYINBAO" interest-free loans, poor families or marginal poor families can better develop production and rapidly increase their incomes. Second, Jingning provides poor families or marginal poor families with funds for business startup and help such families achieve leapfrog development. "ZHENGYINBAO" can be recycled. Specifically, after getting and paying back the loans in the first stage, poor families or marginal poor families can continue to apply for interest-free loans and increase the loan by raising the credit level. Therefore, poor families or marginal poor families can not only expand the scale of agricultural production by using the loan, but also use a part of the fund to take part in other economic activities related to the "small hydropower station, small hotel, and small supermarket", acquire asset revenue, and even take opportunities to start up business, gain higher operating income, get rid of poverty and get rich. Third, Jingning assists most poor families or marginal poor families in winning the opportunities for investment, including investments in capacity building. 4. Jingning helps poor families or marginal poor families develop the concept and capacity of market economy. Poor families or marginal poor families, by undergoing the process of financing—development and production—on-time repayment, refinancing—expansion of production

[21] "Harvest Love Card" is an innovative financial product jointly developed by Zhejiang Provincial Rural Credit Cooperative and Zhejiang Provincial Office of Poverty Alleviation. With a term of less than three years, the credit extension loan can be borrowed and repaid at any time, and can be recycled. The benchmark interest rate is used as the loan interest rate. The county gives interest subsidy to petty loans for poverty alleviation within the term of loan and the credit is offered at an annual interest rate of 3%. The card has functions of the Harvest Debit Card in extending petty credit, and fund payment settlement for poverty alleviation.

scale and equity participation—repayment and refinancing—business startup, etc., have not only realized the positive development of employment—business startup—getting rid of poverty—getting rich, but also enhanced their credit awareness and market idea as well as their capacity of market participation.

Second, Jingning promotes the "Three Rights" mortgage loan project. In accordance with the *Notice of the General Office of the People's Government of Jingning She Autonomous County on Printing and Distributing the Implementation Plan on the Microcredit Discount Program of Poverty Alleviation for Rural Financial Reform* and the *Guideline on Accelerating the Implementation of the Rural Property Rights System Reform and Financial Innovations* issued by the government of Jingning County, the "Three Rights (forest right, rural housing right, land transfer and management right) mortgage loan project was implemented step by step in the whole county, effectively expanding the financing channels for "agriculture, rural areas and farmers", boosting industrial development, and increasing farmer' income. As of the end of 2015, the government had offered mortgage loans for forest right (431 million yuan), rural housing rights (210 million yuan), and land transfer and management right (3.31 million yuan), benefiting 2,774 rural households.

Third, Jingning establishes village-level fund mutual-aid organizations and meets the funding needs of poor rural households in various ways. In recent years, the government of Jingning County has developed and implemented the *Plan on the Implementation of the Demonstration Site Construction Projects of Village-level Fund Mutual-Aid Organizations,* arranged provincial special support policy on subsidized funds and funds from original channels, assisted poor villages in preparing for the establishment of village-level fund mutual-aid organizations, mitigated the shortage of funds for poor rural households, and made innovations in the poverty alleviation mechanism based on financial means. By the end of 2015, there had been a total of 58 village-level fund mutual-aid organizations in the county.

In a word, the poverty alleviation through financial means of Jingning County has solved to some extent the "bottleneck" funding problems of poor rural households in the process of their agricultural production and business startup, increased their income and laid a financial foundation for steady and consistent poverty elimination of Jingning.

3.8 The New Mechanism for Poverty Alleviation Through "Internet + Entrepreneurs + Participants + Government"

The main thinking on the new mechanism for poverty alleviation: the government supports the establishment of an "Internet+" new-type rural service platform, and integrates policies on leading agricultural enterprises, cooperatives, poor rural households and marginal poor households, so as to increase the productivity of rural laborers, increase the level of commercialization of agricultural products of poor rural households, thereby leading them to increase their income, get rid of poverty and get rich. Currently, such platforms as "She Sen Shan" and "Shanshan Shopping Mall" have taken shape.

"She Sen Shan" is a particularly distinctive platform, which, by signing agreements with some towns and villages, rural and agricultural planting and breeding cooperatives, and rural households (including poor rural households) of the county on vegetable cultivation, fowl meat and egg production, and purchase of agricultural products, aims to achieve integrated development of distinctive ecological agricultural products of the She ethnic minority ranging from seed selection, planting, purchase, processing, packaging, marketing, and distribution, thereby enhancing the competitiveness of agricultural products, increasing the level of agricultural operation of rural households, and ensuring that all rural households including disadvantaged groups earn incomes from agricultural operations. "She Sen Shan" has been rated by Lishui Brand Strategy Promotion Committee as "2015 Lishui Famous-brand Product". In 2015, the company achieved a sales revenue of 23 million yuan, 35% higher than that in 2014, directly creating jobs for over 3,000 persons of more than 1,000 rural households of the Shawan area of Jingning, and increasing the annual per capita income of each rural household by about 7,000 yuan.

3.9 Poverty Alleviation Through Subsistence Assistance

Subsistence assistance refers to material assistance or spiritual care given by the state and other entities to those who suffer natural disasters or lose the ability to work or other low-income persons, so as to meet their basic needs in material and intellectual/cultural terms, and ensure that they live at or above the minimum living standard. In 1996, Zhejiang Province took a lead in promoting the system of subsistence allowances for urban/rural residents in China. In 2014, it issued the *Regulations of Zhejiang Province on Social Assistance* and established a sound social assistance system. In 2015, in Zhejiang, the minimum basic aged-care pension benefit for rural and non-working urban residents was increased to 120 yuan per person per month, and the subsistence allowances for rural residents in all counties were increased to above 4,600 yuan, which built a basic safety net and improved people's livelihood. Jingning has taken the opportunity to establish a sound social security system step by step. In accordance with the regulations on subsistence allowances of Zhejiang Province for 2013, 7,616 persons in 4,599 households received subsistence allowances.

In order to implement the requirements on the strategy of targeted poverty alleviation, the government of Jingning County has issued the *Notice on One-to-One Paired assistance to Low-income Rural Households with A Per capita Net Income of 4,600 yuan and Below* and the *Notice on Application for Poverty Alleviation Projects* via *Industrial Development for Rural Households with A Per capita Net Income of 4,600 yuan and Below*, and established the one-to-one paired assistance mechanism for low-income rural households with a per capita net income of less than 4,600 yuan. Meanwhile, by ensuring the basic quality of life of poor people, Jingning County

Bureau of Civil Affairs has established a sound social security system for subsistence allowance recipients in urban and rural areas, childless and infirm rural residents who are entitled to five forms of support (food, clothing, medical care, housing, and burial expenses), orphans, and abandoned children, further improved the social security system covering medical assistance, temporary assistance, sunshine financial aid to students and assistance to homeless minors, and fully protected the rights and interests of disadvantaged groups. In 2015, the government of Jingning County further increased social security benefits, increased the subsistence allowances for rural residents to 4,752 yuan per person every year, basically achieved the integration of the line of poverty alleviation and the line of subsistence allowance, and ensured that all disadvantaged groups can be lifted out of poverty.

It is worth mentioning that Jingning takes a leading position among poverty-stricken areas in dynamic management of poor rural households with an annual income of less than 4,600 yuan. Active explorations have been made on how to accurately identify and dynamically manage people entitled to subsistence allowances and how the government makes surveys and assessments on introducing the third-party intermediary agencies for purchasing social services. Through the above explorations and innovations, the government of Jingning County has initially finished the work of policy making, guidance, supervision and evaluation, not only ensuring the policy effects of subsistence allowances, but also complying with the overall requirements on building a service -oriented government.

4 Targeted Poverty Alleviation in Jingning County: Main Results, Experience and Lessons

To sum up, Jingning has achieved remarkable results in targeted poverty alleviation and accumulated experience with unique value, some of which are of important reference significance to poverty alleviation in other poor areas where ethnic minorities live in concentration.

4.1 Main Results of Targeted Poverty Alleviation in Jingning County

1. The income of the people living in poverty has increased significantly and notable progress has been made in poverty alleviation. In 2015, the goal of "eliminating poverty of households with annual per-capita income of 4,600 yuan and below" was achieved, and 10,512 persons in 4,501 rural households in new-type poverty were lifted out of poverty. According to statistics, in 2015, the per-capita disposable income of permanent rural residents of Jingning reached 13,663 yuan, up 9.9% on a year-on-year basis, of which the per capita disposable income of rural

households in new-type poverty reached 8,567 yuan, up 20.8% on a year-on-year basis, 10.9% points higher than the average growth rate of rural residents of Jingning. As thus, the preset goal of "doubling the income of low-income rural households" of the county was achieved.

2. The level of coordinated urban–rural development has been significantly increased. Targeted poverty alleviation and elimination has promoted the infrastructure construction of poor mountainous areas in Jingning, relocation has promoted new-type urbanization in mountainous areas, and the brand-building program "Jingning, a famous county of She ethnic minority group in China" has seen remarkable results. The working and living environment of rural residents including poor people have been greatly improved, the income gaps between urban and rural residents have been gradually narrowed, and the development level of social programs of rural education, healthcare, culture, science and technology has been markedly raised. Overall, steady and coordinated economic and social development of the county has been achieved. The comprehensive economic competitiveness of the county ranked ninth in 2013, higher than its ranking in all minority autonomous counties of China.

4.2 Experience and Inspirations

1. Jingning makes overall plans on economic and social development by drawing on the joint efforts of all sectors of society.

Jingning, at the time of the implementation of the targeted poverty alleviation, makes overall plans on poverty alleviation, makes targeted poverty alleviation an important political task of the government and makes an overall plan on the economic and social development by drawing on the joint efforts of all sectors of society.

First, the government of Jingning County attaches great importance to targeted poverty alleviation, establishes a leadership system in which the principal leaders of the CPC Jingning County Committee and the People's Government of Jingning play an overall leading role and leaders in charge are responsible for specific duties and corresponding working mechanisms, gives top priority to increasing the incomes of farmers including poor farmers, and makes all efforts to increase the incomes of farmers and lift them out of poverty. In 2013, Jingning established the leading group for the new-round surveying and identification of low-income rural households and key poverty alleviation villages headed by deputy director of the general office of the CPC Jingning County Committee and director of agricultural office, started to implement the "program for income doubling of low-income rural households", and implemented "2014–2016 Special Support Policy on Key Underdeveloped Counties" (namely second-round special support policies). In 2014, Jingning issued the *Notice of the General Office of the People's Government of Jingning She Autonomous County on Printing and Distributing the Implementation Plan on the Microcredit Discount Program of Poverty Alleviation for Rural Financial Reform* (Jingzhengbanfa (2014), No.97) and the *Guideline on Accelerating the Implementation of the Rural Property*

Rights System Reform and Financial Innovations (Jingweibanfa (2014), No. 30). Under the guiding principle of the *Notice of the General Office of the CPC Zhejiang Provincial Committee and the General Office of the People's Government of Zhejiang Province on the New-round Paired Assistance for Poverty Alleviation* (Zheweibanfa (2014), No.8), Jingning carries out the policy on coordinated paired assistance at the provincial, city and county levels, and fully brings out the benefits by establishing the "three-tier guidance and assistance" mechanism. In addition, Jingning, by taking advantage of its status as a minority autonomous county, has developed and implemented a raft of policies such as the *Guidelines on Further Strengthening the Ethnic Work and Deepening the Work of Assistance to Ethnic Minorities for Economic and Social Development Under the New Conditions* and the *Opinions on Strengthening Support for Economic and Social Development of Ethnic Minorities*, so as to boost its economy and promote poverty reduction.

Second, Jingning focuses on drawing on the joint efforts of all sectors of society to accelerate its economic and social development. It involves introducing the most favorable and the best policies on accelerating the development of agriculture, rural areas and farmers, sticks to the overall requirements on coordinated urban and rural development, synchronously advances the industrialization, IT application, urbanization and agricultural modernization, comprehensively deepens reform in rural areas, and does everything possible to promote the "sustained, universal and rapid" growth of the incomes of farmers including poor rural households. For example, in recent years, the CPC Jingning County Committee and the People's Government of Jingning County, by centering on the overall goal of "increasing farmers' incomes, improving people's wellbeing, improving the ecological environment, and enhancing the internal impetus to growth", has effectively implemented two rounds of special assistance programs, of which the second-round special support funds have been used for "agriculture, rural areas and rural residents" and poverty alleviation at a ratio of 81%, more than 30% higher than other special support programs for the county. Specifically, about 30 million yuan is used for petty loan discount, 27 million yuan for economic development of mountainous regions, more than 100 million yuan for building a rural countryside, and nearly 50 million yuan for industrial development. The implementation of a number of special assistance programs has fundamentally addressed the backwardness of infrastructure in rural areas of the county, and significantly improved the working and living conditions of farmers. Meanwhile, the implementation of a large number of projects related to poverty alleviation, industrial development and people's wellbeing has directly benefited the farmers including poor rural households.

Third, to alleviate poverty in a targeted manner, lift poor people out of poverty, and achieve the goal of making farmers' incomes exceed 20,000 yuan in 2020, Jingning has launched "10 major action plans" on increasing incomes, and strives to create a positive environment in which "CPC committees and governments take a lead, departments offer assistance, everyone takes part in the campaign for increasing incomes". The 10 major action plans involve fostering modern agricultural industries, farmers' shareholding, development of rural labor force resources, increasing farmers' incomes through business startup, increasing farmers' incomes through technical training, increasing farmers' incomes by financial means, relocation of 10,000 farmers to urban areas, assistance to farmers through the development of emerging industries, demonstration projects, and doubling the incomes of low-income rural households. The vigorous implementation of the above 10 major action plans make rural residents and particularly rural disadvantaged groups, have a strong sense of benefits.

2. The government, market and disadvantaged groups take concerted actions for targeted poverty alleviation

First, strike a balance between overall economic and social development and targeted poverty alleviation. According to the requirements on targeted poverty alleviation, a key factor to the assessment of economic and social development of poverty-stricken areas is whether the regional economic and social development can increase the self-development ability of disadvantaged groups and whether disadvantaged groups can be lifted out of poverty.[22] As is seen from the practices of Jingning, overall regional economic and social development is basically in line with the goal of poverty alleviation. "Targeted poverty alleviation and elimination" promotes overall regional economic and social development, which can increase the self-development ability of disadvantaged groups and lift them out of poverty. Meanwhile, the implementation of the projects for "targeted poverty alleviation and elimination" has not only improved the working and living conditions of poor rural residents, but also stimulated the vitality of poor villages, creating a new engine driving economic and social development of the county. For example, Jingning carries out poverty alleviation through industrial development and relocation, promoting high-speed development of ecological agriculture and rural tourism and further promoting the overall economic and social development of the county.

Second, strike a balance between local development and overall development. The key to targeted poverty alleviation is targeted identification and assistance. In the process of carrying out targeted poverty alleviation, Jingning focuses on its 148 key poverty alleviation villages, and gives priority to them in the aspects of infrastructure construction, poverty alleviation through industrial development, poverty alleviation through relocation, paired assistance, poverty alleviation, and social assistance. It gives greater policy support to poor villages and poor people of She ethnic minority group. When focusing on key villages and special poor groups, Jingning has broken the limits of key poverty alleviation villages and poor groups and given certain assistance to the development of villages other than poor villages, or carried out relevant programs in different villages, accelerating the overall anti-poverty process of the county.

Third, strike a balance between the government, market and poor groups. As targeted poverty alleviation and evaluation is a complicated systematic project, we must strike a balance between the government, market and poor groups, and give

---

[22] Huang Chengwei and Ye Tao, A Provincial Boilerplate of Poverty Alleviation—A Study on the Models of Targeted Poverty Alleviation and Elimination in Guizhou, Social Sciences Academic Press, 2016.

full play to their respective functions. As the targeted poverty alleviation strategy is being implemented, Jingning creates a "government—market" double orientation poverty alleviation mechanism in accordance with the actual situation of the county. Under such a mechanism, the main functions of the government are to improve public infrastructure, increase the supply and level of public services, create favorable conditions for disadvantaged groups to take part in market competitions, grant people living in poverty with opportunities for and rights of taking part in development and getting rid of poverty, and finally help them get rid of poverty and get rich by market-based means.[23] For example, the financial service platform with "ZHENGYINBAO" at the core provides poor rural households with interest-free loan, not only solving the actual funding difficulties of poor rural households and increasing the investment opportunities for them, but also increasing the opportunities and capability of farmers to enter the market and steadily increasing the incomes of poor rural households. It is noteworthy that these measures have fostered the modern credit awareness of the rural households in new-type poverty of the county and ensure that they repay the loans in due course, and the non-performing loan ratio of petty discount loans of the county is zero. The key incentive mechanism is that the "ZHENGYINBAO" platform of Jingning stipulates that poor rural families can continue to apply for a loan on the precondition of repayment in full and on time. The better their performance in repayment, the larger loan they can apply for. The upper limit of the first loan is 50,000 yuan-100,000 yuan. The specific loan limit is determined by the results of credit rating made by the platform for loan applicants. The results of credit rating will be published at every village so as to play an incentive and oversight role.

Fourth, strike a balance between assistance and self-development. Generally speaking, the driving force of development of an area mainly comes from two aspects, namely internal factors and external factors.[24] Like those poor people in other regions in China, as a result of the rapid economic and social development and sustained poverty alleviation and development, the poor rural people of Zhejiang who currently live in mountainous areas, areas with fragile ecology, areas with concentration of ethnic minorities, and old revolutionary base areas that are far from areas that are economically developed and have better locational and traffic conditions face the "isolated island" phenomenon (rural poverty is relatively concentrated in a few relatively closed areas).[25] Therefore, underdeveloped areas including Jingning are generally considered to have problems such as insufficient internal impetus to growth and lack of the basic conditions and vitality of economic development, and it is essential to advance the development of the county through external assistance. For instance, the central government as well as the governments of Zhejiang Province

[23] Yu Mingjiang: The Building of the Anti-poverty Mechanism of China's Rural Areas: A Study from the Perspectives of Government and Market, Journal of Anhui Agricultural University (Social Science Edition), Issue 5, 2010.

[24] Zhao Qiangshe: A Probe into the Evolution of Poverty Alleviation Model and Countermeasures for Poverty Alleviation in the New Era, West Journal, Issue 2, 2013.

[25] Liu Yansui, Zhou Yang, Liu Jilai: Differential Regional Characteristics of Poverty in Rural Areas of China and the Strategy of Targeted Poverty Alleviation, Bulletin of Chinese Academy of Sciences, Issue 3, 2016.

and Lishui City inject capital into Jingning, assists it in intensifying infrastructure construction, increasing the level of public services, introducing development models of developed regions, and accelerating its modernization process. Of course, external assistance is merely a means and process, and it ultimately needs the government and all ethnic groups of Jingning to seek the fundamental driver of development, enhance their self-development ability, and attain the goal of eradicating poverty and getting rich.

Fifth, strike a balance between "externally-driven poverty alleviation" and "internally-driven poverty alleviation". In terms of poverty alleviation model, Jingning has changed the "externally-driven" poverty alleviation focusing purely on welfare handouts, or "internally-driven" poverty alleviation focusing purely on poverty alleviation and development, but stresses the "effective link" between "externally-driven poverty alleviation" and "internally-driven poverty alleviation", and forms a new mechanism driven by two wheels. It is noteworthy that Jingning takes measures for targeted identification and pursues policies in a classified way in identifying and assisting people living in poverty. For poor people with working capacity but are lacking in fund, opportunities and skills, Jingning, by means of strong policy, project and financial support, provides them with as many as opportunities for employment and business startup. For special groups such as those who have lost their ability to work, childless and infirm rural residents who are entitled to five forms of support (food, clothing, medical care, housing, and burial expenses), orphans, and abandoned children, the government of Jingning gives social assistance. In addition, Jingning keeps up efforts to build a working mechanism for making innovations in targeted identification and dynamic management of subsistence allowance recipients, and introduces the third-party intermediary agencies to assess subsistence allowance recipients based on their purchase of social services. In this way, it has achieved more objective and fair results than ever, relieves government departments of their pressure in handling relevant affairs, avoids various problems to a great extent, and reduces the contradictions between officials and the people. Meanwhile, Jingning increases the standards and scope of its subsistence allowances, and strives to give assistance to all those who are in need. The overall poverty alleviation strategy of Jingning integrates poverty alleviation and development and social assistance, and achieves full coverage of poor rural residents.

At last, the poverty alleviation and development in rural areas is a long-term process. We should not only balance the above relations, but also pay attention to economic and social development, keep increasing the people's living standards, keep widening the scope of poverty alleviation, increase the level of poverty alleviation step by step, and ensure more stable and sustained poverty alleviation. Against the background of achieving the goals of "the basic living needs of rural poor populations are met and that such people have access to compulsory education, basic medical services, and housing" as stated in the *Guidelines of Poverty Alleviation and Development in the Rural Area of China (2011–2020) of Jingning*, on the one hand, the government of Jingning County, in line with the requirements put forward in the *Guidelines* that all local governments need to make policies on poverty alleviation in light of local conditions, increases the standards of poverty alleviation and subsistence allowances year by year. The current poverty alleviation standard is twice higher than the national standard for poverty alleviation. The adjusted standards of poverty alleviation and subsistence allowances designate both the poor groups and low-income groups as the targets of the anti-poverty work of Jingning in the new era, guaranteeing that more new-type poor groups who are in dire need of help can get help from the government. It indicates that the anti-poverty work of Jingning in the new era is not limited to the goal of poverty alleviation, but aims to lift poor people out of poverty and help them get rich. On the other hand, further explorations are made to accurately identify the targets of poverty alleviation, and the single standard for identifying poverty on the basis of the absolute value of income has been abandoned. Multi-dimensional factors such as health, housing, assets and disaster have been considered. The village party branches and villagers' committees take special procedures to select no less than one third of all the households of the village as poor rural households, and select about one third of the above selected households as special targets of poverty alleviation (namely, the low-income rural households in line with the former standard for poverty alleviation as indicated by "eliminating households with per capita annual income of 4,600 yuan and below"). Meanwhile, based on the differences of poverty of different ethnic minority groups in Jingning as well as the goal of assistance to development of ethnic minorities, all She villages and people enjoy priority in actual practices. The above practices indicate that the focus of the anti-poverty work of Jingning begins to shift to narrowing the gap, ensuring equitable distribution and ensuring that poor groups live a more dignified life.

To sum up, the practices of targeted poverty alleviation and eradication of Jingning have made remarkable effects and offered experience that is worthy of promotion, some of which are of reference significance to other poor areas with concentration of ethnic minorities in the future. The most important aspiration is that the development of rural areas must rely on development, which must start with fostering and raising the self-development awareness and ability of poor rural households. For this, the government needs to improve public infrastructure and increase public service supply, and establish a mechanism that can facilitate poor people to integrate into normal economic and social systems, enjoy the fruits of economic development and get out of poverty.

Currently, the targeted poverty alleviation and elimination work of Jingning is still confronted with difficulties and challenges, of which the biggest challenge comes from strong market polarization, causing the phenomena that a number of children, women and old people are left behind by rural migrant workers who work in cities as well as a series of problems such as "hollowing-out" in some villages and aging of rural population, etc. Moreover, the county seat and key towns of Jingning are threatened by the declining population,[26] which leads to poor poverty alleviation effects of some industrial support projects while high-caliber talents are wanted.

[26] Mao Huaqing: *The Speech Delivered at the Forum of "Targeted Poverty Alleviation in Rural Areas"*, The Second Forum on the Development of China's She Ethnic Minority Group in Jingning County, November 27, 2016.

These problems need to be solved in economic and social development and poverty alleviation and development practices in the future.

The manufacturer's authorised representative in the EU is Springer Nature Customer Service Centre GmbH, Europaplatz 3, 69115 Heidelberg, Germany. If you have any concerns regarding our products, please contact ProductSafety@springernature.com

Printed and bound by CPI Group (UK) Ltd, Croydon, CR0 4YY
30/09/2026
02225300-0003